LANGUAGE AND EDUCATION LIBRARY 8
Series Editor: Professor David J. Corson
The Ontario Institute for Studies in Education

Competing and Consensual Voices: The Theory and Practice of Argument

Patrick J.M. Costello and Sally Mitchell

MULTILINGUAL MATTERS LTD
Clevedon • Philadelphia • Adelaide

Library of Congress Cataloging in Publication Data

Competing and Consensual Voices: The Theory and Practice of Argument
Edited by Patrick J.M. Costello and Sally Mitchell
(The Language and Education Library: 8)
Result of an International Conference held at the University of York, March 1993.
Includes bibliographical references and index.
1. Reasoning–Study and teaching–Congresses. 2. Debates and debating–
Congresses. 3. Questioning–Study and teaching–Congresses. 4. Logic–Study
and teaching–Congresses. I. Costello, Patrick J.M., 1959– . II. Mitchell, Sally.
III. Series.
LB1590.3.C65   1995
371.3'7–dc20   95-6553

British Library Cataloguing in Publication Data

A CIP catalogue record for this book is available from the British Library.

ISBN 1-85359-277-3 (hbk)
ISBN 1-85359-276-5 (pbk)

Multilingual Matters Ltd

UK: Frankfurt Lodge, Clevedon Hall, Victoria Road, Clevedon, Avon BS21 7SJ.
USA: 1900 Frost Road, Suite 101, Bristol, PA 19007, USA.
Australia: P.O. Box 6025, 83 Gilles Street, Adelaide, SA 5000, Australia.

Typeset by Bookcraft, Stroud, Gloucestershire.
Printed and bound in Great Britain by WBC Print, Bridgend.

Contents

v

Acknowledgements

The idea of a collection of essays on the theory and practice of argument arose as a result of an international conference, held at the University of York in March 1993, the impetus for which was the work of two research projects conducted at Hull University. The first, entitled 'Improving the Quality of Argument, 5–16', was directed by Richard Andrews and Patrick Costello and funded by the Esmée Fairbairn Charitable Trust. It took place over two years and involved the participation of 20 primary and secondary schools. The second, entitled 'The Teaching and Learning of Argument in Sixth Forms and Higher Education', was a three-year project funded by the Leverhulme Trust. Directed by Richard Andrews, this empirical study was undertaken by the project's Research Fellow, Sally Mitchell. The York conference offered a forum for the discussion of a broad range of issues related to argument, and a number of participants from Britain and abroad have contributed chapters to this book.

We would like to express our thanks to both the Esmée Fairbairn Charitable Trust and the Leverhulme Trust whose generous sponsorship made our research possible. We are also indebted to the many teachers and students who collaborated in the two projects and whose commitment and enthusiasm made them such enjoyable experiences.

As is evident from the above, Richard Andrews was pivotal in the development of both projects. His wisdom, companionship and unfailing good humour during the period we spent together at Hull were invaluable. Richard's own work has added significantly to the theory and practice of argument and we acknowledge his contribution to our common task with gratitude.

Finally, we wish to thank: our contributors for extending and illuminating the argument; Professor David Corson of the Ontario Institute for Studies in Education for his perceptive comments; and Mike Grover of Multilingual Matters for his advice and support in the preparation of the book.

List of Contributors

Jo Backus is Senior Lecturer in Religious Education at Bath College of Higher Education.

Mike Baynham works at the University of Technology, Sydney, where he is Director of the Centre for Language and Literacy and teaches on Adult Basic Education and TESOL teacher education programmes. His book, *Literacy Practices*, is published by Longmans in the Language in Social Life Series.

Audrey Berner is a university teacher/researcher at the Centre for the Study and Teaching of Writing, McGill University, Montreal. She also supervises student teachers and has taught secondary school language arts and history for over 15 years.

William Boswell has over 30 years' experience as a secondary English teacher and is currently a university teacher/researcher at the Centre for the Study and Teaching of Writing, McGill University, Montreal. He is co-editor of *Crossroads*, a collection of Canadian short stories and poems designed for use in secondary schools.

Carolyn Boulter comes from a teaching background and is a lecturer in science education at Reading University, where she works with Professor John Gilbert on the 'Modelling across the Curriculum' project. Her particular interest is in linking discourse with conceptual understanding in science.

Stephen Clarke taught English in secondary schools before becoming a Lecturer in Education at the University of Leeds. With John Sinker, he edited a school textbook, *Arguments*, in the *Modes of Writing* series (CUP), following a similarly co-authored chapter on argument and travel writing in *Narrative and Argument*, edited by Richard Andrews.

Patrick J.M. Costello is Reader in Education and Director of the Centre for Applied Educational Research at the North East Wales Institute of Higher Education, Wrexham. He is co-editor of *Curriculum* and has published widely on the teaching of critical thinking in schools.

Richard Dunne has extensive teaching and research experience in primary, secondary and higher education and was recently a lecturer in education at the University of Exeter. He is now an educational consultant specialising in the design of curricula, courses and instructional materials.

David Fleming is a doctoral candidate at Carnegie Mellon University. His dissertation investigates designers' use of language and pictures in the design process.

Linda Flower is Co-director of the National Centre for the Study of Writing and Literacy at Carnegie Mellon University and author of *The Construction of Negotiated Meaning: A Social Cognitive Theory of Writing*.

Howard Gibson is Senior Lecturer in Language and Literacy at Bath College of Higher Education and co-ordinates the PGCE Primary Course.

John Gilbert is a professor at Reading University and has published in science and technology education world-wide. He has been closely associated with the growth of the Alternative Conceptions Movement in science education.

Maureen Daly Goggin is Assistant Professor of Rhetoric and Composition in the Department of English at Arizona State University in Tempe, Arizona. She has published articles on the history of rhetoric, on the role of history in rhetorical studies, and on the history of the discipline of rhetoric and composition. Her current research examines the role of academic journals in the emergence of post-World War II rhetoric and composition in post-secondary education in the USA.

Gareth Harvard is a lecturer in the School of Education at Exeter University. His teaching and research interests are in student learning, both professional competencies and academic work. In particular he is interested in the development of spoken and written argument and students' interpretation of texts.

Charles A. Hill is Assistant Professor of Rhetoric in the English Department of the University of Wisconsin Oshkosh. He recently completed a post-doctoral fellowship at the Learning Research and Development Centre at the University of Pittsburgh. His areas of specialisation include argumentation, critical reasoning, and writing to learn. His publications include articles in *Written Communication, Computers and Composition,* and *Reading Research Quarterly*.

Elenore Long is a graduate of Carnegie Mellon University's Rhetoric Programme. She has taken a post-doctoral position to continue working with teenaged writers at the Community Literacy Centre in Pittsburgh, Pennsylvania.

Maureen A. Mathison is Assistant Professor at the University of Utah, where she holds a joint appointment in Rhetoric and Composition and Communication. She teaches graduate courses in rhetoric and undergraduate courses in writing. Her research focuses on the theory and practice of critique. Recently, she completed a Charles Phelps Post-doctoral Fellowship at the University of Cincinnati where she conducted research on the role of critique for professionals and students in academic settings.

James McGonigal taught for 12 years in English and Learning Support departments of comprehensive schools, and is now Head of Language and Literature in St Andrew's College in the School of Education of the University of Glasgow. His publications include *Talk About Poetry*, *The Special Needs Pack*, *Hard Words & Fancy Words* and *Sons of Ezra: British Poets and Pound*. He is also, with the novelist A.L. Kennedy, co-editor of *New Writing Scotland* for the Association for Scottish Literary Studies.

Sally Mitchell is a research fellow in the Education Research Unit at South Bank University, London. She was previously the Research Fellow on the project 'The Teaching and Learning of Argument in Sixth Forms and Higher Education', directed by Richard Andrews at Hull University. She is co-author with Malcolm Ross, Hilary Radnor and Cathy Bierton of *Assessing Achievement in the Arts*.

Mike O'Rourke has lectured in Applied Linguistics in Germany, Sweden, Exeter University and most recently at the University of Luton.

Pat O'Rourke has worked as an English teacher in secondary schools and as Head of English in a tertiary college. She was LINC co-ordinator for the East Midlands, where she produced and trialled language materials and worked with teachers and advisory teachers. She is now teaching English to students with learning difficulties in a comprehensive school.

Patricia Wojahn is a doctoral candidate at Carnegie Mellon University. Her area of speciality is computer-mediated communication.

Introduction – Argument: Voices, Texts And Contexts

PATRICK J.M. COSTELLO AND SALLY MITCHELL

The title of this volume, *Competing and Consensual Voices*, has an application to the chapters in this book in two senses. On the one hand, it can be understood as a characterisation of argument itself; or at least of some of its purposes and functions. The distinction it draws is between argument as a means to put forward a position in preference to others and argument as a means to discover a, perhaps shared, perspective: argument to win; argument to arrive at a decision. Competition suggests the work argument does to set a position or person apart; consensus, the work it does to bring positions together. Though these functions seem polarised, both, it will be noted, are predicated on there being more than one voice. Kuhn (1992: 157) makes this point when, having distinguished what she calls 'rhetorical' from 'dialogic' argument (roughly an equivalent distinction to that we have just made), she comments: ' … any reasoned or rhetorical argument in support of an assertion implicitly contains a full dialogic argument.'

Argument, unlike formal logic, is a social operation, a particular mode of communication which is oriented to context and to purpose. It functions, as the terms 'competition' and 'consensus' suggest, both to create and to challenge positions and to form and break apart agreement and identity. It is at once generative and coercive. These are qualities which do not neatly divide between consensus and competition but, we would suggest, are potentially present in each. The clue is in the voices that are heard: who speaks?; to whom?; to what purpose and effect?

In some sense, then, we are suggesting that argument can be defined by what it does, as well as by what it, more abstractly, is. It initiates change, it transforms the significance of material, it enables reflection and action, it brings divergent voices together in interaction, it signals belonging within a certain community, it seeks to persuade, to publicise, to win. So, to answer the question, 'what is argument?' entails asking a number of others: what does argument do? who does it? with or to whom? where? and why? Each of these questions links an understanding of argument not to the realm of the abstract and immutable but to the social, interactional world, or more precisely, worlds. Each points, too, to the way argument is concerned with and to some extent defined by relations of power. Competition between whom and on whose behalf? Consensus according to whose agenda?

As regards responses offered to the above questions by our contributors, these reveal as much difference as similarity. It is here that we have the second sense in which our title can be understood: it reflects the different viewpoints and approaches that the chapters bring to the study and practice of argument. What the chapters share is an interest in the place of argument in education, but this concern is focused in a number of different ways. Some authors, for example, see argument as a means of allowing expression to the student, others as a means by which students generate, qualify and consolidate meaning. Yet other writers take argument to be a goal of the educational process and regard it as, to a greater or lesser degree, determined by pre-given rules; whether of form, content or logic. Frequently, argument is interpreted by writers in a critical way. Some invite us to question its adequacy as a means of learning, either because of its consensual nature (as in Gibson and Backus' discussion of its place within religious education) or, in the case of Boulter and Gilbert, because of its basis in oppositional language. In each case, the premises on which argument is based are seen to be impositions of power.

The chapters represent different academic and pedagogical traditions: philosophy; the Alternative Conceptions Movement; philosophy with children; linguistics; the study of rhetoric and of logic, etc. A number of the chapters (Berner and Boswell, Clarke, O'Rourke and O'Rourke, McGonigal) are grounded in English teaching. It is not surprising that such work occupies a high proportion of the book. In addition to a fundamental concern with the uses of language, it reflects the strong sense in which argument is associated with the self, with passion, with self-determination and with 'voice': these are qualities highly valued within the liberal expressive tradition of education in which English occupies a central place.

Contributors to the book examine the teaching and learning of argument at primary, secondary and tertiary levels. It is notable that, while at the early stages of schooling argument is thought about as an oral, exploratory, philosophical activity, at later levels other factors begin more strongly to shape its nature and practice. At secondary and tertiary levels, learning comes increasingly to be dominated by disciplinary content, by standard forms of writing and ways of doing (speech accordingly is less emphasised and less valued in assessment terms). Subject boundaries at these levels begin to impose rules and limitations on the ways in which language is used and argument shaped, expressed and legitimated. In particular, the role of belief and conviction in argument – the place for the personal – becomes problematic.

We have not ordered the chapters in this book as a chronological progression from primary to tertiary; rather we have attempted to situate them in such a way as to promote a cross-fertilisation of theoretical and practical ideas and instances. In what follows of this introductory chapter we try to draw out the threads which connect chapters and, at the same time, to give the reader a sense of what they offer individually. Our accounts are derived from the authors' own summaries.

We have placed Maureen Daly Goggin's chapter first in the collection because it sets out a framework for recognising that discursive practices – of which argument is one – are learned, dynamic, social processes that are shaped by social, political, cultural, rhetorical and historical forces. It examines the interaction between argumentative practices and different contexts that vary across time and place. In particular this chapter focuses on the historical; it argues that the teaching and learning of argument needs to be informed by three converging perspectives: the macro-plane (history of a general context), meso-plane (personal histories of participants within a context), and the micro-plane (immediate history of a specific context). In setting out these intersecting perspectives, Goggin discusses important implications for how argument should be studied and taught.

The planes Goggin describes allow us, moreover, to situate the work of other authors in this book; Gibson and Backus, for example, take a macro-perspective on the teaching of religious education whilst Mathison and Hill, in revealing the differences between students' and teachers' evaluations of argument address the meso-level. When Berner and Boswell describe their writing classes we encounter the micro-plane. As Goggin points out, however, the planes tend not to be discrete but overlapping and dynamic – and many of the chapters reflect this.

One such is that of Stephen Clarke who argues from evidence generated by the research project, *Improving the Quality of Argument, 5–16*, that some of the best work in argument, especially in the primary sector, derived from placing pupils in a simulated world or dramatic role. This seemed to enhance both the quality of the arguers' involvement and of their speaking, without diminishing the seriousness of debate. On the other hand, although certain topics did not lend themselves to playful encounter, some distancing from direct confrontation seemed to help sustain the rationality of debate. Clarke offers ways of thinking about argument as on a continuum which links the playful with the rational, the artefact (e.g. an argumentative essay) with the activity (e.g. arguing) and again, the literary convention with the enactment of social purpose.

As with Goggin's chapter, what Clarke offers as a mapping of argument finds echoes in other chapters: in McGonigal's account of the use of audio-tape as a medium for the production of argument; in Long's work with teenage children producing anti-drug literature; and in Costello's philosophical conversation with children on the question 'What makes you *you?'*

Mike Baynham's analysis of the spoken language of adult learners takes the exploration of argument into the field of socio-linguistics and asks the questions: How does narrative function in argument? How can narrative be used *in* argument and *as* argument? Baynham examines a number of spoken interactions in which argument is taking place and shows how narrative features are employed in furthering the argumentative purpose. He suggests that the powerful role of narrative in argument is linked to its typical epistemological claims, and to the concepts of 'authority' and 'authorisation' and the 'regime of truth'.

By engaging in close linguistic analysis, Baynham provides insights into the way argument is constructed and given legitimacy in language. His chapter thus provides a useful perspective through which to consider some of the other examples of argument given elsewhere in the book; in particular, perhaps, the attraction of story to the students and teenagers in the studies by Hill and Long *et al.* His suggestion that use might be made of spoken language in developing the writing skills of adult literacy learners may also be compared with O'Rourke and O'Rourke's discussion of Ochs' (1983) continuum between unplanned and planned discourse.

We have placed Gareth Harvard and Richard Dunne's chapter early in the collection because they too offer a way of thinking about argument which can be readily extended to other contexts. They distinguish between dogmatic and critical uses of argument and suggest that, in the context of initial teacher training, the combination of a dogmatic attitude and critical thinking is essential. In exploring this combination, Harvard and Dunne make sense of recent legislation in Great Britain which requires that trainee teachers spend an increased period of time in school. The rationale for this has been phrased by politicians in ways that denigrate theory and that cite the need for trainee teachers to learn from more experienced practitioners. The dichotomy between theory and practice that this implies is rejected by

Harvard and Dunne in their account of the rigorous, systematic techniques and conditions necessary for novices to learn from their own experience and that of other practitioners. For them, argument – a dialectic between belief and reflection – is grounded in 'persistent attention' to actual events. The reciprocity between the dogmatic and the critical is echoed in what other authors have to say about the relationship between stability and change, belief and evaluation, allegiance and doubt. These two impulses are perhaps well expressed by what Mitchell, quoting Ricoeur (1970), refers to as 'a vow of obedience' and 'a vow of rigour'.

Something of these dual but dialectical impulses informs the chapter by Howard Gibson and Jo Backus which focuses on aspects of argument and rationality within the context of religious education and cultural pluralism in British schools. The chapter is divided into three sections. In the first, the authors look at the political, pedagogical and philosophical reasons for the low status of argument and critical rationality within religious education; in the second they develop a rationale for institutionalising dialogue and argument; and in the third, they consider the pressures that this new rationale must make upon current practices. In so doing they offer a re-examination of terms such as 'tolerance', 'empathy' and 'encounter'.

Carolyn Boulter and John Gilbert also uncover difficult tensions when they explore the current state of science education in Britain. They suggest that the prescription of scientific content in the National Curriculum co-exists uneasily with the pedagogical practices employed by many teachers, particularly at the primary level. They consider three models of argument which, as part of the repertoire of a skilled teacher, may help to resolve these tensions. If schooling is to be flexible and effective, teachers should be able to move between different classroom scenarios – informing, questioning and collaborative problem solving – each of which entails different patterns of discourse. Whilst making this proposal, however, the authors are also aware of its limitations and difficulties. These are discussed as the problem of the distribution of power, the relationship of argument to conceptual change and the problem of oppositional language, which may, it is suggested, exclude female thinking.

The view that officially sanctioned modes of operating may exclude as well as enable underpinned James McGonigal's work with the Scottish Examination Board, the aim of which was to give students with dyslexic disabilities and other special educational needs access to the curriculum and to national assessment. In many ways, McGonigal's chapter illustrates what Baynham's argues – the effectiveness of narrative to put forward a case. It tells the story of how these 15- to 16-year-old students were enabled to produce rhetorically powerful argument by means of audio-taping their performance in spoken language. Their achievement, McGonigal argues, has opened up issues which relate to teaching and learning in English for all students. Audio taping bridges the opposition (addressed elsewhere in this volume by O'Rourke and O'Rourke and Mitchell) between the informality and spontaneity of speech and the formal, planned quality of much writing. It reveals the irresistibility of voice and gives it an important role in fostering a more confident and also a more 'political' or social awareness.

Emphasis is also placed on the notion of 'voice' by Patrick Costello, who, in his chapter, suggests that introducing philosophy into schools offers teachers an opportunity to 'extend children's voices'. He uses this phrase to indicate the importance of allowing pupils to articulate areas of experience that are often excluded from classroom discourse. The teaching of philosophy has an important contribution to make both to the theory and practice of argument. In order to substantiate this thesis and to demonstrate the kind of philosophical discussion which may take place with young children, Costello sets out and comments on a dialogue in which he took part with a class of 10- and 11-year-old pupils.

Sally Mitchell's chapter continues the focus on spoken argument, but from a rather different perspective. She uses data from her empirical research in post-16 classrooms and seminars to explore the role of argument in learning an academic discipline. She suggests that argument is an important means by which individuals resist or negotiate positions within discourses which are new to them. By the final year of undergraduate study, disciplinary discourse may, for some students, come to be the basis of belief and personal identity. Nonetheless, even at this level, differences remain in a seminar situation between the discursive behaviour of the students and teacher.

A further observation from Mitchell's study is that the criteria by which argument may be judged in speech are different from those which govern argument in writing. Maureen Mathison develops this point by suggesting what the criteria governing writing in sociology may be. Her chapter reports on the writing of college students who were given an article to critique as part of their sociology course. Mathison analysed the texts for structure, length, type of commentary and support. She then asked four sociology professors to offer their impressions of the texts and to give them a score. She discovered that students were more likely to receive higher scores if they included more negative commentary, if they based their evaluation on disciplinary rather than personal knowledge, and if they interwove their commentary throughout their critiques. In addition, the configurations students employed in constructing their critiques signalled particular internal dynamics; certain configurations of material were more likely to signal a critical stance regarding the source article than others.

It is interesting to note here that whilst interpretations of performance have traditionally been (and in some areas are currently) based on cognitive operations and on the testing of logical skill, in Mathison's chapter success is seen as being dependent on social, rhetorical knowledge rather than on decontextualised (or, in her terms, disembodied) intelligence. As Harré (1983: 137) argues: 'The fact that talk [and writing] displays cognitive properties is a collective not an individual fact.'

The sense, conveyed by both Mitchell and Mathison, that not all arguments are equal, is present also in the chapters by Hill and Long *et al.* Charles Hill suggests that although we have many models for how people *should* evaluate arguments, we know little about how they actually *do* evaluate the arguments that are encountered in their everyday lives. In his study, Hill set out to explore this issue by asking 20 university students and 10 of their instructors to read, evaluate and comment on two argumentative essays. Although the university instructors, it appeared, were more likely than their students to apply 'general' criteria of logic and support, rather than rely solely on idiosyncratic judgements, with some kinds of argument (for example, about the causes of various human behaviours), both groups of readers tended to use their own beliefs in making their evaluations. Hill's findings thus offer a useful perspective on the 'common sense' reasoning that Mitchell describes.

The chapter by Elenore Long, Linda Flower, David Fleming and Patricia Wojahn looks at how teenage writers adapt a typically academic, intellectual strategy – rival-hypothesis thinking – to their own rhetorical purposes. The writers, who were taking part in a community literacy programme, set out to produce a document for their peers which would rival (if not replace) existing anti-drug literature. In constructing claims and evidence for their articles, the writers drew from a range of argumentative norms, strategies and goals; some of these are typically valued in schools, others on the street. What they produced appeared (in a particularly Bakhtinian way) to be shaped by various voices: the comments and questions of adults and peers that merged and collided with internalised voices of teachers past and present; the expectations of teenage readers; the shaping power of available models; the discourse of drugs; and – what the authors suggest, often goes unseen – the writers' own goals, interests and interpretations.

It is precisely these goals that Audrey Berner and William Boswell seek to foster in their writing classes at McGill University's Centre for the Study and Teaching of Writing, where the 'Burning Issue' paper is a highly valued assignment. For this piece of work, students choose a 'real' topic that 'burns' them, and write for 'real' readers who, they feel, need to be convinced. In their chapter, Berner and Boswell describe the procedures they use to help students discover and explore their own 'burning issue' and offer examples of writing produced both as part of the generative process and as a final outcome.

We end the book with a chapter by Pat and Mike O'Rourke, who share with Berner and Boswell a belief in the importance of subject matter engaging the thoughts and imagination of the writer, but who are critical of the notion that argumentative writing is a natural facility. Following Widdowson (1972), O'Rourke and O'Rourke take the view that 'deliberate pedagogical' intervention is needed in learning to write and they show how secondary school children can extend and enrich their 'opinion essays' when they have received focused and reflective teaching. We feel that this chapter offers a suitable conclusion, since it endorses the mutual informing of theory and practice – a theme central to our subtitle.

One note of clarification: a number of contributors refer to the National Curriculum in Britain and this is understandable since it is seen as having significant implications for the viability of teaching argument in schools. To the extent that governments or their representatives either dictate or contribute significantly to the development of educational policy and curriculum provision at a national level, this is likely to have adverse consequences for schools in terms of their ability and/or willingness to provide contexts within which the teaching and learning of argument may take place. The amount of time which is usually devoted to the teaching and assessment of the specified content of a national curriculum, may seriously inhibit the promotion of an activity – argument – which frequently entails the questioning and transformation of content. Oral argument in particular is a potential casualty here, since the increasing dominance of written work within schools may mean that teachers come to regard those activities which are centrally concerned with speaking as an unaffordable luxury.

However, there is another, more positive, way of considering the introduction of a national curriculum. Although, by its very nature, such a curriculum would seem to encourage conformity rather than creativity and innovation, its effect may be – conversely and paradoxically – to encourage teachers to innovate, and to exploit rather than to suppress difference within its strictures. We hope this is so, for this leads us to a strong justification for teaching the skills of argument, namely that such work is likely to counter the effects of doctrinaire frameworks both within institutions of learning and elsewhere. In this regard, it is important to note that when we teach people to think, to reason and to argue well, we are preparing them not only for successive levels of education but also to take on the demanding role of critical, informed and reflective citizenship in the society to which they belong, as well as in the wider world. We offer *Competing and Consensual Voices* as a contribution to both these endeavours.

1 Situating the Teaching and Learning of Argumentation Within Historical Contexts

MAUREEN DALY GOGGIN

Consider the following two vignettes which are drawn from actual cases:

Elaine stops by her English instructor's office; she is confused. Having completed college composition with high marks last semester, she has just received her first major written assignment back from her philosophy professor. It is a ten-page, well documented research paper that was given a grade of D−. The end comment reads: 'Your grade would have been an F if you hadn't provided evidence of so much work. This paper is not up to college-level standards of writing.'

John is a first-semester graduate student in a doctoral programme in linguistics. Fresh out of an MA in literature programme from which he graduated with a grade point average of A, he has just been handed back his first paper from a linguistics seminar. It received a grade of D. The end comment reads: 'This is not acceptable writing in linguistics.'

What do professors in philosophy, linguistics, history, anthropology, engineering or any of the disciplines housed in our academic institutions mean when they say, 'My students can't write'? Similarly what do business, industry and government leaders mean when they say, 'My employees are poor writers'? Perhaps central to many of these assessments are the expectations that some professors and some leaders have for what it means to write in their fields, expectations that have been historically conditioned by their participation in their respective areas. Their complaint should probably be rephrased as 'My students can't write qualitative ethnographic anthropological research studies' or 'My employees can't write effective environmental planning reports'. Such rephrasing would acknowledge that discursive practices – both within and outside the academy – are not monolithic. Rather, discursive practices are multiple, dynamic and at times conflicting because they are both constructed by and responses to particular contexts.

This chapter is concerned with the interaction between discursive practices and different contexts that vary across time and place. In particular, it addresses the learning and teaching of argumentation, and especially of argumentation within disciplines, for most disciplinary discourse emerges from a discipline's efforts at case-building. My arguments are grounded in the assumption that discursive practices are learned dynamic social processes that are shaped by a complex constellation of social, political, cultural, rhetorical and historical forces (Foucault, 1972; LaCapra, 1983). Furthermore, I assume that these practices are bi-directional; that is, discourse is both shaped by and in turn shapes these multi-dimensional constellations. These assumptions hold practical consequences for the way argumentation should be studied and taught. My purpose is to explore the role that multi-levelled historical perspectives can contribute to the learning and teaching of argumentation.

This chapter argues that the study and teaching of argumentation needs to be informed by three intersecting historical perspectives: a macro-plane, a meso-plane, and a micro-plane. The macro-plane is concerned with the history of a context. For example, to appreciate and perhaps comprehend the pluralistic discursive practices within and across disciplines in American universities requires an understanding of how various types of academic institutions, disciplines, faculty and students have changed and become more diversified over time since the rise of the modern university at the turn of the century (Hofstadter & Metzger, 1955; Novick, 1988; Rudolph, 1990, 1977; Veysey, 1965). The meso-plane is concerned with the personal histories of participants in a particular context (e.g. in the case of a class, this plane would consider the histories of the instructor and the students). The third plane, the micro-plane, is concerned with the immediate history of a given context (e.g. the duration of a particular class).

Most of my discussion centres on the practices of academic disciplinary discourses in American post-secondary education because it is an area with which I am most familiar. Yet, disciplinary specific criteria for good writing is not restricted to post-secondary education; it affects how writing is learned and taught throughout the whole educational system, albeit somewhat less distinctly in the earlier years. As the discussion below will demonstrate, the ways in which teachers are trained and the kinds of discursive practices they control influence their construction and evaluation of class assignments. (Also see Wilson & Wineburg, 1988). Moreover, the arguments posed here transcend specific geographical locations precisely because they try to account for how spatial and temporal contexts affect they way discursive practices are learned and taught.

Disciplinary Discourses

Research on writing across the disciplines has demonstrated that what distinguishes one disciplinary academic community from another is not merely its body of knowledge but also its ways of knowing and its modes of discourse (e.g. Bazerman, 1988; Reither, 1985; Russell, 1991; Wise, 1980). Disciplines differ from one another in their assumptions about what topics, problems or issues are worthy of study, which methods are valid to carry out these studies, what information or which techniques need to be justified and which can be assumed as axiomatic, and which rules of evidence and conventions for arguing claims are appropriate. Thus, not only *what* (content) gets said but *how* (rhetorical dimension) it gets said varies greatly across disciplines. Disciplinary practices and disciplinary discourse are synergistically related. This relationship has been explored by researchers such as Karen Tracy (1988), Diane Dowdey (1992), and Sally Mitchell (1992). For example, in studying the nature and function of questions posed in Sixth Form (16–19 year olds) English, Maths, History, Politics, and Sociology classes, Mitchell (1992: 15) came 'to see them [the questions] as at least partial clues to the way the disciplines function, the assumptions about knowledge on which they operate'.

What complicates research and pedagogy on writing in the disciplines is that epistemological and discursive diversity exist not only *across* disciplines but also *within* disciplines. As Kenneth Ruscio (1987: 333) has argued, 'though institutional boundaries conveniently demarcate clusters of academics, the situation is actually more complicated. There is diversity within diversity as different types of professionals exist side by side in the same setting.' Ruscio's argument is supported by Reiff and Kirscht's (1992) study of the inquiry processes of members from social sciences, natural sciences, and the humanities. Their study shows that the process of academic inquiry is dynamic, shifting along personal and disciplinary lines, with individual scholars and researchers often crossing disciplinary boundaries to pursue their research questions (cf. Klein, 1993). These kinds of hybrid moves across fields account in part for the growing diversity within fields.[1]

Complicating the academicscape even more is that in addition to the horizontal diversity *across* and *within* various disciplines is a vertical diversity that spreads through time. Sally Mitchell (1992: 29) makes a similar point when she argues that 'the boundaries [between disciplines] are neither immutable nor timeless but are cultural constructs subject to the effects of choice and change'. The same may be said about disciplinary discursive practices, for it is through an ongoing dialectical process that disciplinary discourse conventions gain institutional acceptance and, thus, author/itative force. As these conventions become accepted, they become sedimented and give the illusion of being fixed and permanent (cf. Gee, 1989; Harré, 1989). Yet, these practices are in continual flux as disciplines shift and reconfigure over time.

Macro-plane

It is this vertical diversity – the historical discontinuities and shifts in disciplines and their discursive practices – which comprises the historical *macro-plane*. Yet there are few histories, particularly of disciplines, that explore the dynamic relationship between discursive practices and contexts. Certainly, a number of histories have been written about various disciplines. However, these have largely been intellectual histories or histories of ideas, concerned with mapping out schools of thoughts, what Wise (1980) calls the 'isms' of history (e.g. Romanticism, Modernism, Positivism). What is problematic about these historical accounts is that they are largely static, compartmentalising and decontextualising major theories, conceptions, institutions and participants. I argue that in their place we need more dynamic histories that account for the discursive interaction between the members of a discipline and a discipline's doctrines, practices, and discourses.

Understanding the historical forces that have influenced the various paths a discipline has taken and the kinds of discourses it practices permits a more sensitive understanding of discourse conventions as adjudicated and flexible. Consider, for example, the discipline of history as it has emerged in American universities. From its inception as an academic field at the turn of the century, history in America has moved back and forth between two conflicting domains in the American academy, namely, the humanities and the social sciences. At first lodged within the parent organisation for the humanities, the American Council of Learned Societies, the American Historical Association left in 1924 to join with other academic associations in the newly formed Social Science Research Council. Throughout this century, as Peter Novick (1988) shows, historians have drawn on a wide range of conceptual frameworks and methodologies, including those from the social sciences (anthropology, economics, political science, psychology, and sociology), from the humanities (language studies, literary criticism, philosophy, and poetics), and from statistics and mathematics (cf. Stone, 1979). As a result, the field of history comprises a number of competing schools of thought and discursive practices.

Gene Wise (1980: 126) points out that these 'schools [of thought] are not inherent in the nature of history; they're created from an on-going dialogue between the materials of historical interpretation and the minds of the scholars who seek to order these materials.' The schools and the discourses they privilege overlap, then, in complex ways. Some historians may share assumptions about reality but not about knowledge or about the appropriate routes of investigation. Others may share methods but not notions about the nature of reality. Because historians vary across ontological, epistemological, and methodological lines, the topography of historiography is richly complex. As Albert Cook (1988: 16) has noted, 'History writing, like philosophy, is not a discourse that conforms just to canons of a literary genre, "historiography". Beyond its literary canons, and in a sense logically prior to them, history writing conforms to its conditions of inquiry.' Given the pluralistic conditions of inquiry in history, it is not surprising that the historian's rhetorical task is conceived in a number of different, and often contradictory, ways by various practitioners in the field.

Tracing one discursive form against the historical background of a particular discipline brings the historical relationship between disciplinarity and discourse into sharper focus. Consider, for example, the emergence of the experimental research article in psychology. Charles Bazerman (1988) has traced the rise of this genre from the turn of the century through to its current codification in the *Publication Manual of the American Psychological Association (APA)*. His study demonstrates how the discourse conventions for experimental research articles have shifted markedly several times over the last one hundred years. Each discursive shift reflects the assumptions governing the dominating *Zeitgeist* of psychology at the time.

First, as psychology moved from a philosophical enterprise to an experimental one at the end of the nineteenth century, the form of the articles changed slowly from reasoned philosophical explorations to descriptions of experimental studies. Under the influence of associative psychology, the descriptions of experiments shifted over time to descriptions that privileged the subjects of the studies, and the genre began to become more standardised. Later, as behaviourism rose to challenge associative psychology, the conventions for the research reports changed slowly again to a form that objectified the methods, the researchers, and the subjects. Concurrently, the conventions for writing these kinds of articles were being codified in the APA manual, beginning with the first publication in 1929 and reaching a somewhat stable state in the 1950s just at the time behaviourism came to dominate the discipline. Though the manual has expanded in size, little in it has changed since the 1950s.

Bazerman successfully demonstrates that the conventions currently prescribed by the APA manual are grounded in behaviourist assumptions, even though those assumptions have been challenged by social and cognitive psychologists, among others, over the last 20 years. Furthermore, the rigid prescriptive guidelines in the APA manual suggest that psychology is and has been comprised of a homogeneous experimental discourse community, and, of course, it is not nor has it ever been (Royce, 1976). The disjuncture between the assumptions behind the rules governing the form and content of the experimental article and the assumptions driving much of the field suggests that not only is there a time lag between disciplinary discourse conventions and the prescriptive advice that codifies those conventions but prescriptive advice is itself misleading and misrepresentative.[2]

Of course, not only do discourse conventions change over time but other equally important matters such as which topics, methods, or analyses require extensive justification and which can be assumed to be axiomatic shift dramatically. Consider, for example, the use in psychology and composition research of think-aloud protocols and verbal reports in which subjects verbalise their thoughts as they work on an assigned task. Early on, cognitive psychologists and composition researchers had to devote a great deal of discourse space to argue the validity and usefulness of such measures, especially in the face of challenges from behaviourists in their communities. In the early 1980s Ericsson and Simon (1984) devoted an entire book to defending and demonstrating the validity of think-aloud protocols. Today, some 10 years later, cognitive psychologists and cognitive rhetoric researchers are devoting less and less space to the justification of such process tracing tools.

Disciplinary histories reveal that these shifts and discontinuities are generational, overlapping in sometimes subtle but always important and complex ways (Messer-Davidow et al., 1993). That is, one set of researchers (or one way of knowing) does not simply displace another set but emerges alongside and overlaps other sets. Consider, for example, that many of the prominent cognitive psychologists and social psychologists researching today were trained in behaviourist psychology. Consider also, for example, Albert Einstein who was never able to accept quantum physics – a set of theories his own work made possible. As he himself admitted, he was at a disadvantage as compared with his students who conceived of quantum physics, for he was not born into an Einsteinian world but into a Newtonian one. Finally, consider that while we are in a post-modern, post-structural, post-positivistic world, many of our theorists (e.g. Foucault, Derrida, Bakhtin) were trained in a modern, structural, positivistic world. It will take their students to challenge their post-modern assumptions and to conceive of a post-post modern, post-post structural, post-post positivistic world.

Conceiving of the *macro-plane* as a series of multiple and dynamic overlapping shifts and disruptions brings us to the next level, the *meso-plane*, for the *macro-plane* is, of course, comprised of layers of *meso-planes*.

Meso-plane

The *meso-plane* is concerned with the individual personal histories of participants in a particular context (e.g. teachers, students and researchers in a discipline). This plane permits us to consider why a student who consistently received high marks in composition one semester received a D on her first paper in a philosophy class the following semester and is told that she does not know how to write an argument, or similarly why a student who received his MA in English literature with an A grade-point average received a D on his first paper for a PhD class in linguistics.

Students unfamiliar with the paradigmatic ways of constructing meaning or arguing as authorised by a particular disciplinary community may at times construct written arguments that seem oddly inappropriate. Yet, simply instructing students in the conventions of a given disciplinary community is probably not adequate enough for making them conversant in those conventions. Rather than learning a static set of rules or conventions, mastering the discourse of an academic community involves learning the processes of how to think, know, and interact discursively within that community. Learning in a discipline, in other words, requires gaining a certain fluency in the ways of thinking and in the ways of discoursing in that field.

The socio-linguist and literacy theorist James Gee (1989: 7) explains that for him 'being "trained" as a linguist meant that [he] learned to speak, think, and act like a linguist, and to recognize others when they do so'.

More than just *learning* about linguistics and its discourses, Gee explains that he had to *acquire* its discourse. Gee's distinction is an important one. Learning involves becoming cognisant of the rules, conventions, and theories; it is knowledge *about* a subject or a discourse. By contrast, acquiring involves becoming enculturated into a discourse; it is knowledge *of* a discourse. Knowledge *about* (or meta-knowledge of) a discourse does not guarantee that one will master or become literate in that discourse. Conversely, one may acquire a discourse but have little or no meta-knowledge *about* the discourse.

The key to the complexity of the acquisition process lies in understanding what Gee means by *discourse*. Gee (1989: 6–7) argues that we all engage in several 'Discourses'. Discourses 'with a capital "D" ... are ways of being in the world; they are forms of life which integrate words, acts, values, beliefs, attitudes and social identities'. Gee's definition of discourse as a multi-dimensional cluster of speaking, acting, believing, and identifying opens up a far more powerful explanatory space than a one-dimensional view of discourse as structural or functional stretches of language does.[3] He distinguishes between what he calls *primary Discourse,* which is the first Discourse acquired through primary socialisation, and *secondary Discourses,* which are acquired through other social institutions or collectives outside the home. Depending on one's experiences, some of these discourses may overlap in ways of saying-doing-being-valuing-believing and others may conflict with one another. Gee's theory provides a useful frame for understanding the dynamism of the multiple disciplinary discourses, which are, to use Gee's phrase, *secondary Discourses.*

Accepting that disciplinary discourses are multi-dimensional and are acquired practices has important implications for the teaching and learning of argumentation. First, as teachers we have been trained in particular kinds of discourses and not in others. Our experiences lead us to ask and value particular kinds of questions, to use particular methods, and to write in particular ways. How we construct assignments and how we later evaluate the ways these are carried out are affected by the kinds of discourses we have been inducted into and continue to practice. Second, the ways in which our students interpret our writing assignments and construct written arguments are contingent upon the discourses in which they have been trained.

In studying the relationships between the context of a graduate seminar in education and its writing assignments, Paul Prior (1991) concludes that the professor's design and evaluation of the writing assignments and the students' negotiation of those assignments occurred in a complex, multi-dimensional context involving the personal histories, socialisation, and disciplinary enculturation of all the participants. That is, what the professor and the students brought to the class by way of discourses, beliefs and experiences affected how they engaged in the discursive practices of the class, and specifically, in writing assigned research proposals and critiques. Similarly, a year-long case study of a first-year graduate student in a doctoral-level rhetoric programme at Carnegie Mellon University points to how the student's personal history influenced how he interpreted and completed writing assignments, and how at times these interpretations clashed with his professors' expectations (Berkenkotter *et al.*, 1988).

Meso-plane histories may permit us a better understanding of these clashes. A recent study of writing in the disciplines conducted by the Center for the Study of Writing at Carnegie Mellon University provides additional evidence for why *meso-plane* histories are important (Spivey *et al.*, 1992). The Center conducted a cross-sectional survey study of faculty and first-year, third-year, and graduate students in psychology to examine how each group conceived of and experienced writing in their discipline. Undergraduate students were asked to explain why they thought their psychology professors assigned writing in their courses; conversely, graduate students and professors were asked to explain the purpose and function of the writing assignments they used in their psychology courses. Most of the students reported that they believed their professors assigned writing for epistemic purposes, to help them learn the material of psychology better. By contrast, most of the professors reported that they assigned writing to help their students learn how to think and write like psychologists, to enculturate their students into psychology.

To gain an understanding of the participants' knowledge of various genres of writing in psychology, they were asked to list all the kinds of writing that psychologists do. Professors and graduate students produced the most comprehensive lists, naming more than 24 different kinds of writing, ranging across research, theoretical, pedagogical, professional and popular genres. Undergraduates identified over half of these same genres which suggested that they had some meta-knowledge about some of the kinds of writing in which professionals in psychology engage. Participants were then asked to list all of the types of writing they had done in the discipline. The professors and graduate students reported having written in most of the genres they had previously named. By contrast, very few of the undergraduates reported having written in *any* of the genres named for their courses in psychology. All but two of the first-year students reported having only written academic research essays – a nebulous genre that is not even part of the disciplinary activity in the field of psychology.

Although a handful of third-year students reported having written empirical research reports in their classes, almost all of them reported that they had also primarily written research essays. Moreover, most of the students did not frame their responses in terms of genres of writing (though they were well aware of various genres) but in terms of paper topics (e.g. 'a paper on issues of co-dependency in chemically dependent families'). This kind of answer suggested that almost all of the undergraduate students held a monolithic view of academic writing (i.e. academic writing is all one genre), seeing course-related writing as separate and distinct from the kinds of writing done by disciplinary members.

The students' responses, then, pointed to a great gulf between what undergraduates knew of genres in psychology and what undergraduates were actually writing in their psychology courses. This gulf is problematic given the professors' reported goals for assigning writing in their courses. Clearly, there was a disjuncture between the reasons professors gave for assigning writing in their classes (*enculturation*) and the kind of writing students reported having completed in those courses (*epistemic*). How can this disjuncture be explained? It may be that some of the professors had indeed designed writing assignments to enculturate their students, that is, designed assignments in one of the genres of psychology, but that their students were not yet well enough steeped in the discourse to interpret the assignments as such. Or it may be that some of the professors fell back on their own experiences as undergraduates and designed the ubiquitous academic essay or term paper. Or it may be that there was some combination of the two. Whatever the reasons, it is clear that most of these undergraduates had not had any experience writing in any of the genres in psychology that they could name. In other words, they had some meta-knowledge of some of the various discourses in psychology, but they evidently had not had the kinds of experiences needed to acquire these discourses.[4]

Thus, while students may be aware of various forms of writing, they may not be able yet to construct those forms, and may therefore construct arguments that are very different from what the professor expects. These brief illustrations suggest that as teachers we need to examine our own goals for assigning and studying disciplinary discourse; we need to look closely at our expectations for writing assignments and at how our personal history has shaped our expectations. At the same time, we need to consider how our students' personal histories have shaped their interpretations of our assignments. We need, in other words, to become more self-reflexive in the classroom. These *meso-plane* histories may in turn help us to understand the next plane, the *micro-plane* (e.g. what goes on over the course of a semester).

Micro-plane

While the *macro-plane* and the *meso-plane* permit important insights into the constellation of forces that work to shape discourse, there may be a temptation to see the forces as uni-directional, a view that is often promoted by a social constructionist theory of discourse. However, such a view cannot account for the changes – the shifts, the anomalies, the disjunctures – in history. If the process were simply one of social forces shaping individuals and their discourse, there would be only a circular pattern of reproduction; there could be no change. Historical change can only be accommodated by a theory that accounts for a reciprocal relationship between discursive practices and contexts. In other words, a bi-directional model of discourse and context is needed to explain how conventions (e.g. argumentative patterns) change. The *micro-plane* permits a way of examining the dynamic interaction between individuals and contexts as these individuals negotiate conventions and adjust them to construct their arguments. It is this plane that permits an understanding of how those practices are put into action.

Throughout life, an individual may acquire a number of discourses. The various *discourses* an individual controls may at times work against each other as values, beliefs, and attitudes conflict from one to the other. Thus, Joseph Harris (1989) argues that we ought not view discourse communities as homogeneous discourse groups. Classrooms, for example, are not composed of two coherent and contradictory discourses – that of teacher/academic discourse and that of students/non-academic discourse – but rather of many conflicting and overlapping discourses. The cacophony of discourses – what Bakhtin (1981) has termed *heteroglossia* – may be played out in a range of contradictions and intersections. It is at these points of intersection that the bi-directionality of discourse may manifest itself. And so it is to these points that we need to turn our attention.

Recently, researchers have begun to examine the dynamic relationship between individual cognition and the socio-political contextual forces that constrain and shape the rhetorical situation in which the individual constructs meaning (e.g. Hull & Rose, 1989, 1990; Flower *et al.*, 1990, 1993). Long *et al.* (see Chapter 12 of this volume), for example, examine the relationship between academically successful college mentors and inner-city high school students over the course of a semester as they collaborate to produce community documents, tracing the points of conflict and negotiation that emerge as these disparate pairs work together. Other work in socio-linguistics, for instance, also offers some promising directions that will enhance understanding of the dynamism of discursive practices (e.g. Jacoby, 1993). This research suggests that as teachers, we need to help students find strategies that will permit them to negotiate unfamiliar contexts and to recognise those instances when they are confronted with such contexts.

Conclusions

Discursive practices constitute such a complex and complicated phenomenon that no one line of inquiry can possibly address the subject adequately. Multiple vectors of inquiry – rhetorical, sociological, anthropological, psychological, for example – are needed to explore and understand this vital activity. What I offer here is an argument for one methodological vector, namely, an historical one. In mapping out the three intersecting historical planes – macro, meso, micro – I have had to separate them for the purposes of my discussion. These are not, of course, three separate planes but three intricately and dynamically intersecting dimensions. Considered together, they point up the richly complicated and multi-dimensional nature of discursive contexts as intersections of social, political, cultural, rhetorical and historical forces. Taken together, they make salient the dynamic reciprocal relationship between discursive practices and context and help to account for codification and change, for consensus and diversity among participants within shifting contexts, and for multiple approaches to writing assignments students take within and outside our classrooms. Finally, together they raise some issues and directions for research and teaching.

First, on the *macro-plane*, we need to encourage histories that map the discursive practices in various disciplines or other contextual settings. And we need to use these histories to inform how we study and teach argumentation. Second, we need to find ways to map on a *meso-level* our own discursive histories and those of our students. Longitudinal studies and ethnographic techniques point the way but we need to find other methods. We also need, as I have argued above, to become more self-reflexive and we need to help our students to become so. Finally, we need to map on a *micro-level* the histories of our classes to better understand the dynamics of teaching and learning argument in the classroom. While we cannot possibly control all of the diverse kinds of discourses our students will need to master, we can become more sensitive to the ranges of diversity, the conflicting and overlapping of multitudinous discourses, and we can try to find flexible ways to help our students become inducted into various kinds of discursive practices.

Notes

1. The diversity is, of course, not new; it may be expanding somewhat but we are also becoming more sensitive to it. Moreover, the diversity is not and has not been restricted to the human sciences or the humanities but is central to the physical sciences as well. For example, according to Koch (1976: 529):
   None of the currently institutionalized sciences form single, homogeneous language communities. Physicists in one empirical area do not necessarily fully 'understand' physicists in another; pathologists do not necessarily understand electrophysiologists, and so on. And within each scientific area, even when cut rather finely, one may distinguish disorderly 'hierarchies' of language communities: in the extreme case, there may be quite definite and unique observable properties and relations which only two men, perhaps working in the same laboratory, may be able to perceive, and denote by some linguistic expression.
2. In a recent study, cognitive, social, and developmental psychologists were asked how useful they found the *APA Manual*; nearly every respondent wrote disparaging remarks against the manual (Spivey *et al.*, 1992). Given the disjuncture between the current cognitive and socio-cognitive assumptions and behaviourist assumptions, their acrid attacks are perhaps not so surprising.
3. Like Gee, Rom Harré (1993) also problematises the definition of discourse in his functional conception of language as operating on four-dimensions – a temporal manifold, a spatial manifold, a moral manifold, and a social manifold. Elsewhere Harré (1989) argues that rules and conventions are not a priori mechanisms but rather rule-following is a practice that one must be trained in and inducted into. He further argues that the source of a practice is in the forms and customs of a culture; that is, practices are cultural constructs, one of which is discourse.
4. Let me point out that I am not suggesting that all assigned writing in college is discipline-specific. See, for example, Schmersahl and Stay (1992: 142) who interviewed a score of college professors in an American liberal arts college and found that: 'Writing is used in ways that are more imaginative and less discipline-defined than we expected. In fact, much of the writing assigned at our college serves general instructional purposes without conforming to the conventions and practices of specific disciplines.' But I am suggesting that if the function of writing assignments is to introduce students to the ways of knowing and writing in a discipline, then students need to do disciplinary-defined writing tasks. Moreover, even if the purpose of a writing assignment is for 'general instructional purposes', the assessment of that writing may be affected in subtle, but important, ways by the kinds of discursive practices the instructor has been trained in and engages in.

2 Ushering in the Tigers of Wrath: Playfulness and Rationality in Learning to Argue

STEPHEN CLARKE

Introduction: The Terms of Antithesis

The evidence drawn upon in this chapter derives from *Improving The Quality of Argument, 5–16*, a curriculum project, founded upon and developed through the work of teachers in and around Humberside and Lincolnshire, but inspired and run by Richard Andrews and Patrick Costello, at the time, both of them, of Hull University. This project, funded by the Esmée Fairbairn Charitable Trust, was begun in 1991 and its final report was published in March 1993 (Andrews *et al.*, 1993). It worked through teachers from 10 primary and 10 secondary schools who met twice at the university, initially, to think together about how to improve and extend argument work in the primary curriculum generally and in English in the secondary sector. During the next year, in their individual schools, the teachers devised and carried out programmes which fulfilled ideas about the construction and enactment of arguments. My involvement, following work on the topic of argument (Clarke & Sinker, 1992), was as the project evaluator, and in that role I came to understand some of the ways in which the teachers thought about argument; I had also the privilege of seeing what work had been developed with their classes.

The title which I have chosen derives from William Blake, poet and visionary who, when he wrote, as one of the 'Proverbs of Hell' that: 'The tygers of wrath are wiser than the horses of instruction' set up an antithesis between instinct and reason. Whatever ambiguity surrounds the precise educational implications of Blake's saying, tension between the wrathful tigers and the instructive horses seems clear. The tigers are instinctual in their wrath and the horses seem, by contrast, rational, and in their rationality, dull. I draw upon this antithetical image because of its power to illuminate tensions that surround the teaching of argument.

All the teachers who participated in this project required argument to extend the thinking capacities of their pupils, and their abilities as language users. Some also required that it served a further function, not a psychological one, but cultural and political, namely to demonstrate that some issues are necessarily contentious, and thus dependent on argument in order to be properly understood. These two functions are not particularly oppositional, but in order to fulfil one or both several teachers presented their pupils with other people's arguments as having formal properties of their own which could be demonstrated, and thus 'argument' came to mean a kind of cultural artefact rather than an activity. Tension could easily grow between doing and analysing. On another facet, the tension is between modes of encounter that are open-minded, speculative and playful with subject-matter that does not, by its immediacy and seriousness, seem to invite much in the way of a ludic response, or at any rate an extended play of the mind.

Tensions such as these were, I think, felt by some of the teachers involved in the project. My own substitutions for Blake's wrath and instruction, playfulness and rationality, seem tame and abstract compared to their originals, but in that there are antitheses at work, then I want to elucidate what I understand, from the Esmée Fairbairn evidence and experience, are the essential elements of those antitheses. In any case at least one of Blake's tigers can be readily understood as playful, and that is the smiling glass-eyed creature, anything but fearful in its symmetry, used as the accompanying illustration to the poem *Tyger Tyger*. Perhaps this tyger is a classroom version of one of the tygers of wrath, every inch a tiger, but not one to harm a child.

Arguments as Games

Let us start with playfulness. I want to illustrate the achievement of two particular primary teachers within this project, and to see how their work relates to the idea of play. Argument has always been conceived of as an enjoyable language game, although the teachers involved eschewed for the most part the public show elements of the game of argument. In place of that, many of them drew upon the concept of the simulated world, the place or time where arguers can engage with problems that are not immediate, and via personae that release them from a constraining self-consciousness but which allow them to retain their own sense of moral and critical reasoning. Teachers, primary or secondary, have always known that classrooms are value-riven places as well as forums for the clash of personality. From that point of view we can see the importance of setting arguments in simulated, dramatic or playful contexts, places in which you can rehearse the opposition of ideas whilst pretending not to be yourself, free of the constraint to seem, at least, consistent in public. The clash of value-positions is central, but each arguer has an experimental space in which to try out ideas and explore how to formulate a point of view.

When I encountered 10-year-olds arguing about whether or not they should declare war on Germany in their roles as Prime Minister Chamberlain's Cabinet members in 1939, and when they recorded themselves and lent me their tapes, then I saw how play and argument, skilfully linked by the teacher, could do far more than co-exist, but be positively each enriching of the other.

Voice 1 (male):	We made this promise (interruption, 'yeah but ...'). Yeah but we made this promise to Poland and the thing is we can't get out of it. None of us want to declare war, but we just can't get out of it.
Voice 2 (female):	We'll have to do something ...
Voice 1:	We'll have to say, 'get out'.
Voice 2:	Give an ultimatum.
Voice 2:	We can't make Germany think we're weak.
Voice 3:	Why not?
Voice 2:	I mean if we ...
Voice 3:	By not declaring they could think they could get away with it.
Voice 1:	If we, if we declare war on Germany there comes a point, you see, when this could be treacherous because you could kill 40 thousand men, just kill them.
Voice 3:	But maybe people are dying at this moment in Poland.
Various:	Yeah, yeah, that's right.

The pupils enjoyed the element of pretence, relating what they had heard about in other history lessons to the present chance to act important. Their talk developed not only ideas that were oppositional, but developed too the mutuality and social encounters necessary for the production of those ideas, and also an improved understanding of what the dilemmas were that faced the pre-war administration. I do not think that verisimilitude to the precise historical details matters too much in the context of teaching argument like this, any more than it matters whether Shakespeare's *Julius Caesar* reproduces with documentary exactness the events in ancient Rome on the Ides of March. Instead what ought to count should be the strength of argument that derives from speaking in role, the tonal assurance of the statements, the intellectual sharpness of the questions and the degree to which the participants find the issue worthwhile. These criteria are best summed up, perhaps, in the Cox Report, (DES/WO, 1989).

It is when we consider the nature of the assigned roles that we can see how problems can begin or possibilities be created. The Cabinet member quoted above who insists that, 'we made this promise to Poland and the thing is we can't get out of it' has learnt more than simply how to enjoy focusing the minds of his fellow pupils (though that is a good lesson to learn and highly germane to argument). He is determined to persuade a bunch of indecisive colleagues of the size and nature of the threat that they face and of the judgement that history will make on the appeasers of Fascism. Perhaps I push the thesis a little too far , but the speaker at that moment had discovered how to turn his view of an historical moment into a personally endorsed moral position; it was driven by a moral force, or, if you prefer, by a philosophic force, a reminder of what move you make in the language game if you promise something. This is so even if view and moral or philosophic stance are only borrowed for a while and later statements do not seem to be entirely consistent with earlier ones. The matter is so important that the speaker is unlikely merely to say his piece and then dry up (as happened once or twice to different children in other contexts). The Cabinet had begun to explore how to act in the right way and what the likely outcomes of their decisions would be.

The children, aged 10 or 11, think together on the tape, building on each other's contributions but prepared to qualify previous statements as well. Thinking together like this can properly be called arguing in that each member of the group was subjecting the ideas of others to critical thoughts of their own and submitting their own thoughts to critical evaluation by the rest. The simulated meeting might have been more combative if each contributor had been concerned to win, with the aim being to make the rest of the group finally accept his/her original and immovable position. Political debate, after all, can be and often is like this. It is not hard to see how this is commonly regarded as argumentative, but it is not like conversation; it lacks the susceptibility to shared thinking and the resolution of difference. Conversation is essentially about testing ideas rather than thinking how to win against other speakers. The moves may not be oppositional but they can be highly persuasive.

I was most impressed by the boy who sat there, in a different discussion group to the Cabinet, one of a group of four who began by saying, 'You've got to convince me why I should go and fight in Yugoslavia.' This seems to me both excellent practice in learning to argue, in that you are not only argumentative in yourself, but the cause that argument is in others, a kind of Falstaffian dialectician, and, at the same time, a disastrous lesson in how to cope in the real world. Imagine saying, 'You've got to convince me', to the recruiting officer in a time of conscription. I do not think that he would see that statement as the call for a fully argued and rational defence of the concept of a just war! Nevertheless, I have no doubt he might say some very convincing things.

Other occasions and contexts from which we can note the power of playfulness in establishing and creating sustained argument would have to include the extraordinary (I use the word with care) achievement of one teacher and her children. One of the most memorable sights on the series of 18 visits that I made to schools involved in this project was that of one class of 6-year-olds discussing how they were going to survive on a desert island. There they were, sat in a slightly elongated circle, the whole class, listening, talking and concentrating. Nearly everyone joined in, while I was there, 30 to 40 minutes of sustained and relevant discussion in which the infants imagined difficulties, offered solutions, questioned assumptions and stated their abilities to rely on empirical testing when the exigent should come. There were also thoughtful pauses between speeches. However, the most memorable words that day were about a crab's claws. You could chop trees down with them, said one boy, very certain of this. His classmates wanted to know how you could get a claw off the crab, a fully rational as well as moral question, I think. They also wanted to know what use a bent crab's claw was on a tree; a fully rational and empirical question as a follow-up to the moral one.

Despite the 30 to 40 minutes already mentioned, on the day of my visit, I think I did not realise until over a year later quite how extraordinary the capacity of this class was to sustain serious discussion; even though I was impressed by what I saw, I was later to read the evidence of even more acutely argued positions. I understood this finally as a member of Pamela Rose's seminar at the Dissemination Conference of this project, held at Hull University in January 1993 to allow teachers and researchers to see, in a day's lecture and seminar programme, what the Esmée Fairbairn Project had achieved. In that seminar we read the transcript of a different session from the one I saw, and in that transcript the full extent of the children's capacity for sustained thinking became evident. The work was wonderfully managed, and what it fixes from now onwards is a standard (if I dare invoke a term that the educational right tries to monopolise) of how 6-year-olds from ordinary backgrounds are able to discuss. What is present in the transcript of their discussion is argument, a logical series of deductions, a well-derived series of propositions, individual thoughtfulness, an often unsuspected articulacy and logical challenges to a prevailing viewpoint. All are driven by an earnest imaginative entry into this other place, an island, probably tropical, out there in the uncertain and imagined world that borders the known limits and horizons of a 6-year-old's mind, a world dense in possibilities, I think, a kind of layer surrounding the world of their current and previous experience, but a good locus for an argument.

There are two further issues to be defined here, and the first and simpler is that this topic and approach was yet another example of children arguing well when they have been guided by their teachers to something that is worth arguing about, even, in this case, the pretend world of an island. This topic of worthwhileness is a problematic one, of course, since it is not always possible to predict what issues will catch the imagination and concern of a class; but questions deriving from issues of social justice, and problems posited on the existence of sentient as well as thoughtful individuals tended to be the subject of good arguments. Instant topics for debate, or insufficiently realised fictive worlds for role-playing tended to have poorer outcomes. What had gained the attention and respect of these children, what had come to be worth arguing about at such length, was how they should run their affairs on an island, what forms of government and power they should create or allow; behind such questions and suggestions about procedures and structures lay a basic impulse not so different from that which drives and informs Plato's *Republic*.

Games as Provokers of Thinking

It is hard to see quite how this idea of worthwhileness, for all its importance, hooks up with the tigers and the horses; but how about looking at it from this angle? In Blake's horses of instruction we can understand the National Curriculum for English, in England. This was commissioned in its original form, in 1989, under Kenneth Baker, Secretary of State for Education, but a subsequent Secretary of State for Education, John Patten, instructed that the provisions for English were to be revised. The currently proposed revisions (SCAA, 1994a) emphasise correctness in spoken English in a way that the originally proposed National Curriculum in English, known as the Cox Report, did not. The words, 'Argument and debate' are currently listed as a single bullet point in a fusillade of brief statements about a range of purposes for speech, but Cox, in the earlier proposals (DES/WO, 1989) had talked of, for example, trade union meetings and thereby suggested a political world, anticipating the 6-year-olds above. The horses of instruction, hired by the state, have become plough horses, plodders, aiming across a field of endeavour in straight lines that repeat but never cross, flat and level by attainment, neatly planned by an owner in advance, and all ready for the right quantity of instructional seed to be planted. Neither the rhetoric nor the deeper instincts of this proposed revised National Curriculum for English deal in intellectual excitement or in the idea of the conflict of values, perhaps the fierce conflict, about such fundamental issues as how we should govern ourselves and in so doing constitute a just state. If these things can happen as they did, then perhaps official curricula would do well to anticipate them and to signify the greater importance of excited, involved, extended utterances over those with the right kind of formal linguistic markers.

Any national curriculum dealing with the mother tongue must, if it is to be respected, cope with children constructing propositions, wondering out loud, listening to each other with thoughtfulness and criticality, challenging the logic of opponents, attempting to gain and deny power, and generally behaving like political animals. Young political animals play at ideas much as their elders and betters do, and like the adults they speak, at times, for no better reason than to gain power and to assert their authority. Insofar as the playing is almost entirely constituted in speaking, and insofar as the nature of the speech acts is such that it brings about the kind of intellectual and social development that probably is not happening at home (if only because children do not get together in groups of 30 in order to conduct formal arguments), then the nature of the speaking requires a framework in which to be valued, or evaluated, and in which due recognition can be set for what the children have achieved, in arguing. What this project provided are profoundly valuable examples of young children's speech, based on the subtlety and intellectual strength of their best attainments. It is around these that curriculum discourse needs to be constructed, not around context-free instances of correct and incorrect speech.

I say this not because I think that we have in general underestimated the speech abilities of young children, but the kind of evidence that Tizard and Hughes (1984) presented some years ago about home and school speech differences left me wondering whether school had as much capacity to develop the speaking of young children as parents did; some of the replies to well-meant questions on the teacher's part were very brief. This project left me wanting to make serious claims on behalf of the school. Argument, taught as it was with this class of infants, had the power to extend connected and logical thinking even at this tender and robust age. Fundamentally what these debates were doing was teaching the children to converse, not just with parent or teacher, but with one another, and thus to think together.

So much for worthwhileness. The other important element in this work that I need to draw attention to is that of the power of imagination, a common enough item in the rhetoric of junior school education, but in its softer varieties unsupportive of the concentrated, focused and cerebral activity which characterised the children's approach in this class. The teacher had, I think, presented the idea of this island by shaping her class's discussions so that their imaginative efforts could bring it closer to the prospect of belief. After all, only when the place had been imaginatively (and incidentally, in model form) constructed, and only when the possibility of survival on it had been established could discussions start to grow about how best to order and govern it. I am not necessarily saying that the first activity, giving the place a local habitation if not an actual name, was less argumentative than the second, talking about government, or that the second was less imaginative than the first, but in general terms we can agree that argument can be properly rooted in imaginative ground. Argument and imagination, in this case as in Blake's, were close allies, and though this alliance may also need to be understood in terms of playfulness and logic, we can see in the teacher's work how each drew upon and contributed to the other. If this sounds a little bit heavy on description rather than encounter, then let me ground my argument in a reminder of how these children argued:

William (talking of democracy) : *I don't think that's a very good idea because if people had silly ideas, what would you do then? What if everybody didn't have good ideas? If everybody didn't agree with each other, what would you do then? What would you do without a boss? Suppose you didn't have one, all you'd be able to do is, everybody would be arguing. Everybody would think they had better ideas than everybody else. They'd always be arguing.*

Ironic, is it not, that in lessons devoted to argument, the prospect of eternal argument seems hellish, but perhaps that is only true in the mind of a would-be boss. Someone else, unnamed, in the transcript, but possibly lacking a sense of the ironic, replies: *I agree with you.*

So far, in pointing to two projects, I have listed how playfulness and an imaginative approach created and sustained good learning of argument, though in one case the instruction of history was present, and in both cases the statements were as rational as one could hope for. I could add to my list by recounting how history was taught in another school through argument and role-play, how indeed the playful and the instructional were combined; but there are limits on space. I do not, in fact, wish to suggest that all the teaching of argument could or should be as simple, directly playful, or humorous as the two examples relied upon so far, examples of arguing which I have tried to render as versions of a pedagogic Eden, spaces in which the tigers and the horses are at one, lying down together. The degree, however, to which full seriousness, rationality and playfulness were united was remarkable, and is surely well worth repeating in different versions and in other contexts.

Games, Real States and Rationality

Richard Andrews (1992) wrote, concerning the Fairbairn project, about the effects of the differences in traditions between primary and secondary schools, something which the project was well able to illuminate. Although I subscribe entirely to what Andrews said about the relatively contained modes shaping the work in secondary schools, I want to suggest that if we dwell for a while on what a primary and a secondary school shared and had in common, we can see how these different curricular traditions shared in the solution of the difficulties that are faced by any teacher who sets her pupils to grapple with a problem that is subject to contention in the world outside school as well as within it.

If we compare the work in a Hull secondary school with that of a primary school in Lincoln then we can see the validity, yet again of tackling issues that the pupils found worthwhile, and some of the difficulties too, in working outside the fictive, and inside the immediate and fully political realm of rights. In the work on animal rights that went on in Hull, we noted that some of the pupils were unable to play very freely with ideas that came too close to offering a threat to the kinds of animals of which they were fond. From that point of view not only was the playfulness inappropriate as far as the arguers were concerned, but so was the rationality within the debate also under threat. An issue close to home is not so easily taken up as a simulated re-enactment from history whose outcome is known. This suggests that there is all the more need for argument, perhaps, in an area that our society finds difficult to resolve; the children of a democracy need to try to understand the contentiousness of things. The two secondary teachers, working together for this special summer term project, opened up by their skill a space for thinking, free of unresolvable contention and immediate or personal conflict.

Some of the sharpest minds among the 12- and 13-year-olds were able to formulate strongly rational questions. David Bellamy, a popular television enthusiast for the scientific study of the natural world, was seen on a video, shown to the class, to defend scientific testing of medicines on laboratory animals. The boy who wanted to know whom Bellamy included in his significant category 'all' and who quoted his line from the video, 'All I want all of us to do is live without pain and die without pain', had used his scepticism to good effect as an arguer. If animals were not included in 'all of us' then Bellamy's formulation and sympathies were inadequate. For other pupils, equally sceptical about the pro-experimental line conveyed by Bellamy, such articulation was less obvious. I do not remember hearing it to quite the same quality, but it takes a while to discover that you may as well listen hard to an argument you dislike because it will probably contain flaws. You can call that attentiveness and detection a cognitive strategy, or *pace* Postman and Weingartner (1971), crap detection; but how you teach that is what we need to look at next.

One of the teachers strove to persuade the class to look at the quality of argument being offered from different and conflicting sources, from pro- and anti-experimentation groups, and the other encouraged them immediately they had finished watching Bellamy's video, to ask questions. In the example of Roy, quoted above, we see the synthesis of both teachers' approaches. Looking at the nature of other people's arguments and asking questions, as opposed positively to formulating a position, amounts not so much to a kind of detachment from the immediate and hard-to-resolve nature of the issues, as to a suspension from having to find an answer. It also helps to show how arguments are about words. They are not exactly playful moves, these teacher strategies, but they are rational, critical, aimed at continuation and openness, and very much predicated upon the idea that what is essential for the construction of classroom debate is the quality of individual thinking. No formulas are given as to the form of outcome; you do not have to make your speech moves in any particular genre and the category 'questions' is wide enough to be, in effect, an encouraging space rather than a prescription. These teacher strategies, then, could be highly instructive, showing the pupils how to think. Neither teacher seeks to effect a result, answer, resolution or closure. I am not sure what follows from this except to note that this form of classroom argument-game is signally different from the form of the essay; the speaker debates but the writer concludes. How the individual writer carries over the speaking into the writing, the openness into closure is a key area, I think, for further research.

Possibly a parallel issue in a primary school to that of animal rights in the secondary sector is that of bullying. This issue, taken up in a Lincolnshire primary school, like the other, looks towards action as an outcome. In both cases an injustice is addressed, and what might emerge from the debate is the idea that cruelty cannot be tolerated. Perhaps from the pupils' perspective, argument would be secondary to a practical outcome; it is perhaps more important to stop bullying or cruelty to animals than to argue about them. However, in a rational world the children could see the benefit of discussion preceding action, so that quite what constituted bullying could be established and defined, and then what was the right course of remedial action could be equally the subject of debate. They were constructing a rational world in the course of arguing. In both contexts, secondary and primary, the issues generated considerable spoken argument in class, were felt to be important by teachers in developing thinking within the pupils, and in both cases writing as well as speaking was seen as appropriate in terms of its capacity to further this thinking. What they have in common too is that the issues were seen by the arguers to be fairly urgent, yet in each case the teachers constructed ways of working that showed the pupils how to broaden their thinking and construct through it something of the full complexity of what was involved in coming to a decision about how to act.

The Lincolnshire children had, when they came to discuss bullying, weeks of experience of talking about such problems as whether someone who kicked a football over a fence should buy its owner a new one. This preparedness to reason through everyday problems had been instructive at the level of thinking calmly, of reflecting on the emotional elements within the argument and of needing to consider feelings in any interactive situation. It is not like a game in that there is no element of pretence or simulation, but, in more than adequate compensation for the lost fun element, this approach allows a greater understanding of how complex the world is compared with any simulated version of it. All the same, I want to argue, the notion of playfulness remains important even in this kind of context and discussion. The seriousness of the issues, coupled with the wisdom and sensitivity of the teaching, opens up a breadth and depth of thinking that must have given the children pleasure in discovering that what is difficult can be fascinating. The act of clarifying what bullying is emerges from the data (the speaking and the writing) as something greatly significant. It is hard to think that such reflections on the experience of seeing bullying or being bullied, can do other than help individual children at the level of self-esteem. Argument, sensitively handled, can illuminate not only unresolved social problems, but painful experiences on the part of individuals.

Conclusion: Resolving the Antitheses

I have drawn upon two examples that utilise the directly playful, but in a fictional or imagined world and two examples which show equally well conducted and well constructed arguments, but which are less obviously based upon a simulated version of reality. These essential differences, between topics for argument being presented in a simulated context, and topics presented in actuality, can in fact form categorical headings for nearly all the work that I saw in progress as evaluator of the project. I raise the question of the distinction here partly because I wish to suggest that it is a theme for further exploration and partly because so much work in English in any case is grounded in the study of literary texts, and thus, if they are fictional texts, in a secondary world. Where I think we need to go next, immediately, in developing argument in English, is with study of, or at any rate engagement with, written argument as an art form.

I have written elsewhere (Clarke, 1994) about the nature of the relationship between reading and argument, but, in few words, we need our understanding of what it is to argue to be deepened and broadened by encounters with the passionate coolness of Swift, the absurd logic of Groucho Marx, and the strange poetics of visionaries who paint tigers that contradict their word-portraits. All this invocation of playfulness has not been in advocacy of the trivial or faintly amusing; we need to see how, for the children, the compelling issues are not necessarily best explored through the most sensible modes of writing. In the projects I have described each of the issues is acutely important, yet the treatments of these topics can, to great point, involve the sustained dwelling on them through the structure of a game.

3 Narrative in Argument, Argument in Narrative

MIKE BAYNHAM

In this chapter I approach argument through its relation to narrative. I take two perspectives. The first has a practical orientation and relates to the role of spoken language in adult literacy and to the extension of the repertoire of adult writers in the more public discourses of which argument is one. It may seem odd to include development and extension of spoken language as one of the aims of an adult literacy programme, but in fact time after time, the gains self-reported by adult literacy students include not only gains in reading and writing but also increased confidence in participating in public discussion and debate, where argument is clearly a key component.

My second perspective relates to an interest in understanding oral narrative from a linguistic point of view, not just in the relatively well understood internal textual organisation of narrative, but in the ways that narrative functions in wider discourse contexts. What are the purposes to which narrative can be put in ongoing discourse, and in particular in the rhetorical staging of argument?

I will be drawing on the work of Kress (1989: 12) which treats narrative and argument as two distinct modes of cultural textual organisation:

> Argument provides, in culture-specific textual forms, the means for bringing difference into existence. At the same time, it provides conventionalized textual forms not just for maintaining and tolerating difference, but for culturally productive use of difference. Yet where there is only difference, the cultural group cannot attain stability, cannot reproduce itself or its values. Narrative, as a textual form, provides means of resolution of difference, of reproducing, in an uncontentious mode, the forms and meanings of a culture. Narrative serves as a major means of the reproduction of social and cultural forms

and values.

Narrative, in other words, is a form whose fundamental characteristic is to produce closure; argument is the form whose fundamental characteristic is to produce difference and hence openness.

While it has been convincingly argued (e.g. Andrews, 1989; Kress, 1989) that narrative and argument are two distinct modes of discourse which should not be conflated, it has equally been argued that these modes of discourse are frequently interrelated in textual practice. Narrative can count as argument and argument can be seen to have narrativity or narrative features. According to Parret (1987: 165):

> Nobody can deny that argumentation and narrativity overlap in many sequences of discourse, and that there are units of fictional, poetic, scientific and philosophical discourses as well as of everyday language that can be interpreted from the argumentative and the narratological point of view. On the one hand, there is without any doubt in many contexts argumentation in narrative: protagonists in stories argue within dialogues, conversations; dialogical and conversational sequences in narratives are dominated by argumentative motives and moves; and it makes surely sense to put the problem of argumentation in narrative communication (communication by means of narratological units). On the other hand, there seems to be narrativity in argumentation as well.

Hill and Zepeda (1993: 212) echo this when they ask in a study of narrative and argument in oral language: 'Why do argumentative moves often include embedded narrative?'

Labov and Fanshel (1977: 105), who analysed the discourse of a therapy session, had this to say about the function of narrative in the ongoing therapeutic discourse:

> The fact that many narratives carry with them their own justification does not mean that they can be introduced into a conversation at any point. In the therapeutic sessions that we will observe, narratives play a tightly integrated role in the conversation, and they function as equivalent to such single speech acts as *response, putting off a request, challenge* and so forth. Frequently their function is as responses, refusals, challenges, or whatever is enhanced by their evaluative or affective central point: a request that the patient turn to her aunt for help will be rejected by an anecdote showing that the aunt's behaviour is extraordinarily, astonishingly, incomprehensibly unreasonable.

Narrative here is a move in a dialogic argument sequence.

In this chapter I will try to ask 'how' and 'why' questions about the interpenetration of narrative and argumentative modes: how does argument operate in narrative, how do narrative and narrativity features function in argument and, by extension, why are these effects rhetorically powerful? These questions take us beyond the traditional view of narrative as supplying 'vividness' to argument. It is here that I think concepts like *evidence, authority, authorisation* and *regime of truth* in discourse are useful. The concept of 'regime of truth' that I am drawing on derives from the work of Foucault (1980: 131):

> Each society has its regime of truth, its 'general politics' of truth: that is, the types of discourse which it accepts and makes function as true; the mechanisms and instances which enable one to distinguish between true and false statements; the means by which each is sanctioned; the techniques and procedure accorded value in the acquisition of truth; the status of those who are charged with saying what counts as true.

The regime of truth construct raises related issues of truth, evidence, authorisation and authority in discourse – who is authorised to speak what is held to be the truth in a given context? Whilst Foucault examines how regimes of truth are constructed in discourses like medicine, the law, education, in this chapter I shift the focus a little, and ask: how do speakers/writers construct truth claims in discourse?

The following example is taken from the argumentative front-line of family life. Tom, a 7-year-old is leaving the house to go to school with a large plastic dinosaur given to him by his friend Theo, in his school bag. In the past a number of precious things have been taken to school and lost; the school has also made it clear that children should not bring toys. Dad therefore attempts to head off Tom's move and the exchange is played out as follows:

Dad: I don't want you to take Theo's dinosaur to school.
Tom: Theo did.

What makes Tom's move a powerful one, an argument within the power play of family relations? One of the reasons is that he introduces as fact a proposition that contradicts the directive, a proposition which is authorised by his own knowledge and experience. Tom's response shifts the exchange into another mode, that of narrative, in which factuality and authorisation (this is my experience not yours) constitute the epistemological space.

Tom's 'Theo did' can be seen as what Eco (1979) calls a 'virtual narrative'; it has the potential for expansion into a fully played out narrative: e.g. 'When Theo took his dinosaur to school, the teacher didn't say anything, he didn't lose it, etc. etc.'. In terms of the exchange structure, Tom's response counts as a move which rejects or challenges Dad's directive.

Fairclough (1992: 204–5) in a reanalysis of data from Liebes and Ribak (1991) looks at the ways in which the mother of a family uses narrative to support a critical reading of the news and authorise a position in argument. This is the narrative that Fairclough reanalyses:

As I was saying, no Arab ever threw a stone at me, but some Jew did. On a Shabbat I got hit by a stone on my car, and they threw a garbage bin at me, and they almost jumped at us; she's [*i.e. the daughter*] my witness; here, just next to the house. I believe more in the Arabs than in the religious Jews. I am more afraid of them. I don't know, this is my opinion. In the morning I sit in the kitchen and I hear under my window, 'shabbes!' [*Sabbath*] and 'pritzes!' [*whoring*]; here under this window is the problematic street Yam Suf, and they want to close it [*to traffic on Saturdays*]. If I got into my car I don't know what they would do to me. They would come in the tens and hundreds, and would anybody pay attention? So they arrest them, and in the evening they let them go. On Lag Ba'omer [*a holiday when bonfires are lit*]: I was at a friend's today, and she told me that she went to see a bonfire in the centre of town, not in Mea She'arim, not Mea She'arim but closer to the centre of town, and she said that the religious started a bonfire there, and burned the Israeli flag.

The speaker uses narrative in complex ways to articulate and support with evidence her argument that the ultra-religious Jewish groups taking various forms of direct action to protest against the breaking of 'Shabbat' are more of a danger to the social fabric than the Arabs. Fairclough points out the different kinds of narratives that are in play, such as the narrative of personal experience, whose evidential claim is that this once happened to the narrator:

On a Shabbat I got hit by a stone.

This narrative is authorised by the narrator as first-hand witness and supported by her daughter ('she's my witness'). The next narrative sequence is again authorised by the narrator as first-person participant, but the evidential claim is here a generalising one (this is what typically happens to me) and the narrative is told in the generic present ('In the morning I sit in my kitchen').

What follows is according to Fairclough a hypothetical narrative: a reconstruction of what would happen if she tried to get into her car on the Shabbat. The concluding narrative is a third-person narrative embedded as reported speech in a first-person narrative. ('I was at a friend's today, and she told me … ') in which the authority of the narrator is supported by the authoritative first-hand account of her friend.

Fairclough in his analysis emphasises the polyvocal, heterogeneous nature of such discourse, in which different voices are interpolated and play off each other. Through these narratives, with their rather different evidential claims, a complex texture is built up which serves to authorise from a number of perspectives the narrator's argument that ultra-orthodox Jews are more of a problem than Arabs.

The argument in narrative, as this example shows, is not always explicit and I think it is useful to think in terms of *virtual arguments,* in the same way that Eco (1979) describes the narrativity of non-narrative texts as their virtual narrative. In the narratives that we will consider, the argument is not always explicit, but remains virtual to be reconstructed pragmatically by the interlocutor. When we come to consider the pedagogical implications of this kind of analysis, I will argue that unpacking and making explicit the virtual argument may be an important component in oral work on argumentative discourse in adult literacy classes.

Argument in Narrative

In this section we will look at argument in narrative, analysing data from both non-educational and educational contexts. The data here will be narratives of everyday experience.

The following text was recorded off air from a radio phone-in on literacy. The caller, who identifies herself as having literacy problems, briefly describes her school experience to the phone-in host:

(Caller = C, Host = H)

C: I couldn't read or write and with those forms you know … worse than a piece of blank paper. But I put the blame on the school where I started. When I was a little girl at school, I was – um – I was taught by how clever you was, you know if you was backward or clever or … you know.

H: Yeah.

C: They taught you by how clever you was. And when I was seven, I had to go to another school and when I went to that one they taught you by your age, you know, how old you was.

H: Hhmm.

C: And from that day even now I still blame the second school what I
started at because instead of teaching by what you knew they didn't
they taught you by your age if you know what I mean.

The caller's argument, which turns on why she did not learn to read and
write at school as a child, is authorised by her personal, autobiographical
experience, which is brought forward as evidence to support her initial
argument statement:

I put the blame on the school where I started.

This explicitly marks the discourse as argument and she then immediately shifts into narrative:

When I was a little girl at school …

The narrative carries a contrast, which is intrinsic to the argument,
between the first school which taught you by how clever you were, and the
second, which taught you by your age (notice the use of the inclusive,
generalising 'you' as a systematic way of creating a certain dialogic
relationship between speaker and audience).

The argument remains virtual. The contrast is not even marked, as it
might be, by the adversative conjunction 'but'. There are of course certain
clues in the discourse texture, not least the striking structural parallelism
between the treatment of the two schools, in terms of grammatical and
lexical repetition. In this juxtaposition of the terms of her argument,
though, there are areas of uncertainty: is she blaming the methods used in
the second school, or the fact of being moved from one school to another?

The argument is concluded within a narrative coda. The coda in Labov's
analysis of narrative (Labov, 1972) signals the conclusion of the narrative,
returning from narrative time to current discourse time and highlights the
significance of the events narrated:

And from that day even now I still blame the second school what I
started at …

The coda provides the opportunity for a slightly more explicit reformulation of the argumentative contrast between the first and second school,
which somewhat resolves the uncertainty in the argument mentioned
above:

… because instead of teaching by what you knew they didn't they
taught you by your age if you know what I mean.

The following are extracts from an interview, which took place in the
office of a Moroccan community association (data from Baynham, 1988), in

which Mr Ch., a Moroccan parent, critiques the British education system for failing Moroccan children:

(I = Interviewer)

( ) = taped material that could not be transcribed

Mr Ch: I see three children just last week.

I: Yeah.

Mr Ch: You know the cigarette e doing something, I dunno what, this white small one, put it inside on the cigarette and when um he ask him, "'scuse me what you doing the cigarette' I said to him, no just ( ) something I ask him, 'you Morocco?' He said to me yes.

I: You asked the b – the child?

Mr Ch: Yeah 'you Morocco?' He said to me yes. I ask him, my language, 'this this no good for you what you doing like this? I dunno, one colour boy, another one English. Why this boy, [*hits table*] if this boy going good for school, how can e going e doing this?

The discourse of which this is an extract has a serial structure, with Mr Ch. providing a series of narrative instances followed by rhetorical questions, which forcefully hammer home the virtual argument contained in the narrative:

... if this boy going good for school how can e going e doing this?

The argument turns on Mr Ch.'s perception of the failure of the British school system to provide an adequate education for Moroccan children.

What authorises this question, providing its rhetorical force, is precisely the narrative effect, in particular the evidential claim of personal narrative: 'I was there, I witnessed this'. Mr Ch. is harnessing the power of the narrative effect to give his question (almost literally) its punch.

Mr Ch: And every year, when he finish the school last term July, he give to him the certificate. What the, what the, snu yaqulu l-hisa:b? [Moroccan Arabic = how do you say maths?]

I: Hisa:b? [Moroccan Arabic = maths]

A. el G: Hisa:b, I don't know.

Mr Ch: You know er that one this three four zero this one?

I: Maths, we say maths.

Mr Ch: One good, he give to him, this nice, if this writing no good, he give to him only three or zero, he writing here they you no no very good for a writing or no very good for this one. When he bring this one the father and the father he looking this one, 'oh my son what's the matter with you you no looking for this eh writing look teacher what he said to you and headmaster'.

I: Yeah.

Mr Ch: But, in here I see, 'no worry', or 'you how old are you? Four years,
         five years, you going another class, six years, you going another
         class.' When he have sixteen, when he have sixteen 'oh you can e
         going a college or you can e going to look for the job'.

If the evidential claim of the first narrative was derived from personal,
first-hand experience, here the claim is a generic one: 'this is what is
typically true in these circumstances'. Mr Ch. is contrasting different
approaches to schooling in Morocco and England. In Morocco, if a child is
not doing well at school, the teacher informs the parents who take steps to
improve the situation. In England, the school tends, he argues, to take a 'no
worry' approach, masking any deficiencies in the child's education until
he or she is 16 and then can't get a job or go on to college because they can't
read or write.

The argument is mounted through contrasts between the child who does
well in Morocco and is praised in the report, and the child who fails within
the British system. The narrative dramatises the concern and involvement
of the parent, setting up a contrast between this and the situation in the
British school, marked by adversative 'but', which again is a generic
narrative, with the British school's perspective dramatised through direct
speech:

but, in here I see, 'no worry', or 'you how old are you? Four years, five
years, you going another class, six years, you going another class.'

The texture of this argument is almost entirely created by the juxtaposition of narrative sequences and, throughout the extended argumentative
sequence, Mr Ch. neatly makes the argument dialogic by turning peri-
odically to the interviewer (British, educator) and saying, that's why I'm
very happy that you've come to talk to us. Now you can tell us why this is.

What made Mr Ch.'s strategy for presenting his argument powerful in
this discourse context? (That it was powerful, I can vouch for, since, as
interviewer, it had me at a loss for words, even though there was a
significant difference between Mr Ch. and myself in terms of command of
English.) I think it was partly because he was using the resources of
narrative, including its closure in Kress's terms, to present argument as
fact. The evidential claim of personal and generic narrative is precisely that
it is factual and based on the speaker's own experience, thus authorised
and vouched for by the speaker. To challenge the argumentative position
is to challenge the speaker's factual knowledge and experience.

In the next extract we find a participant's account of a series of dealings
between Alaa, a professionally qualified job seeker and the Australian

Commonwealth Employment Service (CES), in the form of narrative and recount discourse, all highly evaluated and providing interesting evidence of the speakers' ideologies and values as well as of the organisational and literacy practices of the CES. The implicit presentation of these ideologies and values can be interpreted as an implicit or virtual argument.

In the first part of the extract, the speaker is describing what he perceives as the casualness of the CES in giving him travel expenses to attend an interview in another state. The most telling point for him was that the evidence he submitted to prove he was in fact going to a bona fide interview referred to him by a name other than the one under which he was listed at the CES. In the extract, narrative features that I will go on to discuss are in **bold**.

(**S** = interviewer, **A** = Alaa)
( ) = material that cannot be transcribed from the tape

S: So … what was the CES's reaction when you went to the CES about getting the money for the fare?

A: Er.

S: OK?

A: **Incredible,** I mean.

S: Was it?

A: Yeah.

S: What were they difficult?

A: **Even they didn't** try to make sure what I'm saying is good.

S: What **they didn't even** ask you for a bit of paper or anything?

A: **Nothing** at all. **All they have** what I have it here, **just** the covering letter which I sent it with the ad.

S: So you wrote your own covering letter?

A: I wrote my own covering letter and I sent it to them.

S: Right.

A: No, to the company the first covering letter …

S: Ohh. The first covering letter you sent with the ad, so **you didn't even** have to get confirmation from the er.

A: I tell you one more **amazing** thing. My name in the covering letter as you know is Alaa S.

S: Yeah.

A: My official name in the CES is Abdullah Al S.

S: Right and **they didn't even** worry about that?

A: But they know this story and I told to them and I told to them before and what.

(Data collected by S. Roy)

In this narrative, the virtual argument is that the behaviour of the CES is somehow amazing in its lack of responsibility. The narrative is, if not jointly constructed, at least jointly evaluated, with both Alaa and the interviewer cooperating.

What does it mean to talk about evaluating a narrative? Evaluation is an element of the schematic structure of narrative (e.g. Labov, 1972) making clear what the point of the narrative is, what makes it significant, worth telling in a given discourse context. Evaluation is not a sequential component of the narrative structure, but is diffused through the text, via a whole range of textual effects. Some of the most obvious evaluative effects, indicated in bold, are: lexical choices ('incredible', 'amazing'); the grammar of modality to indicate that the CES didn't come up to minimal acceptable organisational behaviour ('didn't even', ' nothing ... all they have ... just').

The use of 'even' and the semantics of counter expectation, examples of which are also highlighted, is another feature that contributes to the overall textual effect. 'Even' in linguistic terms is an interpersonal adjunct that implies that what is stated is somehow odd, surprising, contrary to expectation (cf. Quirk *et al.*, 1972; Martin, 1992) The expectation that is countered here can be understood as a should/ought of obligation: this is how the CES ought to have behaved. The expectation against which the semantics of 'even' is set, can be understood as a series of should/ought statements, such as the following:

Even they didn't try	(they should have tried)
They didn't even ask	(they should have asked)
You didn't even have to get	(you should have had to get)
They didn't even worry	(they should have worried)

The arguments of everyday life mostly involve what people and organisations do or ought to do. The participants here jointly construct an ideological perspective on how things ought to be, the virtual argument of the narrative. Interestingly, although there is argument (that is *dissent)* implicit within the narrative, between the practice of the CES and how it ought to be, the narrative is constructed *consensually* between the partici- pants in discourse. This is one of the properties of narrative as social practice: that it projects consensual participation between co-participants in discourse. If argument is fundamentally predicated on dissent, narrative is predicated on agreement between co-participants in discourse. This is perhaps a way of explaining why narrative as argument is powerful: it discursively enforces agreement between co-participants (in Foucault's terms, its regime of truth). It is therefore more difficult, though not of course impossible, to struggle out of a narrative, with all its density of implicit epistemological claims into a position of dissent, than it is to disagree with an explicitly stated proposition.

Alaa then tells a narrative in which the CES has sent him a pro forma to fill in asking him to show in what ways he has fulfilled his 'contract' with the CES to engage in further study or to search for work in return for his benefit.

S: You've been in and out to that CES office quite a few times haven't you?
A: Yes.
S: They know you.
A: Yeah, as a matter of fact last er …
S: They must be your good buddy now.
[*S & A laugh*]
A: As a matter of fact what happened last … at the beginning of this year they send me a letter.
S: Right.
A: No no no … sorry … er what I have done to still get paid.
S: To still get.
A: To get paid the benefits.
S: Oh benefits, right, OK.
A: Not only to write just what I have done, just to tick squares.
S: Right, right.
A: Just have you done what we did agree? Yes or no?
S: Right.
A: If I said yes I still get paid. If I said no they will cut the pay.
S: Right.
A: I called them I said look it does not make any sense everybody would say yes I am attending to it.
S: Yes, right.
A: The lady who (   ) she told me just write yes and send it us – to us.
S: We don't want to see you [*laugh*].
A: Yeah, I won't do that, I need.
S: Help.
A: I need to make an interview because the contract which I did sign with you said to both of us to do something. I have done my part, you haven't done your part.
S: Oh good on you [*laugh*] and what did she say?
A: She said 'OK, I er, what's your name?' 'My name is Abdullah' (   ) started with A they classify the people over there with the surname. 'You have to go, a certain, certain person will interview you.'

S: Yeah, right.
A: 'All your files is there.'

(Data collected by S. Roy)

This narrative embeds an argument between Alaa and the CES which again turns on the question of what counts as reasonable behaviour on the part of the CES. This time the argument is explicit, in that it is recounted, first through Alaa's summarising of the contents of the letter from the CES. Alaa recounts his response through a dramatisation of his telephone conversation with the CES, which results in a successful outcome: the lady at the CES modifies her position and calls him in for interview.

The narrative's closure (in Kress's terms) is precisely the successful outcome of the argument in Alaa's terms. Again we find joint construction of the narrative by co-participants, once the interviewer picks up on Alaa's intention in telling the story, for instance when she completes a turn of direct speech reporting that Alaa has initiated:

A: The lady who ( ) she told me just write yes and send it us – to us.
S: We don't want to see you [*laugh*].

This indexes that she is on the wavelength of his narrative intent.

The interviewer also provides an explicit evaluation of his argumentative strategy, followed by a prompt for the continuation of the narrative:

S: Oh good on you [*laugh*] and what did she say?

which shows how she is actively constructing the consensual regime of truth on which the narrative is based. Argument is of course based not on consent but dissent, on the competition between truth claims (cf. Lindstrom, 1992) and within the framework of dissent constructed by the narrative, she places herself on Alaa's side. Here the discourse of dissent is nested or embedded within a discourse of consent.

The next extract is from a discussion in an adult literacy class on child abuse:

(**T** = teacher, **C** and **K** = students)

T: And there's this thing about not interfering isn't there? That neighbours don't like to.
C: Well not like they used to do, they used to do, they used to do didn't they?
T: Do you think so?
C: The neighbours used to be more friendly than they used to be nowadays.
K: Mmm.

C: They used to come and have a cup of tea with you and sit on the doorstep and sit and have a natter and sit and watch television till 12 o'clock in the house with, you know, your neighbours.

K: Like Coronation Street [*laughs*].

C: But now, its very very rare you see your neighbour

K: Yeah.

C: You know, you'll be lucky if you see your neighbour one day t'next only she's going to the shop.

T: Mmm.

K: And a lot of people think if you sort of say 'and are you all right' and you go around and say 'do you want any help?' They think you're being ...

C: being nosey now.

K: Or funny but you know, you know ...

T: Whereas before people were lived in each other's pockets that ...

K: That's it, that's right.

C: Yeah, yeah.

T: Yes, I suppose that gave the children a bit more protection, cos you couldn't hide behind closed doors as much.

(Data collected by Wendy Moss)

The argument in this text is conducted through generic narrative. The argument is all in the contrast between the THEN narrative and the NOW narrative. To that extent the argument is implicit or virtual, although we can see the teacher's contributions as tending towards making explicit connections.

K.'s interjected comment:

like Coronation Street

itself completely topic coherent, is also very interesting from a pedagogical perspective. In making an explicit reference to a well-known soap opera, whose organising theme is precisely to portray a society of neighbours, living in each other's pockets, in each other's houses till 12 o'clock, K. is adding a dimension of intertextuality to the discussion, the locus of which is in a kind of proto literary discourse.

The discussion, in itself tending towards different kinds of abstraction, trails the possibility of a number of more abstract discourses (the sociology of neighbourhoods in the late twentieth century, soap operas as a genre). In an everyday conversation these little theoretical flashes would normally go unnoticed, but in the framework of an educational discourse they serve as nodal points through which entry into more abstract discourses becomes possible.

Conclusion: Pedagogical Implications

So, what are the implications of the ideas presented in this chapter for adult literacy teaching? Recent research on language and writing development in adult education classrooms, such as Gardener (1986) while emphasising the importance of discussion also recognises the need for transitions into other modes of discourse. This is only possible through an increased understanding of the nature and organization of oral discourse and the kinds of situated theorising that can go on in even casual conversation. This situated theorising can be made the basis for a more explicit introduction of theoretical discourses, for example in a Return to Study course for mature students wishing to return to formal study: how would a sociologist talk/write about these issues, how would a literary theorist or semiotician deal with the presentation of neighbourliness in Coronation Street or other soaps?

The strategy for writing development here would be to make explicit the virtual argument in narrative, or the ways in which issues raised within one discourse/epistemological space can be readdressed in other discourses, other epistemological spaces. The situated generalisations on social life, then and now, achieved through the harnessing of generic narrative to construct positions in argument, can be reframed as sociological discourse or as discourse on the representations of idealised stereotypes of social life in a soap opera like Coronation Street.

There are also implications for the teacher's own language awareness. It is important for the teacher to be aware of the complex textual organisation of spoken language, for example the features of narrative in argument and narrative as argument that we have been discussing here, because it is through spoken language that the classroom itself is constituted. It follows that spoken language in the classroom provides a set of opportunities for language development, both spoken and written, which the teacher needs to be able to recognise. For example, being able to see and develop the virtual argument in narrative may be a way into the development of the basis for argumentative, expository writing. (As an illustration of what I mean by this, you might want to take one of the texts from this chapter, perhaps the phone-in text or Mr Ch.'s argument about British schooling, and try to summarise in your own words what the speaker's argument is.)

There is a potential for teachers to extend their students' range of writing by picking up on the virtualities and possibilities present in spoken language and work on them as written text, as part of a shift towards more dominant modes of written argument. (The need for a writing pedagogy that extends the range of students' writing across text types has been powerfully argued by the genre theorists; cf. for example Martin, 1989).

This relationship between spoken language work and writing development is one issue that arises from close analysis of the relationship between narrative and argument in spoken language. But as I mentioned at the beginning of this chapter, the development of spoken language in more public formal contexts is itself a potential goal in adult literacy work. The emphasis on spoken language work in literacy classrooms leads many students to report increases of self-confidence in speaking out in public settings. For students, in dialogue, to explore the interrelationships of narrative and argument, may be a way to increase control of the more public dominant modes of discourse both spoken and written.

Acknowledgement

I am grateful to my colleague Chris Nesbitt for discussions on 'even' and the semantics of counter expectation.

4 Argument as a Key Concept in Teacher Education

GARETH HARVARD AND RICHARD DUNNE

Introduction

The initial training of students for teaching in Great Britain has for many years emphasised the value of experience. Educators have sought to increase the number of occasions and lengths of periods that students engage in classroom teaching; student-teachers have attested to 'teaching practice' as the site of their most useful, fulfilling and relevant learning (Bennett and Carré, 1993); and recently legislators have secured an increase in the proportion of initial training courses that is spent on a school site (DFE, 1992). As teacher educators we have argued that it is 'a mistake to assume that classroom experience automatically provides the most appropriate learning ... [and that there] is a need for closer attention to be given to the purposes of classroom experience and the deliberate work that can meet these purposes' (Dunne & Harvard, 1993: 117).

We have been concerned about the implicit trust that is invested in first-hand experience and have developed an approach to the training of teachers (Dunne & Harvard, 1992a, 1992b, 1992c) that specifically challenges this assumption, especially its tendency to close down the possibility of conceptual change. We have remained unimpressed (Dunne, 1992) by the assumption that recourse to the idea of the 'reflective practitioner' (Schön, 1987) rescues 'experience' from its limitations. We have emphasised, in contrast, how carefully designed experiences, limited in number and in duration, should be the subject of persistent attention. In this context, we discuss in this chapter how Ryle's (1949) notion of 'intelligent practice' can be related to Popper's (1963) distinction between a dogmatic and critical attitude, and how both have direct practical implications for the initial training of teachers. We will show how it is useful to distinguish between *critical thinking, dogmatic thinking,* a *critical attitude* and a *dogmatic attitude.* In doing this, we will make a claim for argument as a central feature of learning to teach. This will involve an exploration of the *conditions* necessary for student-teachers to learn from school-based work, an outline of the idea of a *knowledge object* and clear advocacy of the crucial idea of *breaks with experience.*

Critical and Dogmatic Attitudes; Critical and Dogmatic Thinking

Popper (1963: 52) distinguishes between a critical and dogmatic attitude, arguing that the critical attitude is not so much opposed to the dogmatic attitude as superimposed upon it: criticism must be directed against existing and influential beliefs in need of critical revision. He argues that 'logical argument, or deductive logical reasoning, remains all-important for the critical approach, not because it allows us to prove our theories, or to infer them from observation statements, but because only by purely deductive reasoning is it possible for us to discover what our theories imply, and thus to criticise them effectively.'

In seeking to apply Popper's distinction between a dogmatic and critical attitude to student-teachers' professional learning, we have concluded that it is necessary to make a more careful distinction between the attitude and the thinking of the learner so that distinctions among the dogmatic attitude, dogmatic thinking, the critical attitude and critical thinking are of central importance. Our distinction recognises the value of criticism (appropriately developed and acted upon) but emphasises how this critical thinking is productive when based on the secure knowledge of a situation that is achieved via a dogmatic attitude. Our intention in making this distinction is to avoid encouraging a development in student-teachers that we commonly see, that is, a tendency rather easily to offer criticism as a matter of course, to seek to find something 'wrong'. It is this almost instinctive reaction, the assumption that the major task is to identify errors, that we characterise as a critical attitude, and it is this that we want to avoid. Equally, we would be concerned to find evidence of what we have called dogmatic thinking, this being a tendency always to avoid consideration of the conflict that exists between consolidated experience and new evidence.

The dogmatic attitude sets out to reinforce existing schemata by applying them and confirming them with the use of data, and this creates a tension when critical thinking requires a determination to change them — to test them, to refute them, to falsify them if possible. We must show

how these competing aspirations can be developed such that productive tensions can be generated and resolved by individuals, but we will first make the point more clearly about attitudes and thinking. Table 4.1 emphasises the salient points.

Table 4.1 Dogmatism and criticism in attitude and thinking

	Dogmatic	*Critical*
Attitude	Useful in certain contexts	Not helpful
Thinking	Not helpful	Useful in certain contexts

Popper (1963: 316) argues that criticism is, in a very important sense, the main motive force of any intellectual development: 'Without contradictions, without criticism, there would be no rational motive for changing our theories: there would be no intellectual progress.' He reminds us that criticism consists in pointing out contradictions and in not putting up with them because this would no longer induce us to change them: it is the resolve not to put up with contradictions that promotes development. We look for a new point of view which may enable us to avoid them, a resolution that can be justified. He also points out how dogmatism is to some extent necessary: if we accept too easily the logic of the contradictory evidence we may prevent ourselves from finding out that we were nearly right. It is this tendency to dogmatism of a certain type, which we refer to as a dogmatic attitude, to which we pay considerable attention.

Specifically, it refers to a tendency to be tenacious about existing beliefs in the face of contradiction rather than immediately to accept the new evidence as superior or conclusive. It involves an analysis of the extent to which current assumptions can be modified to incorporate the new perspective, that is, how the case for the existing perspective can be strengthened by further reference to the data on which it is based. It demands a knowledge base that is sufficiently well developed to provide the confidence and flexibility that is necessary for such novelty. It is this that we see as a major purpose of training: to induct students into well-formulated knowledge about teaching and to convince them of its validity (that is, to establish the conditions for developing a *dogmatic attitude*). This is in contrast to a *critical attitude*, indicated in Table 4.1 as being unhelpful, which is the tendency immediately to reject current ideas when confronted with a contradiction or logical inconsistency or contrasting example: in this case, the potential for clarification and development of the current notion is lost. What this means is that there is no development, only replacement of one viewpoint by an immediately more palatable one.

If training were conceived only in relation to a dogmatic attitude, a severely impoverished experience would result. A second major purpose of training is the provision of the conditions necessary for the development of critical thinking. In stressing the importance of a dogmatic attitude we assert that this is valuable only when at the same time *critical thinking* is developed: this thinking is to be exercised in relation to ideas which are sufficiently understood, internalised and cherished to be worth challenging (i.e. when the learner's attitude to current knowledge is dogmatic). It is contrasted with *dogmatic thinking* which would seek merely to use new data to confirm existing viewpoints.

We identify the combination of a dogmatic attitude and critical thinking with Ryle's notion of 'intelligent practice' which he contrasts with 'habitual practice'. Ryle (1949: 42) states that 'It is the essence of habitual practices that one performance is a replica of its predecessors. It is the essence of intelligent practices that one performance is modified by its predecessors. The agent is still learning.' In linking this with Popper we have concluded that Ryle has insufficiently emphasised how habitual practice is an essential component of intelligent practice, and our approach with novice teachers reinstates this repeated practice as an important training element. Although this implies that some processes are to be practised until they become automatic, this does not reduce them to mindless routines: students still have to decide where, when and how these routine procedures or processes can be appropriately applied.

It is our contention that, in those cases where a dogmatic attitude and critical thinking are combined, it is possible for argument to be generated in useful ways: it is the co-existence of these dispositions that establishes the conditions for argument.

Argument is Central in Learning to Teach

We have indicated above that argument is comprised of the several elements of description, explanation, justification and reformulation. We have also noted that it is necessary to provide students with an outline of the nature of argument so that they are clear about how their work should be constructed: they do not do this in relation to their own practice even if they exhibit the capacity to do this in the accepted disciplines. We express argument as being comprised of four elements, each further elaborated in three levels that need to be addressed progressively. The four elements are not all of the same kind: whereas description, explanation and justification can to some degree be thought of separately, the notion of reformulation is in important senses lacking in substance without being conceived alongside, incorporating, the other three. But it would be wrong merely to consider the sum of description, explanation and justification as being the totality of reformulation. This is expressed in Table 4.2.

Table 4.2 The criteria for argument

	Reformulation
Description (1) Provide an account which contains sufficient points to represent the work accurately. (2) Provide an account framed in own words and using verbatim quotations for specific illustration. (3) Reorganise the sequence to improve coherence and make connections with supportive items from other pieces of work.	(1) Specify similar examples
Explanation (1) Identify and cite appropriate points for explanation (2) Orientate the reader to an appropriate basis for the explanation and explain succinctly. (3) Support the explanation by applying it to other relevant evidence.	(2) Identify similarities and differences across several examples
Justification (1) Make relevant claims for the significance of selected items. (2) Relate claims to established concepts and empirical data. (3) Challenge established concepts or empirical data.	(3) Examine purposes and principles

It is fundamental to our approach to course design that the development in students of a dogmatic attitude is not just a personal matter for each one: it is a wider matter of publicly known, understood and utilised methods and vocabulary. It is a dogmatic attitude that underpins development of creativity in teaching: we do not accept that the cultivation of creativity or idiosyncrasy involves an initial encouragement of personal responses. Rather it is based on a disciplined process of induction into publicly understood ways of representing and talking about teaching. The difficulty is that the development of pedagogy in the United Kingdom does not exhibit these paradigmatic features (Kuhn, 1962). It is for this reason that we were not easily able to engage in a programme for the development of argument as a central competence in learning to teach. We had first to establish certain shared ways of representing the work of a teacher and introduced a number of features into our courses in initial training that need some description. Central to the students' work is a category system (the nine dimensions of teaching: see Appendix 4.1) that serves as an outline of classroom work for them to attend to. Each of the nine dimensions is further elaborated in eight criterial levels (see an example of this in Appendix 4.2), representing progression from relatively simple levels of performance to more complex expressions of competence. This description of teaching is not assumed to be a complete description of what is possible in classrooms: it is the version that, widely accepted, forms the basis of the students' training. It is this description of teaching about which they develop a dogmatic attitude, in the sense that their successive attempts at teaching are consistently appraised by themselves (with assistance) against these dimensions and their criteria. In order to illustrate this, we can refer to the criteria for *structured conversation* outlined in Appendix 4.2. A student who had been observed for structured conversation during an episode of classroom work would subsequently examine this in detail. This examination might, for example, include reference to the requirement that the student should 'listen carefully to what children are saying' (Appendix 4.2, level 1) and to what evidence there is that this was done. This would involve citing appropriate evidence, examining what kind of evidence is possible, what would need to be done to produce more evidence, and so on. It would not be acceptable to dismiss the idea of 'listening carefully' because it was not particularly apparent in a particular episode, or because the student did not agree that it is important, or because it is so obviously a teaching skill that it can be taken for granted: one of the major purposes of this work is to train the disposition of dogmatism of attitude that underlies the visible behaviour of persistent attention.

However, in seeking to develop a dogmatic attitude in that sense, we seek simultaneously to develop critical thinking because the criteria are deliberately designed not to be clear statements of competence but, rather, as problematic statements to be elaborated by the students in the light of their own practice. In the case of the example, above, of the need to 'listen carefully to what children are saying', students would give attention to the questions of when this is important and when unnecessary; how and to what extent it is possible in classrooms; what effect it might have on children's learning to listen or not to listen; whether it is appropriate for them to be encouraged to listen to each other rather than putting the onus on the teacher, and how the teacher might keep track of this; and so on. This elaboration is crucial and is undertaken in two contexts. Firstly, in a setting known as a supervisory conference, the work focuses on a particular representation of the student's classroom work (an annotated agenda: see Appendix 4.3) and is tested for conformity to the criteria in the category system of the nine dimensions of teaching. This particular requirement that students engage in description, explanation and justification resembles Fenstermacher's (1991) notion of 'practical reasoning'. It is persistent attention to the annotated agenda, the observer's record of what actually happened during a short episode of classroom work, that is crucial in progressively developing the dogmatic attitude.

This conference work is a rehearsal for the second context in which the student is expected persistently to attend to description, explanation and justification, and it is this second context that most explicitly demands the refinement of ideas that is involved in principled reformulation. This second context is a written evaluation that follows each of the conferences.

In each context there is a requirement to construct an argument in a formal way. Initially, in the supervisory conference involving a student and a tutor, the student is helped to develop an argument orally, the assistance being provided by the manner in which the tutor conducts the conference. The subsequent written evaluation requires the student specifically to attend to the criteria (Table 4.3) that define the nature and quality of argument. Our emphasis here is on ensuring that the student returns to teaching events and re-represents them in practical action and oral and written argument. This requirement reinforces the cyclical nature of oral and written argument because in each context the students are not merely repeating what they have already said but bring different understandings to the ideas. They are constantly refining and reformulating their ideas and, in doing so, meet the formal requirements of practical rationality as defined by Fenstermacher (1991: 10): 'Practical rationality may be defined as the capacity of a person to reason in some relatively coherent and logical fashion from action to the grounds for that action and back again.'

In recognising the need for students to develop a dogmatic attitude we have designed their courses so that they are inducted into a framework for construing classrooms, the nature of teaching activity and their own actions. This framework, the nine dimensions of teaching (Appendix 4.1) and the associated criteria (Appendix 4.2), frame but do not completely prescribe the possibilities for effective action. We actively encourage a necessary dependence on ideas from sources outside the students' own teaching experiences, and put equal emphasis on, for instance, readings and experiences in other kinds of context. We believe that such dependency represents the possibility of growth because it discourages the sole use of experience, which novices are insufficiently knowledgeable to interpret and adapt in isolation as the basis for their learning. In our work with students it is an explicit principle that different kinds of relevant knowledge should be used in learning to teach, including the practical knowledge and understanding that is gained from working in the classroom and from central organising principles and concepts in more theoretical knowledge. We have already explained how we use these sources of knowledge to promote a dogmatic attitude that can be tested with various critical thinking strategies. We have established that the difficulty in achieving this with students is in the nature of knowledge about teaching: it is all too easy to avoid the persistent attention that is necessary for both dogmatism and criticism, especially criticism that consists not only in pointing out contradictions but in resolving not to put up with them. We try to overcome this difficulty by emphasising the idea of knowledge *objects* and how they can be used for criticism, particularly the pointing out of contradictions.

These 'objects' consist of summaries of articles, lectures, seminars and so on and, crucially, the annotated agenda of classroom episodes. The theoretical and research background to this is drawn from Talyzina (1981) and described elsewhere (Dunne, 1994); suffice it to say, here, that in concentrating on a material object (usually written, but including sequences on video), persistent attention is achieved both by the requirement to re-represent these in different ways and by the requirement to re-examine them in relation to each other (Harvard, 1994).

The term 'object' is not being used here as a metaphor for the multi-dimensional and gradual awareness which represents the full experience of understanding. We report elsewhere (Harvard & Dunne, 1992; Dunne & Harvard, 1992a, 1992b, 1992c) how successive levels of integration come from the repeated rehearsal and reconstruction of teaching episodes through persistently attending to various 'objects' in material and materialised forms. This involves deeper levels of understanding in which students make explicit links across nominated dimensions of teaching and construct various constellations of criteria to test and validate actions and achievements. The detail of the criteria we use offer direct visualisation and a permanent record of knowing about typical teaching events.

An agenda (Appendix 4.3) contains the essence of what we refer to as a knowledge object. In its most simple and concrete form it shows the relevant content, sequence and teaching dimension for observation. Its subsequent annotation prevents the loss of important detail so often experienced when recalling events, and ensures that data is available in a form and within a structure susceptible to critical comment and more intensive study. The annotated agenda, as a schematic for learning, also serves to remind students about related information and ideas both at the centre and at the margin of awareness. Although the choice of particular dimensions offers a sharp focus for conducting and analysing teaching, they invariably invoke other related detail, in a manner similar to Polanyi's (1967) 'focal' and 'subsidiary' awareness.

An explicit emphasis on knowledge objects offers students a logical structuring of knowledge about teaching; it is in the supervisory conferences and written evaluations that tutors encourage a personal *restructuring* of knowledge about teaching in which students envisage other possibilities. In other words, knowledge becomes increasingly strategic. Eventually, students use their knowledge of the logical relations among objects in physical, material and materialised forms, within the general theoretical framework of the dimensions, to apply to specific situations. Agendas, as the materialised form of teaching activity, play a crucial role in developing students' understanding of their own and others' teaching. In this way students learn how to use their own structures to control their actions and explanations, especially when the various components and structures of selected objects can be quickly invoked with minimal prompting.

In one sense, argument is endemic to teaching, in that teachers are constantly having to confront pedagogical dilemmas. Such dilemmas invite argument but do not necessarily provoke it. For this purpose, we have proposed a model of mentoring (Harvard & Dunne, 1992), which involves teachers and tutors in visibly demonstrating argument for students to model. Informal *in situ* conversations and structured conversations in conferences can be important features in promoting argument provided the necessary conditions are in place. It is important not to assume that because there are identifiable features of reasoning in informal conversations about teaching that these will automatically be enhanced by encouraging such conversations. We do not seek merely to elicit students' practical reasoning but actually to develop the capacity to engage in argument. In constructing argument there is an element of systematic confrontation that requires persistent attention to specific aspects of students' actions and reasoning.

The course structure and the various techniques focus students on increasing control in practice through self-evaluation, a prominent feature of which is confronting a pedagogical dilemma as an argument with oneself. We have described how a common set of criteria, with the requirement continually to examine practice in that context, contributes to a dogmatic attitude; we have also indicated how certain conditions are necessary to provoke an examination of this tenaciously observed outline of teaching, namely, that a variety of learning objects are developed in order to focus that deliberation; and we have indicated that the crucial arbitrator between these is the critical thinking implied in 'argument'. The use of 'argument' is in itself the subject of deliberate attention: its occurrence is not left to chance. The students' work at every stage is guided by an outline, with criteria, for the structuring of an argument; and their understanding of this outline is itself gradually developed and scaffolded by university tutors in the various contacts in conference sessions and in the marking of the students' work.

From the first day of the course 'argument' is introduced as comprised of description, explanation, justification and reformulation, summarised in Table 4.2. Early assignments for the students serve as an induction to these generally applicable criteria; but they are assisted in their use by the provision of explanatory notes that refer to the specific items in the current assignment. For instance, when students are provided with a profile for a child, with examples of the child's work, and asked to analyse this, to comment on difficulties and to construct an exemplar which shows how they might expect to respond in the classroom, they are given the task-specific criteria in Table 4.3 (see next page).

It can be seen from the task specific criteria that students are required to make reference to certain concepts, these being those contained in specified readings. In the early stages of the course these readings will already have been intensively analysed and written about so that the students have each committed themselves to a point of view. Each committed viewpoint represents a knowledge object for that student: it represents how the student knows those ideas in a certain sense. It is the subsequent requirement to make specific reference to that knowledge object (essay, notes, video sequence, etc.) in a new context and to modify the earlier understanding that provokes 'knowing' it in a new sense. The cyclical nature of the work, guided by the central notion of argument, is designed to establish teaching as an intellectual, speculative and uncertain activity.

Table 4.3 Developing argument with task specific criteria

Categories and criteria	Task specific criteria
Description	
(1) Provide an account which contains sufficient points to represent the work accurately.	Select one subject area from the profile and describe the nature of the work ...
(2) Provide an account framed in own words as using verbatim quotations for specific illustration.	... make your description authentic by using specific quotes.
(3) Reorganise the sequence to improve coherence and make connections with supportive items from other pieces of work.	Avoid simply repeating the chronology of the account you have selected: refer to other subjects from the profile where similar or dissimilar evidence may be available.
Explanation	
(1) Identify and cite appropriate points for discussion.	Say which are the most important points for attention ...
(2) Orientate the reader to an appropriate basis for the explanation and explain succinctly.	... and say why this is the case by referring to National Curriculum demands.
(3) Support the explanation by applying it to other relevant evidence.	
Justification	
(1) Make relevant claims for the significance of selected items.	Describe what assistance you can give to the child, relating this to your exemplar.
(2) Relate claims to established concepts and empirical data.	Refer to 'assisted performance', mediation or 'scaffolding' as appropriate.
(3) Challenge established concepts or empirical data.	Suggest where 'assisted performance', 'mediation', 'scaffolding' are not helpful in this circumstance.

Table 4.3 *cont.*

Reformulation	
(1) Specify similar examples.	Relate your personal experience or your observation of a child during school experience.
(2) Identify similarities and differences across several examples.	
(3) Examine purposes and principles.	

Our work with the initial training of students for teaching has increasingly drawn us to the idea that students need instruction that enables them to confront and go beyond the limits and distortions of the conceptions of teaching that they bring with them. We have been impressed by the manner in which Buchmann (1993) has expressed this as a need for *breaks with experience* in learning, and we have adopted this idea to characterise how it is necessary to ensure that students experience some conflict with existing conceptions of teaching, rather than having them continually reinforced. This is not merely a case of offering them hints or new ideas or methods, but requires that they acquire an abstract conceptual system so that when links are made with experience they are made within that system. The outline of teaching that we provide (the nine dimensions: Appendix 4.1) and their associated criteria (see example: Appendix 4.2) constitute just such an abstract system. The requirement to make links with experience is encapsulated in the demand to engage in argument in relation to that abstract system. The approach to learning to teach that we have designed exhibits those features referred to when Floden and Buchmann (1993: 40) explain that:

> students can transcend given ways of thinking and acting by first acquiring habits whose components they can imitate and practice but whose purposes they initially do not understand. Such transcendence requires schooling that breaks with the natural attitude and everyday understandings. While this separation may forfeit immediate relevance, there are distinctive educational gains.'

Conclusion

Teacher educators, and teachers as they play a greater part in the initial training of students for teaching, need constantly to examine just what it means to be the kind of person who is becoming a teacher, thinking as a teacher about what to do, remembering that proposals for action can be more or less effective or ineffective, and acknowledging that if other, incompatible conclusions can be drawn from the same argument, choices cannot be unequivocal. The theoretical model adopted in our studies recognises how argumentative discourse works so that it calls for various levels of integration of actions, discourse and analysis for informed professional judgements. Students need to manage interconnected operations rather than separate ones: to move flexibly between descriptions, explanations and justifications, as a means of reformulating existing ideas and offering challenging new ones. We emphasise the 'outer-directedness' of mental activity by identifying appropriate 'objects' of teaching and persistently attending to them. Further work is needed on factors that are not directly explored in this study, in particular an analysis of the dynamics of dialogue, especially the way in which participants start from initial agreement and how they move towards final agreement, or how they qualify partial acceptance of a viewpoint as a way of not moving toward consensus. It is our intention as teacher educators to ensure that student-teachers learn to analyse critically what they do, especially at a time when doing more school-based work is considered to be a sufficient condition for teacher training. But we also need to consider that:

> Attempts to represent teachers' arguments should capture some of their moral, personal, conflicted, interpretive and open-ended nature, which involves beliefs and desires in all of these aspects, and striving for goodness in the concept of teaching itself. Analyses should seize on what is characteristic about teaching: its objects ... and its conversational nature. (Buchmann, 1988: 212)

Appendix 4.1: The Nine Dimensions of Teaching

The criteria for the nine dimensions of teaching shown below represent progression from relatively simple levels of performance to more complex expressions of competence. The first three levels approximately illustrate the kind of work we would expect students to be doing at the end of initial training, being the essential teaching skills the accomplished teacher demonstrates on a more or less continuing basis. The achievement of more sophisticated levels is seen in the daily work of some teachers, but on the whole these levels are achieved from time to time as they are judged appropriate. That is to say, they are within the repertoire of the experienced teacher but are called upon in response to a professional analysis of what is needed.

Although we have indicated that students are able to achieve approximately level three in each dimension at the end of initial training, it is important to recognise that this is variable. The idea is that an appropriate record of what has been achieved is central to further professional development. This, of course, is consistent with staff development or staff appraisal schemes that schools already use.

Dimension 0: Ethos

Being a teacher demands attention to the characteristic spirit, the ethos, of the classroom. There will inevitably be different views of what is an appropriate ethos: the whole question is value-laden. Yet we have a responsibility to make our view explicit and to indicate the way in which such a spirit can be developed.

Our view of an appropriate ethos entails mutual respect between teacher and taught, a shared sense of purpose, a spirit of co-operation. It involves, on the part of the teacher, a commitment to developing individual autonomy within a co-operating community; striving to equip and enable children to hold power and take initiative whilst recognising the rights and interests of others; minimising bias, discrimination and stereotyping, maximising security and independence.

This view of the classroom is ambitious. Progress towards it is so important that it comprises not only the first of the dimensions of teaching which we describe, but is the one to which each of the others contributes in ways which we expect the developing teacher increasingly to make sense of.

The ethos dimension outlined here lists the points which should progressively receive attention. You will notice that this is the only one of the dimensions which is not numbered: this is because we do not feel that it is appropriate to predict a 'level' at which you should be working at the end of school-based work. However, you will be expected to show increasingly mature consideration of the relationship between the other dimensions and the ethos of the classroom.

Dimension 1: Direct instruction

The repertoire of teaching skills includes the ability to tell, describe, demonstrate and explain. There is a sense in which the successful performance of this ability could be demonstrated in front of a video camera when it would be possible to judge clarity of speech, speed of delivery and so on. But the development of this ability demands an increasing awareness of and responsiveness to the audience, including selection from a range of options in order to clarify a point and the use of simile, analogy and metaphor.

Dimension 2: Management of materials

This dimension refers to a basic, vital aspect of the teacher's work: the preparation, provision, selection and design of consumable materials, hardware and visual aids.

Dimension 3: Guided practice

The memorisation of facts and the practice of skills, processes and routines are not ends in themselves. Those which are selected for attention are those which have utility or lead to the development of important concepts, but a selection does have to be made, and then the teacher has to design and conduct appropriate practice tasks. These tasks require sequencing; they need to be presented in a variety of modes (e.g. oral, written, word-processed); attention must be given to reinforcement; children's responses need observing and interpreting. And there must be sensitivity to the dangers of inappropriate practice and of an over-emphasis on practice. The guided practice dimension illustrates how you should progressively attend to these aspects.

Dimension 4: Structured conversation

Learning begins with uncertain understandings which need refining. The mature learner can test that emergent understanding by e.g. posing alternatives, testing against experience and seeking elegance. Children need experience of these processes and a model of them in use. The beginning teacher needs to develop the ability to elicit children's perspectives, enable them to listen to each other, draw attention to conflicting ideas, provide conflicting ideas, ask for examples, support children in their attempts to report their thinking, and remove the stigma generally associated with making a mistake. This complex set of skills we summarise as structured conversations. It is not expected that the entire range of activities under this heading will be brought into play every time structured conversation is attempted, but the beginning teacher should be aware of the variety of useful strategies. This dimension of teaching, structured conversation, is summarised below. The first four levels illustrate the fundamental requirements of using this approach; the remaining levels indicate that structured conversation, drawing on the range of strategies, should be attempted in increasingly complex settings. It is this development – deliberate use of certain aspects followed by the selection of appropriate aspects in more demanding contexts – which we expect you to undertake.

Dimension 5: Monitoring

Our view of successful teaching is one which emphasises the actively thoughtful role of the teacher in collecting information about children on a moment-by-moment basis, sensitively interpreting this information and using it to guide action. This action must be directed towards maintaining an orderly working environment and developing understanding. This process involves observing and listening to children; creating hypotheses to make sense of their reactions; and testing these hunches.

Dimension 6: Management of order

In a classroom which is orderly, busy and productive you may well notice sensitive teaching, efficient management of materials and respon-sive monitoring. You may also notice how the children take responsibility for their own work, co-operate and respect each other. It would be easy to assume that these visible features are those which produce the orderliness of behaviour since the teacher is giving no explicit attention to the management of order. This would be wrong. The orderliness is there because the teacher has paid explicit attention to it, to the extent that it is now part of normal classroom life, with the children needing perhaps only a quiet reminder from time to time. The beginning teacher must pay attention to this dimension of teaching. The development outlined below clarifies how we anticipate you will progress towards an orderly class-room.

Dimension 7: Planning and preparation

Effective planning is very demanding. You must plan to enable children to learn in a classroom with an appropriate ethos, which requires that you pay attention to the variety of modes of teaching, to the management of materials and order, and to the monitoring of children's work. You will need to draw on your earlier analyses of these dimensions and your progress in them and on the subject knowledge and curriculum knowledge studied in your university course. Our view of the way in which you will make progress in this dimension is indicated in the successive levels shown below.

Dimension 8: Written evaluation

This dimension has close links with the 'monitoring' dimension: both stress the importance of the collection and interpretation of data and the development of constructive, practical consequences, from analysis. There will be a need, therefore, to show thoughtfulness in the context of the other dimensions including, of course, monitoring. The outline of the evaluation dimension shows how we expect you to make progress in becoming deliberately reflective about your work.

Appendix 4.2: The Criteria for Structured Conversation

Dimension 4: Structured conversation

The introduction included under the above heading is followed by:

(1) Listen carefully to what children are saying and respond supportively.
(2) Attempt to elicit children's responses; recognise and attempt to analyse difficulties.
(3) Use planned and unplanned opportunities to hold conversations with children to challenge their perspectives.
(4) Focus on challenging children's ideas by drawing attention to and providing conflicting ideas; by asking for examples and supporting children in reporting their thinking.
(5) Experiment with planned conversational teaching on particular aspects of the curriculum.
(6) Experiment with small-scale and limited duration conversational teaching as an occasional feature of the classroom work.
(7) Plan for and experiment with conversational teaching in many curriculum areas by maintaining the children's engagement in exploring a variety of directions raised through conversational teaching.
(8) Adopt a chairperson's role in fostering thoughtful consideration of appropriate concepts and issues.

Appendix 4.3: The Annotated Agenda

We have found two major difficulties in securing persistent attention to classroom events:

(a) beginning teachers find it very difficult to recall in any detail what has happened during their teaching;
(b) typically, observers make notes in general terms that focus on criticism or praise.

We have developed an approach to classroom observation that is designed to secure the persistent attention that is of crucial importance. This involves the following features:

(1) The class teacher and the student work closely so that the intentions of any episode are understood by both.

(2) The class teacher is the person who observes the student at work so that what is intended is understood by the observer and what is possible is also appreciated.

(3) The focus for observation is agreed before the session takes place.

(4) Only a short episode (15–20 minutes) is the subject of close observation.

(5) The observer makes notes of what the student and the children actually say and do.

In order to ensure that an appropriate object is generated for subsequent scrutiny, the student and the class teacher prepare for the observation by co-operating in producing an agenda for the short episode that is to be observed. The agenda, produced on one side of a sheet of A4 paper, is derived from the lesson plan and is a summary of the content and sequence of what is intended in the episode. It must carry sufficient detail to make clear how topics will be introduced (the actual words), how resources will be accessed, and so on. It is important that the agenda is thought out in detail, but it is not expected that the episode will necessarily conform to this. In the subsequent analysis, it is of as much interest if the episode did not go as planned as if it did. The important thing is to be able to examine intentions and actual events extremely closely. The agenda, together with the observer's notes on the same sheet, comprise the annotated agenda that is given attention in the subsequent supervisory conference.

5 Argument, Dialogue and Religious Pluralism: Reflections on the Current State of Religious Education in Britain

HOWARD GIBSON AND JO BACKUS

In this chapter we consider aspects of argument and rationality within the context of religious education and cultural pluralism in British schools. In the first section we examine some of the political, pedagogical and philosophical pressures that place doubt upon the feasibility of institutionalising argument within the religious curriculum, and develop the position that uniting the principal approaches to religious education in British schools is a common epistemological bond, a clear rationale for the diminutive status of argument and a disregard for the status of critical rationality. In the second section we assemble a rationale for institutionalising dialogue and argument and here draw from a number of diverse philosophical traditions – Mill, Gadamer, Feyerabend, Habermas – and by so doing develop the concepts of dogmatism and relativism in an attempt to clarify the notion of dialogue. Our third section is tentative, for here we try to review the pressures that our epistemological stance must make upon current practices and so move towards a re-examination of commonly used terms such as 'tolerance', 'empathy' and 'encounter'.

Argument

Current pressures upon the status of argument within religious education in Britain come from a number of directions; from legislative and assessment frameworks that determine permissible discourses; from pedagogical patterns and associated conceptual difficulties, such as the question of personal commitment or whether a teacher can approach 'the ineffable' *qua* rationalist; from the realities of cultural pluralism and the concern for 'tolerance'; and from philosophical assumptions that underpin the principal approaches to religious education in British schools. These might be seen to do with politics, pedagogy, pluralism and philosophy, although the points we make below overlap.

Although the Education Reform Act (ERA) of 1988 prescribed no nationally based content for religious education in Britain there was an explicit preference for Christianity. In line with developments in other areas of the curriculum, notably English and History, where government agencies were giving increasing credence to the transmission of 'cultural heritage' (DES, June 1989), the Act instructed Local Education Authority (LEA) Agreed Syllabuses to 'reflect the fact that the religious traditions in Great Britain are in the main Christian' (ERA, 1988: Schedule 1, Section 8, 3). This move amounted to a migration from previous practices that had involved not only the inclusion of non-Christian faiths but also, in certain LEA syllabuses, secular 'world views' such as Humanism and Marxism (e.g. City of Birmingham Agreed Syllabus 1975). While this explicit preference for Christianity proscribed the inclusion of catechisms and the like, it permitted the *study* of denominational teaching within Agreed Syllabuses (ERA, 1988 Schedule 1, Section 1, 3). As a result, it became 'legal to teach that such and such a group believes certain things, or even takes things to be true, but illegal to imply or suggest that such things are true.' (Cox & Cairns, 1989: 27)

It could be argued that this ingenious detail demonstrated little sensitivity for the chemistry of classroom interaction, for we take it as self-evident that few teachers outside a religious school would expect their more mature pupils to accept denominational formulae without critical discussion, and yet this is what the Act seemed to imply was possible. Our point is that the distinction the 1988 ERA wished to make between *teaching* denominational formulae and teaching *about* such formulae left unclarified important epistemological issues regarding the discursive nature of learning, the significance of dialogue, and the relevance of empathy and argument within those processes. It is these issues that we will be discussing in this chapter. Also, and more obviously, the Act also left a huge question mark over the preference for Christianity and what amounted to the legislative parameters of permissible discourse within the religious curriculum – which is why some have re-assembled argument outside and against the legislative framework itself.

In contrast to the ERA, the adopted framework for the General Certificate of Secondary Education (GCSE) assessment throughout the 1980s and 1990s has not been Christocentric but, on the contrary, oriented towards a candidate's application of 'evidence and argument' to support 'a personal opinion':

> Candidates are encouraged not only to be aware of differences of opinion in matters of religious belief and practice, but also to express an opinion of their own, based on the use of evidence and argument at a simple level. In this case, it is the evaluative process that is being assessed. *It cannot be emphasised too strongly that this element in the assessment objectives is in no way intended to test the validity of any viewpoint held by the candidates, but only to assess the extent to which they are able to express and support an opinion coherently.* (GCSE: National Criteria, 1985; London East Anglia Group: GCSE Examinations June 1990/January 1991; see also School Curriculum and Assessment Authority, 1994b)

By implication argument is defined here as that which is used to support a subjective judgement, a personal preference, a point of view, and the reason for awarding a candidate such-and-such a mark depends on criteria in some way divested of content – coherence, consistency, cogency, the absence of contradiction, and the like. And if it is the inherent purity of the individual's belief system that is being countenanced here, one would presume that a candidate's reasoning, measured instrumentally (Horkheimer, 1974), would enable him/her as Christian, atheist, pagan, or anti-semitic to be assessed in principle as equally first rate. But to assess an argument without reference to its content assumes that an examiner can disengage sufficiently from its substance and examine merely the clarity of its presentation; it ignores the monotheistic preferences within other parts of the syllabus that may well set the agenda within this; and for us more importantly, it leaves unquestioned the links between knowing and intersubjectivity by implying that the knowable 'owner' is an autonomous rational agent and that the procurement of knowledge is akin to the acquisition of private property.

Thus while the clauses pertaining to religious education in the ERA have chosen to circumscribe the areas of permissible discourse, the framework for GCSE assessment admits no preference for any specific denomination and, in contrast, celebrates neutrality. We have implied though that both contrasting frameworks are laden with epistemological difficulties. The former, anticipating the revival of Christian culture, is unsubtle in its approach to 'truths' other than Christianity and insensitive to the nature of the links between dialogue and learning. The latter, favouring a relativistic stance, relegates argument and commitment to the ability of autonomous rational agents to articulate personal preference without reference to 'truth'.

Pedagogical matters complicate the issue further. Teachers have always needed to select from competing interests when adopting teaching strategies and devising methodologies and, with regard to religious education, three concerns compound the problems of engaged dialogue and argument within the classroom. The first concerns the vulnerability of young children – their limited life-experiences, their inability to argue cogently or to do so in certain contexts, questions of parity, problems of making explicit an understanding in language, insufficient time, and so on – and the ways these factors combine to produce problems of equity and to make young children relatively less powerful in dialogue. Thus some have advocated that the negating effect of argument and critical reasoning should arrive in this area of the curriculum only after faith has been nurtured: 'Children should not be confused by being taught to doubt before faith is established' (HMSO, 1967: 207). But by presupposing the very notion of spirituality and the value of transmissive pedagogies – by advocating a confessional or instructional stance on the part of the teacher – there is an avoidance of the issues of religious *education*. Indeed it could be argued that it is the very vulnerability of young children that is being exploited here.

Second, one might question whether a teacher *qua* rationalist can do justice to an investigation of 'the ineffable'. The issue here, and one to which we shall return in our final section, is whether the tradition of questioning, argument and negation provides an appropriate dialogical context for exploring complex religious phenomena, no matter what the age or life experiences of the pupil, in that it is possible to negate the very subject matter in an attempt to appropriate it rationally. What is at question is not the justification for an affective or empathetic component in this area of the curriculum, but how it is conceived that these areas are to be linked with the cognitive, reflective and critical. The use of 'empathy' as an affective device in religious education, for example, is habitually and unintention- ally conflated in Agreed Syllabuses with 'sympathy' and 'agreement' (see Knight, 1989).

Third is the question whether a teacher can or should deliver a religious curriculum in which they can find no truth. The debate about procedural neutrality is well rehearsed, as if it were possible for teachers to purge themselves systematically of preferences and interests in the processes of education and cleanse themselves of judgement before entering the classroom. From Warnock's position on moral relativism one can extrapolate the difficulties of playing an apparently neutral game within religious education:

> Moral relativism may be a fact; but it is not a fact that we feel while we are forming moral judgements. If we really believe that any moral view were as good and worthy to be adopted as any other, then we would of course make no moral judgements at all. And the same is true of all other non-moral evaluations. We cannot evaluate and accept another evaluation at the same time as equally sound. Moral views, then, are not prejudices; but they are also totally distinct from matters of opinion. (Warnock, 1975: 111)

Hulmes would extend the notion to religious judgement in education:

> (The) personal commitment to truth as I see it takes me again and again into that potentially disturbing area of encounter with people from other religious traditions. There is no question of trying to compel assent to that which I hold to be true. It is more a matter of revealing my commitment so that any one who is sufficiently generous to take it seriously may criticise and question it. Yet it would be dishonest if I pretended that by expressing my commitment I did not retain the hope that eventually some may even come to share it. (Hulmes, 1978: 29)

If a religious belief has this effect on its spiritual adherents, in what way are we to interpret the position, common throughout the 1970s and 1980s in LEA Agreed Syllabuses, that a teacher's personal stance on any religious issue is irrelevant to their task as an educator or assessor? As Hirst argues:

> To understand beliefs or actions does not necessitate that one either accepts or approves of them and to teach for such an understanding demands acceptance or approval of them by neither teacher nor pupil. (Hirst, 1971: 9; see also Hull, 1982, 1984)

But as long as the teacher's role is said to present any religious matter objectively, 'regardless of his faith or lack of it' (City of Birmingham Agreed Syllabus, 1975), the value of and criteria for engaged argument remain unexplored. The LEA position may not only exaggerate the possibility of 'bracketing out' one's interests and judgements – the question of neutrality – it may also fail to recognise the problem of relativism, of side-stepping truth claims, of neutering engagement and leaving unacknowledged the epistemological advantages of participants clarifying their ideas in dialogue.

The growth of many of these epistemological/pedagogical complexities correspond with the growth of cultural pluralism, especially since the mid-1960s and with the need to rethink the way of religious education in Britain (see Thompson, 1988). Until then it was possible to retain the impression that Christianity was the only influential religion and the only one that needed to be dealt with extensively in religious education (see Cox & Cairns 1989: 18). But Britain had become more obviously a complex heterogenic mix and this raised real concerns regarding the teaching of religious and moral issues. Some schools retained a singular religious or 'confessional' approach and assumed that the aim of religious education was 'intellectual and cultic indoctrination':

> (Confessionalism) is often linked with a belief that any other kind of religious education is valueless and unworthy of the name. This has been the traditional view of the Roman Catholic Church in this country. (Schools Council, 1971: 21)

In contrast, state run or 'county' schools responded through LEA Agreed Syllabuses by developing a phenomenological approach (see Smart, 1968) where children were not instructed what to believe. The aim was to expose children to the 'facts' of various religious practices, to the 'experiences' of the faithful, and to engender their engagement in religious phenomena 'empathetically' (see Westhill Project, 1990). Here children were invited to 'bracket out' their currently held beliefs and values, attempt a postponement of critical judgement, place themselves in the shoes of another and so reconstruct the psychic state or world view of the religious believer by re-living their experience vicariously. Thus the phenomenological approach was said to view the aim of religious education as:

> the promotion of understanding. It uses the tools of scholarship in order to enter into an empathetic experience of the faiths of individuals and groups. It does not seek to promote any one religious viewpoint but it recognises that the study of religions must transcend the merely informative. (Schools Council, 1971: 21)

Ultimately it was necessary for pupils as individuals to 'determine and justify their own positions' for to believe or not to believe was seen as a matter for personal judgement: 'It is no part of the responsibility of a county school to promote any particular religious standpoint' (see Hampshire Agreed Syllabus, 1978; Northamptonshire Agreed Syllabus, 1980).

But in our description of both contemporary practices it would appear that the very nature of discourse – as *intersubjective* – has become a withered or apparently unproblematic concept. From the *confessional* standpoint religious and moral truths are to be delivered into seemingly unquestioning and uncritical minds, and if the aim of religious instruction – *contra* education – is to foster an attachment to a particular set of religious truths, discussion about their respective merits becomes an unwarranted concern, or for some, as we have seen, a handicap. On the other hand, from the *phenomenological* standpoint common in county schools, if religious truths are to be experienced as if through the eyes of a believer and children are to emerge from school justifying their own religious positions – and are to be assessed at GCSE on this basis – critical contact with truth claims is systematically avoided and questions regarding the validity of various religious stances are again not raised.

In this section we have suggested that while the ERA may be read as an attempt to support a return to Christian confessionalism, and while the county syllabuses and national assessment frameworks have become firmly entrenched in what we shall call relativism, both polarities are connected in their consistent undervaluing of the links between dialogue, argument and learning. We have acknowledged that this may have been provoked by a real concern for the vulnerability of young children, the desire to promote religious tolerance in a pluralist culture, the problem of approaching certain complex religious phenomena within a liberal-rational framework, the dilemma of personal commitment and the question of teacher neutrality. However, what has been withered in the process is regard for the status of critical rationality that had at its core the free and open rivalry of divergent elements of knowledge and, as its telos, the quest for 'truth'. In essence, what we may have in religious education in Britain is evidence of a Cartesian Anxiety for the only epistemological choices that inform current practice are, seemingly, *dogmatism* on the one hand or *relativism* on the other. It is the philosophical assumptions that underpin these approaches that we investigate in the next section.

Dialogue

Philosophical *relativism* rests upon the conviction that when we examine those concepts that philosophers, scientists, theologians, etc., have taken to be the most fundamental – rationality, truth, right, justice, values, etc. – we are forced to recognise that in the final analysis they must all be understood as reactive to a specific conceptual scheme, theoretical framework, paradigm, form of life, society, or culture, and that there is no way one can rationally arbitrate between the competing claims or alternative paradigms (see Bernstein, 1983: 8–16). Because human rationality is thought to be incapable of acting as a value-free adjudicator over particular positions there is, in practical terms, a reticence to engage or a scepticism as to the outcome of argument, for there can be no final assurance. Such a position implies an essentially functional or instrumental view of reasoning, one that can be isolated from value and commitment, so that the acceptance of ideas, the criteria for action, leading principles of ethics, political, educational and religious matters, are necessarily matters for 'personal opinion'. Once rationality has been disinfected of its potentially impure or false elements, the domains of opinion, belief, commitment and conviction are left to fend for themselves:

> Reason, once it is particularized, is assigned to the level of subjective consciousness, whether as the capacity for the empirical verification of hypotheses, for historical understanding, or for the pragmatic control of behaviour. At the same time, interest and inclination are banished from the court of knowledge as subjective factors. The spontaneity of hope, the act of taking a position, the experience of relevance or indifference, and above all, the response to suffering and oppression, the desire for adult autonomy, the will to emancipation, and the happiness of discovering one's identity – all these are dismissed for all time from the obligating interests of reason. (Habermas, 1963: 262–3)

Moreover, from the relativist's stance, inter-subjective communication or dialogue, that is the free and open rivalry of divergent values, views and elements of knowledge, becomes purposeless discourse, for it has lost its telos.

On the other hand, if *dogmatism* may be described as a passivity to what is epistemologically questionable or a willingness to protect from judgement assumptions that lie beneath the construction of claims to truth, then some have taken the very model of scientific rationality, the dominant framework guiding Western thinking since the early Enlightenment, as illustrative of a paradigmatic dogmatism, and an illusory solution to the Cartesian Anxiety. Such epistemological features issuing from the Enlightenment would include the dominance of 'scientific enquiry' in the construction of knowledge, the dissociability of subject from object, the idea that autonomous rational beings should trust to no higher authority than human reason, the conviction that human reason can free itself of bias, prejudice and tradition and so transcend its own historical context, and so on. Here Feyerabend (1975, 1978) has been incisive in ridiculing the notion that there are free-floating standards of rationality detached from actual historical practices to which we can appeal in order to decide who is and who is not 'scientific'. Similarly Husserl (1954) has suggested that European sciences since Galileo have been predicated on the premise of the mathematisation of nature and a dogmatic refusal to reflect upon this 'pre-logical a priori', a pre-scientific premise. The accusation of dogmatism within the Western paradigm of scientific enquiry can of course be replicated in other arenas of human rationality, from the false assurance of the bar-stool bore to the dogmatic Christian theology of Barth. What is unifying is the suspect but dogged conviction that there are permanent, ahistorical frameworks to which one can appeal in determining what is 'true' and what is not.

We would suggest that it is in the work of Gadamer, Mill and Habermas and their reflections on the notion of *dialogue* that a more subtle and secure solution to the traps of relativism and dogmatism may be found. All three are agreed that if reasoning is both a *reflection of* and a *reflection on* reality then the very processes of knowing must become transparent. For Gadamer this would involve rehabilitating the concept of prejudice expunged by the Enlightenment in favour of an attachment to an illusory rationalism:

> The overcoming of all prejudices, this global demand of the enlightenment, will prove to be itself a prejudice, the removal of which opens the way to an appropriate understanding of our finitude, which dominates not only our humanity, but also our historical consciousness. (Gadamer, 1975: 244; see also Horkheimer & Adorno, 1944)

For Gadamer the key prejudice of the Enlightenment was the belief that reason could free itself from tradition and then, from the side so to speak, examine these traditions in the clear light of reason (see Mendelson, 1979: 60). In *Truth and Method* he uses the metaphor of an 'horizon' to clarify the knower's attachment to tradition, to a standpoint which affords only a certain range of vision, and he warns that 'if we fail to place ourselves in this way within the historical horizon out of which tradition speaks, we shall misunderstand the significance of what it has to say to us' (Gadamer, 1975: 272). But for Gadamer it would also be an error to consider that 'otherness' can *only* be viewed as if from one's own fixed ground, for the horizon in which we operate is being constantly reconstructed by our reflective involvement. This he terms 'effective historical consciousness', and concerns the processes of unearthing assumptions, the 'testing of prejudices', the 'fusing of horizons', and the emergence of a truth which, he suggests, 'transcends the subjective opinions of the partners to the dialogue' (1975: 272–3, 330–1). In many respects Gadamer's emphasis on the significance of dialogue as a central epistemological category is no different from the stance of classical liberalism. J.S. Mill, for example, shares the assumption that to exist historically means that knowledge can never be completed and is inevitably partial; that to risk and test one's ideas is a constant task and not a final achievement; that the notion of truth is provisional and can only be warranted by argumentative discourse. As he says in *On Liberty*:

> There is the greatest difference between presuming an opinion to be true, because, with every opportunity for contesting it, it has not been refuted, and assuming its truth for the purpose of not permitting its refutation. Complete liberty of contradicting and disproving our opinion is the very condition which justifies us in assuming its truth for purposes of action: and on no other terms can a being with human faculties have any rational assurance of being right. (Mill, 1859: 145)

But both Gadamer and Mill's claim for dialogue as an ontological structural element in understanding minimalises the import of the social context in which dialogue is to function. It says nothing concerning the intentions or aims of those in dialogue, it seems to ignore the social power of contenders and refuses to raise questions regarding the reasons why participants would choose – or choose not – to validate practical discourse, and we are left with a philosophical model dissociated from praxis. For Marx, the case liberals made for the free exchange of ideas was inexorably tied to the social and economic world, to the free exchange of commodities, so that with the development of capitalism the reality of free exchange in either domain became patently illusory for the majority: liberalism, he says, gives us merely an 'abstract model of existence of free individuality' (Marx, 1858: 163–5, 649–52). Gadamer too has been accused of leaving his epistemology incomplete and merely at the level of philosophical abstraction insofar as he forsakes the very social and political fabric that can enable or distort encounter. Philosophical hermeneutics, as with all philosophy, can solve neither social nor political problems, and in describing 'what always occurs' in understanding, it rejects any attachment to a specific methodology or social theory. In stressing that dialogue is underpinned by notions of mutuality and respect, that it can result in genuine novelty in understanding, and that it demands an openness to risk and to the testing of one's opinions, Gadamer presupposes or at best underplays the social contexts which make this sort of ontological encounter a reality. In a way he presupposes the existence of the very sense of community that dialogue is intended to develop (see Bernstein, 1983: 162, 224).

However, the practical and political implications that Gadamer fails to pursue have been taken up by Habermas and developed into a critique of the social contexts that would distort dialogue: 'The ontological illusion of pure theory behind which knowledge-constitutive interests become invisible promotes the fiction that Socratic dialogue is possible everywhere and at any time' (Habermas, 1968: 314; see also Habermas, 1979). Drawing on diverse traditions, Habermas emphasises the need for a theoretical framework that can interpret the possibility of structural barriers that might distort free communication, where the subjective meanings of contenders are veiled or corrupted by the social relations of participants. Whereas Gadamer's framework is incapable of dealing with Marx's notion of ideology as 'false consciousness', or with the Freudian idea of the unconscious motives of contenders, or with aspects of structural inequality that would effect the distribution of social power in dialogical contexts and prevent mutuality, Habermas's work constantly draws our attention to features of social life that inhibit, deform or prevent dialogue from being concretely embodied in everyday practices (see Holub, 1991; Bernstein, 1983: 224; Mendelson, 1979: 64). Thus what Habermas has attempted to do is to construct a theory for the purpose of explaining how the understanding of meaning can be distorted. And this we believe is necessary if we are to understand dialogue-in-practice within the classroom.

We conclude this section by drawing out four elements of our argument so far and, by so doing, attempt to set the agenda for the next. First: in contemporary British culture there exists a plurality of traditions and horizons; that particular individuals are reflections of particular traditions is unavoidable and is encapsulated in Feyerabend's provocative description of pluralism as cultural relativism:

> Being a tradition it is neither good nor bad, it simply is. The same applies to all traditions – they become good or bad (rational/irrational; pious/impious; advanced/'primitive'; humanitarian/vicious; etc.) only when looked at from the point of view of some other tradition. 'Objectively' there is not much to choose between anti-semitism and humanitarianism. But racism will appear vicious to a humanitarian while humanitarianism will appeal vapid to a racist. RELATIVISM (in the old and simple sense of Protagoras) gives an adequate account of the situation which thus emerges. (Feyerabend, 1978: 8–9)

Second: it is only dialogue or argument or 'conversation' that can mediate between horizons; dogmatism and philosophical relativism are philosophical traps. Third: not every dialogue is the expression of unforced consensus; that dialogical contexts are inherently social contexts implies that when dealing with intersubjective interaction – within a classroom say – there is a need not only for a philosophical description of how understanding may occur, but also for a theoretical interpretation of the distribution of social power so that one may decipher fear, force, reticence, coercion, inequity, and the like. Fourth: we also need to admit the possibility that the very model of liberal rationality and argument that we have been developing in this section and that underpins our notion of dialogue, as well as the whole framework of education in liberal-secular communities, may simply be part of *our* horizon, or 'our rationality' in Peter Winch's terms (Winch, 1972). Thus, if in this section we have implied the prospect of inter-faith encounter, we might anticipate problems of appropriating 'the other' within *our* scholarly tradition.

Encounter

In the first section of this chapter we suggested that phenomenology arose in the mid-1960s as a counter to confessionalism and as a response to cultural pluralism. We argued that the Agreed Syllabuses of state schools and GCSE criteria for assessment end up neutralising claims to truth by relativising them, that they demand that pupils should choose from paraded alternatives and emerge from school with their own 'personal' views about faith. Phenomenology has responded to the accusation of appearing to recommend merely superficial glimpses of religions, a fleeting 'Cook's Tour' (DES/Welsh Office, 1985; see also Jones, 1986) of them all, by insisting that not merely the superficial gloss of observable phenomena, the beards, beads and bangles, but the deep enduring truths, the mysteries, the dogmas, the experiences of adherents, and so on, must be approached by the teacher if they are not to distort the very substance of religious belief. Phenomenology has also needed to stress the ability of teachers to objectify their own life world and so, in the context of the classroom, set aside their own particular horizon so that, irrespective of their own faith or lack of it, they may tackle the spiritual depths of diverse religions in a scholarly way, 'objectively':

> This openness to the possibilities of alternatives is not the only condition for objectivity in religious education. Criticism is required too. It is not sufficient to parade alternatives before the eyes of the imagination and leave it to that, as if there were no objective ways of judging their relative truth or adequacy. The special function of academic communities is to create schemes for the critical evaluation of interpretations originating in non-academic communities, whether the interest be economic, social, military, political, or religious. Although the various disciplines study different aspects of experience, they are united in a common loyalty to this principle of criticism, the search for consistency and adequacy in their interpretation of data. That search must form an integral part of religious education in schools. (Schools Council, 1971: 26)

That this is a sound basis for scholarly enquiry and underpins the study of art, mathematics, movement, literature, etc. is not at question in this chapter. The concern here is whether the tenets of rational reflection, argument, criticism and objectivity can be exported to permeate religious education sufficiently to make it 'sound scholarship' (Schools Council, 1971: 22). If the educationalist's role is to engender a dialectical cycle of adopting, commenting upon and criticising informed opinions, into which new experiences will enter that will lead successively to the negation of previously held positions, and so on, then in such an educational climate naively held views, poor judgements, unreflected opinions and dogma may have a limited history for knowledge claims will appear in constant succession. The push to interpret interpretations, to gain perspectives on perspectives, to scrutinise revealed truths, must all aim at dislodging dogmas for there must be room for argument to find 'objective ways of judging their relative truth or adequacy' (Schools Council, 1971: 26). But while attempting to maintain the rigorous criteria of 'objectivity' during the study of religions there is an unclarified desire to portray religious education as somehow both the *same* and as something qualitatively *different* from all other subjects:

> The objective study of religion is only a special case of the objective study of any subject whatsoever. There are, of course, features of religious inquiry that differentiate it from the study of other matters. Still, the same fundamental canons of sound scholarship apply in the field of religion as in other fields of investigation. (Schools Council, 1971: 22)

It is the uneasy proximity of religion and education that is at issue here. It is the interface between a dogmatic, revelatory epistemology on the one hand, and scholarly conduct that aims at the negation of dogma on the other, that is unclear. We wish to examine it at three points. First, through the notion of 'tolerance'.

Attempts to bridge the conceptual gap between the demands of religious pluralism and the Enlightenment tradition of 'sound scholarship' have spawned notions like 'critical openness', 'critical tolerance' and 'tolerant understanding' (Hull, 1984: 209, 114, 115; see also Rowe, 1986) that do little to clarify the status of dialogue and argument within religious education. For in answer to Hull it could be said that when one is *critical* one is intolerant of wrong opinion and that when one is *tolerant* one is uncritical. If tolerance is more than the rhetoric of the pluralist, then its setting in religious dialogue needs careful attention because the notion pertains to both the contexts of interpersonal exchange as well as to the veracity of truth claims. To allow argument to proceed equitably is quite dissimilar from tolerance of untruth, for a fair say *and* a genial but utterly condemning reply are compatible in liberal dialogue. Thus Hull's formulation begs the question: should a teacher be tolerant in the sense of allowing an equal say to divergent thinkers while maintaining their procedural right to remain naive, partial, or bigoted? Unperceived by Hull, the rhetorical notion of tolerance in fact straddles the domains of both Gadamer and Habermas, and for coherence one would need to develop a much stronger theoretical framework that could hold within it both the ontological claims of dialogue as well as an explicit critique of social barriers that would distort free communication within and beyond the context of a classroom. We surmise that only then might one discover why the anti-semitic GCSE student that we mentioned in our first section, despite his/her scholarly endeavours and the cogency of his/her argument – that is his/her 'ability to formulate a coherent argument to support an opinion' (GCSE, 1985; LEAG, 1990/1) – may not in fact be tolerable.

Second: we have already noted that 'empathy' is a central tenet of phenomenological inquiry. In our first section we suggested that the aim of empathy was to foster understanding at the experiential level, that pupils in this encounter would be invited to 'bracket out' their own prejudices, stand in the 'shoes of the believer' and so come to experience a different horizon. The mechanism is said to have the potential for mutuality between the horizon of the pupil and the adherent of another horizon so that understanding may occur when one 'feels as the believer does'. A possible scenario for this empathetic encounter might be that the pupil acquires an acquaintance of the religion from a variety of sources – from texts, meeting the adherents of the religion, visiting places of worship, by sharing in the worshipping experiences of the believer – and that at different stages the pupil would check his/her understanding against that of the faith community. Through empathy a pupil would then begin to acquire more than just a superficial understanding such that s/he begins to hold the truths of both his/her own and the other horizon. Krieger (1991: 50) refers to this as a 'conversion' experience, that is, one where the pupil experiences a conversion to both horizons. But the phenomenological model does not allow for this mutual conversion to occur. Empathy in this model has become an end in itself and its telos self-referential. The direction of the framework prevents convincement into a tradition, for pupils can know but are not to be encouraged to believe, for the potentiality for 'unscholarly' conduct is prevalent. A potential for inter-religious dialogue, of the kind that Krieger talks about in his description of 'jumping in between' (Krieger, 1991: 35–6) horizons, cannot be acknowledged to be happening, for while pupils are acquiring various kinds of understanding of religions, it is then demanded that they refer them to a scholarly, liberal-rational model. In effect they are encouraged to 'jump back' from an empathetic experience into this model despite other possible consequences of encounter. The uses of empathy to effect perceptual change, the possibilities of investigating metaphor and symbolism, the conceptual links with reflection and encounter, and so on, are arguments well rehearsed within drama in education (see Neelands, 1992; Bolton, 1979).

Third: we have implied that phenomenology was a relativistic response to cultural pluralism and to the limits of dogmatism expressed as religious confessionalism. The point we wish to make here is that it chooses to mediate religion through a liberal/secular dogma and in so doing distorts the very subject matter. The 'scholarly' model is, in other words, a hybrid of both relativistic and unreflected dogmatic elements. It is dogmatic insofar as the methodology underlying the model assumes a clear preference for the production of autonomous rational agents who defer to no higher authority than themselves. Here the telos of rationality is very definitely fixed within an 'horizon', an Enlightenment tradition that abhors the prospect of indoctrination and – in theory if not in practice – refuses to admit the veracity of any authority apart from individual free will and intellect. The model may in principle allow a pupil to be converted to a faith but in fact precludes this happening by anticipating its own telos, for the aim to which it is directed and which it hopes for is the emergence of individuals who know about religions but who make autonomous and 'personal' judgements about whether or not to believe. In short, phenomenology gives pupils a view of religion *mediated* through an alien horizon, a model which usurps religious claims to truth and thus deforms their nature in the process of scholarly appropriation. Moreover, it does not offer its own horizon for critical scrutiny.

The Rushdie affair may be taken as illustrative of the clash of horizons when conflicting frameworks encounter the other, and the example may be taken as illustrative of classroom encounter. In Krieger's terms the affair was an example of what he would call 'jumping back' from plural encounter for it encapsulated a desire to withdraw from the possibility of dialogue into the 'comfort and security of one's original tradition' (Krieger, 1991: 35) or horizon. On the one hand deeply held Muslim beliefs were offended by the publication of *The Satanic Verses* (Rushdie, 1988) and so, motivated by Qur'anic injunction to carry out Jihad or spiritual struggle against all those who would present an ideological and moral threat to their religion, Muslims were led publicly to destroy the book in protest and proclaim a Fatwa on the author that to this day still stands. At the heart of the demonstrations was a deeply felt unease at the lack of support for their sensitivities by the majority of non-Muslims. On the other hand, one found authors, the press, secular humanists and other non-Muslim groups, defending the publication under the fundamental liberal rhetoric of the right to free speech, and that this right was being challenged by vociferous militants. Argument and dialogue, which may have helped clarify the position of the other, did not occur, for both communities were securely grounded in their own horizons so that rules for engagement could not be agreed. That is to say, both positions were predicated upon the confines of particular horizons so that the criteria of meaning and 'truth' ascertained in one could not be applied to another (see Jones, 1985: 223–4; 1986: 107–12). In essence, the Rushdie affair may be said to exemplify the challenge of religious pluralism and the ever-present possibility of 'jumping back'.

The affair also points to the instability of different horizons in proximity and to the power of the dominant horizon to assert itself. We have interpreted the 1988 ERA as a legislative first step towards returning schools to Christian confessionalism. But we have also suggested that phenomenology too revolves within a paradigm that participants are required to share, an educational framework that mediates belief systems as if they were objective facts and where the essences of different religions and their claims to truth are devoured. For some, the answer would be to remove the subject from the curriculum of schools and reposition religious education within faith-based communities. For others, this would need to be resisted, for in partitioning religion from education it would herald not merely the demise of 'religious schools' but also destroy a platform for plural encounter and the contestation of truth claims.

6 Argument and Science Education

CAROLYN J. BOULTER AND JOHN K. GILBERT

This chapter considers the uses of three forms of argumentation in the teaching and learning of science, particularly within the traditions of primary schooling in Britain. It develops the idea that the strategies of informing, questioning and collaborative problem solving form the repertoire of skilled teachers who are able to move between classroom scenarios for different purposes using different patterns of discourse. Flexible use of these strategies may be a way successfully to mediate the tensions present in science education. The chapter raises three issues in particular: the distribution of power in discourse; the relationship of argument to conceptual change; and the problem of oppositional language. Each of these is common to both science education and the study of argument.

The Tensions in Science Education

Within the tensions inherent in primary educational practice (Berlak & Berlak, 1981) there are several that are particularly important for primary science education. The first of these concerns the way in which children are to meet science (Figure 6.1).

A tension exists between communicating to pupils the facts of science, the content, and providing experience of the process of experimentation. This has affected how science is taught (Harlen, 1978). Over the last century, whether process or content was considered most important has varied.

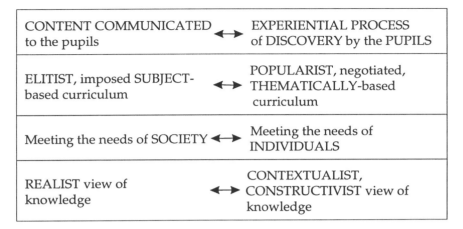

CONTENT COMMUNICATED to the pupils	◄─►	EXPERIENTIAL PROCESS of DISCOVERY by the PUPILS
ELITIST, imposed SUBJECT-based curriculum	◄─►	POPULARIST, negotiated, THEMATICALLY-based curriculum
Meeting the needs of SOCIETY	◄─►	Meeting the needs of INDIVIDUALS
REALIST view of knowledge	◄─►	CONTEXTUALIST, CONSTRUCTIVIST view of knowledge

Figure 6.1 Tensions in primary school education

Science, rather than nature study, really only emerged as an important component of the curriculum in British primary schools as a result of the Plowden Report (CASE, 1967). Even then, it appeared only as the seventh heading in the chapter describing aspects of the curriculum. 'Discovery learning', one of the catch phrases of the Plowden Report, described first-hand experience and children's questions and understanding as forming the starting points for investigations which the teacher guided through dialogue. The Nuffield Foundation took this discovery learning ethos and produced teacher and pupil material for process-based courses, starting with Nuffield Science 5–13 (Schools Council, 1974). Discovery learning went hand in hand with the child-centred approach to teaching and learning and focused on the concerns and stage of development of the pupil. Since the Black Papers of 1977 (Cox & Boyson, 1977), however, the child-centred discovery learning approach has been under attack. In particular, it has been undermined by the progressive redefining of the science National Curriculum, with its emphasis on assessment and the objectification of pupils into products of a system. It is clear that, in the National Curriculum, content is regarded as the more important part of the science that children do in school. Despite this, child-centred discovery learning is still strongly adhered to in principle by primary teachers.

The notion of science for all gathered strength in the egalitarian climate of the 1960s and continues to be deeply held. It was probably one of the justifications for the high profile of science in the National Curriculum. At the same time, however, elitist views of science continue to prevail (Fensham, 1985) and these are equally embedded within the National

Curriculum. Elitist science has an emphasis on factual recall with experiments to confirm those facts and with social aspects being merely illustrations. The curriculum is structured on the lines of individual subject disciplines and the pupil is completely dependent on the teacher for the content knowledge and structure. Control is entirely in the teacher's hands. Compared with this is the use of practical activity, exploration through questioning, using themes and social aspects as starting points and a curriculum based on pupils' experiences and interests. In this popularist science, the student has some control and is able to negotiate how he approaches the content. This approach to science is attractive, especially to pupils of middle and lower ability (Cowie & Rudduck, 1988), but has less status.

The resulting tension – if the science is too elitist then it fails to appeal to all; if it is too popularist it is not taken seriously by society (Fensham, 1985) – informs such debates as that over topic work in the primary school. At present, the elitist view of science, which tends to narrow the focus of topic work to a single subject and to reduce student control, appears to be winning the debate (Alexander *et al.*, 1992). But whilst this brings about a rise in the formal status of science within the curriculum at primary level, it is accompanied by an inevitable tarnishing of the appeal of science in the early years.

Part of the argument for the high profile of science in the National Curriculum has been the perceived need for a more scientifically qualified workforce to drive the economy to become more internationally competitive. This is a utilitarian aim for science education: meeting the needs of society tends to stand against the individual's need for a personally relevant scientific education. The coherence of the National Curriculum from ages 5 to 16 means that it is no longer possible for primary and secondary science to be other than a continuum geared to the perceived needs of industry and commerce. This tension between utilitarianism and the needs of the individual is especially acute in the primary school with its child-centred inheritance.

The last tension is in many ways the most significant and concerns the very nature of science itself and how its knowledge is perceived. During the 1970s, a major movement in science education arose, which became known as the Alternative Conceptions Movement (Gilbert & Watts, 1983). Both discovery learning and the approach to science teaching and learning that believes that information must be transmitted imply that there is a single external reality which exists as we observe it. Although in the transmission approach reality is communicated directly to the pupils, and

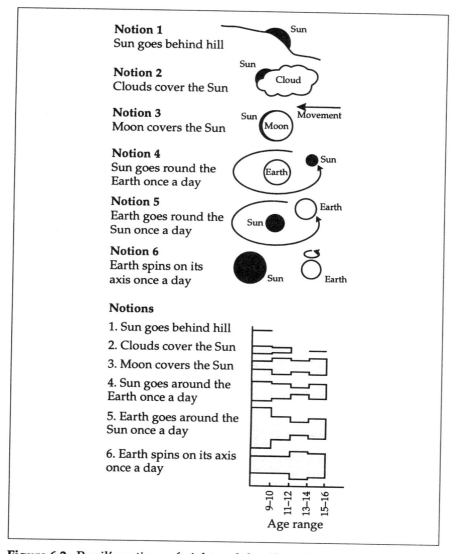

Figure 6.2 Pupil's notions of night and day (from Baxter, 1989)

in the discovery approach reality is discovered and mapped, both approaches are fundamentally realist. The Alternative Conceptions Movement, however, is contextualist and sees all knowledge as being personally and socially constructed: reality may exist but all knowledge is made in context. Recent research shows that most teachers at secondary level hold realist views of science (Lakin & Wellington, 1991) and this causes a tension with developing understandings of how science is constructed in laboratory settings (Latour & Woolgar, 1979) and with the way in which teachers view their pupils' failures to learn science (Fox, 1983). In addition, the lack of philosophical underpinning to the National Curriculum in science has strengthened an implicitly realist approach to science.

The Alternative Conceptions Movement is founded on the research into the scientific understandings that children bring with them into the classroom, for example (Figure 6.2) about how day and night form (Baxter, 1989). Since 1970 such work has gone on all over the world (Carmichael *et al.*, 1990). It has given rise to research into how these conceptions can form the basis of classroom work (CLISP, 1990; SPACE, 1991) and to new materials for classroom use. Increasingly the term *constructivist* has come to be used to describe the approach to science education which takes as its basic assumption the view that knowledge is personally and socially made and that all the theories that learners construct of the world are therefore provisional. The characteristics of constructivist pedagogy follow this basic premise (Figure 6.3). Constructivism is about how knowledge is built: it is seen as constructed.

- Knowledge is PERSONALLY AND SOCIALLY CONSTRUCTED
- Theories about the world are PROVISIONAL
- Every learner has PRIOR CONCEPTIONS
- Learners actively CONSTRUCT MEANING
- New experiences initiate CONCEPT CHANGE
- Meaning is constructed in INDIVIDUAL, COMMON AND PUBLIC DOMAINS
- Teacher DIAGNOSES and MEDIATES between domains

Figure 6.3   Characteristics of constructivist pedagogy

From a constructivist viewpoint, the teacher mediates the evolution of the children's meanings until they develop into the official publicly agreed framework of science. The teacher is seen as being able to take on the role of diagnosing the personal knowledge of the child, allowing it to be voiced in the building of common understanding in group interactions and mediating its relationship to publicly agreed understanding. The teacher is no universal provider of ready-packaged official understanding with a pupil dependent all the time on her unchanging pearls of wisdom. Nor is she content with only the understanding that the pupil can discover, as the

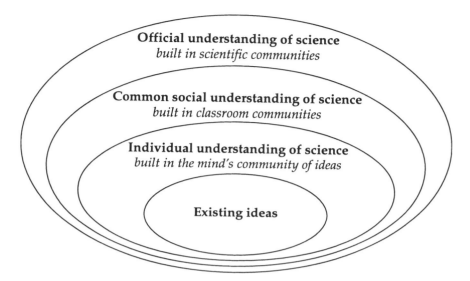

Figure 6.4 Domains within which understandings of science are built

child-centred ideology would dictate. Her role is to mediate and catalyse the development of understanding where reality is seen as the meanings we agree. To do this, she must sometimes take an interdependent view of learning which, unlike the transmission and child-centred approaches, is interactionist rather than individualist. That is, she must allow the private knowledge of the individual to emerge and to become common knowledge through social interaction (Edwards & Mercer, 1987), choosing the right time for the public official understandings of science to enter. In each domain the knowledge is built in the context in which it arises: within the individual, in social classroom groups, and in the scientific community (Figure 6.4) .

Constructivism can therefore be seen to have a contextualist and not a realist view of science itself and stands firmly within the tradition first established by Kuhn (1962). Conceptual change occurs within each domain. Within the individual, new experiences interact with existing ones and the result is a new conception. How this change takes place is often described as being a result of the challenge to the existing framework that is seen not to accommodate the new experience.

One might expect that constructivist pedagogy would sit uneasily with a prescriptive National Curriculum. It is opposed to implicit realism, tends to have affinities with the popularist, thematic curriculum and naturally has the teacher in a less controlling role. In terms of the tensions elucidated above, those aspects on the right-hand side of Figure 6.1 tend to go together just as the National Curriculum tends to be described by the aspects on the left-hand side of the diagram. Science education in the primary school is, therefore, at an important stage, influenced by constructivism yet controlled by the National Curriculum.

It is this complex situation which a framework relating argument and science education may help to explain and develop. It must attempt to encompass the tensions in the themes of: the learning process, the science curriculum, the purpose of learning and the means by which knowledge is acquired. To be effective, such a framework needs to be based on what happens in classrooms or in what might be called classroom scenarios.

Classroom Scenarios and Types of Argumentation

The way in which teachers teach is currently under scrutiny. Primary teachers are being exhorted to do more whole-class teaching (Alexander *et al.*,1992). Evidence from the ORACLE report (Galton *et al.*, 1980) suggests that teachers see the management of children as a whole class or in smaller groups as strategies concerned to balance the need to save time with the desire to talk to each child face-to-face (Galton, 1981). For the teacher who sees the purpose of whole-class grouping as primarily to socialise children and to transfer the knowledge that she has decided should be covered, the whole class is a highly efficient and convenient arrangement and allows for a receptive audience.

In such a scenario the teacher is likely to employ a style of argumentation, similar to that defined by Andrews *et al.* (1993: 16): 'a process of argumentation, a connected series of statements intended to establish a position (whether in speech or writing)'. In this definition the emphasis falls on the speaker (or writer) whose crafted statements link to others without another voice being heard. The thinking of the audience (reader) is not considered. Kuhn (1992) terms this 'rhetorical' argument: its purpose is to persuade its tacitly receptive audience of a position; its structure is relatively simple and linear. We refer to this kind of argumentation as didactic; it is the kind we usually mean by teaching and is reflected in the Greek word *didaskein* meaning *to teach*.

Discussion is another term often used within teaching. Here the root of the word is the Latin *discutere,* meaning *to break up*. However, in school, although the children are allowed to speak in this scenario, the pattern of their interactions is very stylised and the typical question-answer-evaluation pattern is what is most commonly seen (Figure 6.5). The child-centred aspirations of the teacher mean that the questions are directed to different children. The remaining pupils are expected to form the audience. The purpose is, as it were, to map out the schema that is in the teacher's mind of the content to be covered. The meaning no longer flows directly from the teacher but takes a somewhat devious route leading both to a number of blind alleys and to a fair degree of cognitive confusion in the audience. Often the teacher reformulates her question so as to obtain the answer she expects. This type of argumentation, found in the child-centred questioning scenario, can be referred to as socratic discovery in question-and-answer form.

Teacher (initiates the exchange):
'What do you think the weather is going to be today, Susan?'
Pupil (responds to the teacher's question):
'Cloudy.'
Teacher (evaluates the response):
'That's right, cloudy. I think it's going to be cloudy.'

Figure 6.5 Child-centred questioning

In both these classroom scenarios the assumption is that the teacher knows the facts of the content as they really exist and that her task is to transmit or encourage the discovery of them. There remains at least a third scenario, which may be called collaborative, where the teacher's purpose is to build an understanding for that time and place and with those children. Here the aspiration of the teacher is that the children themselves will raise the questions and discuss their investigation. This is more important than any knowledge she may have of the facts. The structure is complex as the children interact not only with the teacher but with their classmates and the wider audience, since the end product of their interactions forms a matter for broader discussion. It is perhaps in this constructivist scenario that true dialogical argumentation will be found. Dialogue comes from the Greek *dialogos*, meaning *through words*, and suggests that here the meaning is emerging and flowing between speakers rather than being imposed. Kuhn (1992: 157) points out that this is the sense in which we usually use the word 'argument', as: 'a dialogue between two people who hold opposing views'. The purpose of argument here, she suggests, is to move towards a resolution between the assertions; both parties are active and the complex cognitive conflict between opposing ideas is out in the open. Billig (1987) considers this interactive dimension of argument to be a crucial component of thinking.

Table 6.1 Classroom scenarios

	Informing	Questioning	Collaborative problem solving
Argument type	DIDACTIC ARGUMENT	SOCRATIC ARGUMENT	DIALOGIC ARGUMENT
Intention	Meaning flows. TRANSMISSION	Meaning mapped. DISCOVERY	Shared meaning. CONSTRUCTIVIST
Structure	Traditional rhetorical tools.	I-R-E Reformulations. Implicit rules.	Framed deliberations. Rules explicit.
Audience	Pupils passive and receptive. Internal conflict hidden.	Pupils listen when not questioned. Internal conflict hidden.	Wider sense of audience. Cognitive conflict shows in deliberations.
Role of teacher	Represents public understanding of science persuasively.	Provides a scientific concept map and access to it.	Mediates the transitions between conceptions of science.

This first look at argumentation and classroom practice which takes into account the tensions in primary science might give the framework outlined in Table 6.1. Juxtaposing the three types of argument in this way allows some of the tensions with which this chapter began to be seen in a new light. The teacher may use argumentation with, or enable argumentation between, the children within these three scenarios. Knowledge may be communicated, discovered and built, and a teacher may perhaps sometimes take a realist and sometimes a contextualist view of scientific knowledge. Such flexibility is, in fact, seen in the expert teacher (Boulter, 1992) who is able to use each of these scenarios, changing her style of argumentation and indeed her whole style of discourse as appropriate.

Similarly, children are able to adapt to such changes in scenario. The flexibility of the expert teacher will only work if appropriate language is used for a particular classroom scenario. Such language emerges from the role that the teacher chooses to adopt in relation to the public understanding of science at that time, in that place, with those students, and with that content focus.

The implications of the three scenarios for argumentation can be developed by looking at a number of issues which are common also to the learning of science in the primary classroom.

Shared Issues 1: The Problem of Power

Power in the classroom is invested in the teacher both because she is generally regarded as an expert and because she has the position of a teacher (Russell, 1983). The effect upon speech in the classroom is extreme. Numerous studies of a wide variety of classrooms show that when the teacher is present in class discussions or small group work speech usually has the characteristics shown in Figure 6.6. This is what Janda (1990) calls the 'default mode' and it makes the building of understandings in a constructivist manner almost impossible if it is what happens all the time.

- Teacher defines the fine grain of the content
- Asymmetrical control – the teacher's role is to control
- Focus on content
- Talk disembodied from pupils' experience
- Teacher talks most
- Teacher reformulates the question until she gets the expected answer
- Pauses minimal
- Interactional rules are not explicit and are learnt through participation
- Children's initiatives are ignored
- Planning is the property of the teacher

Figure 6.6   Characteristics of child-centred questioning discourse

To take the children's viewpoints seriously and to enable them to voice their ideas, the constructivist teacher needs both to be able to switch off this default pattern and to operate in more collaborative forms of speech (Figure 6.7).

- Teacher defines the general content frame
- More symmetrical control – the teacher guides and summarises
- Focus on investigative and interactional processes
- Pupils' individual and shared experience are valued
- Teacher listens within the frame set
- Teacher's probing is to clarify the pupil's voice
- Time is allowed for reflection
- Interactional rules are explicit and strongly teacher-directed
- Deliberations initiated by both teacher and pupils
- Planning is made explicit and sometimes shared

Figure 6.7 Characteristics of a collaborative problem-solving discourse

In each scenario, informing, questioning and problem solving, it is the amount of control over the content that determines the sort of knowledge that is expected to emerge. It is argued here that to be successful learners and teachers we need to be skilled in each scenario and to use it according to the purpose we intend. The same is true for argument. We need to become skilled at the three forms of argument – didactic, socratic and dialogic – and be able to use them appropriately, realising their strengths and weaknesses. Janda (1990) suggests that far from being confused, pupils learn as quickly to operate in their 'collaborative self' as they learn to operate as a socratic student or as a child with their parents. Perhaps we should turn our minds to developing the use of such 'multiple selves' and investigate how learners pick up the mode in which they are expected to operate. Perhaps even within the three domains of scientific understanding – individual, common, and official – the three forms of argument exist and could be made to function more effectively for the benefit of science education.

Shared Issues 2: The Relationship of Argument to Conceptual Change

The process by which children change their conceptual frameworks has been the source of much debate by constructivists. Generally this is seen as taking place through a conceptual conflict set up in the learner's mind (Posner *et al.*, 1982). The teacher is seen as providing these opportunities for conflict, diagnosis of existing frameworks, and the presentation of official science at appropriate moments. As has been shown, neither didactic nor socratic argument allows the possibility of the pupil taking the initiative because it would involve being in opposition to the teacher. The pupil may rehearse the teacher's rhetorical argument in his head or join in with the teacher's ideas as a chorus, but he does not have the opportunity to voice his own ideas. Such arguments deal only with the ideas in the teacher's mind and do not explicitly engage with the pupil's ideas. For it to be possible for learners to engage in genuine dialogue, they must do so in the belief that either the person with whom they talk has roughly the same knowledge base as they do or that the person is not going to reveal superior knowledge (Grannott, 1991). This is critical both for a constructivist building of understanding and for dialogic argumentation.

In a recent case study the teacher saw investigative science as being contextually constructed in the classroom. She used strategies to elicit the questions which the pupils wanted to investigate. As the term progressed, it became clear that she saw her role as being that of the director of an action research-like process which went through sequences (Figure 6.8). In this process the pupils accepted that the teacher's role was to direct the process and that any knowledge she might have was not revealed. This teacher did, however, present a number of situational challenges during the work to selected groups of children and she was present to evaluate their outcomes. From a constructivist stance, this was interesting as she allowed several different conceptions to sit alongside each other in the classroom even when there was inconsistency.

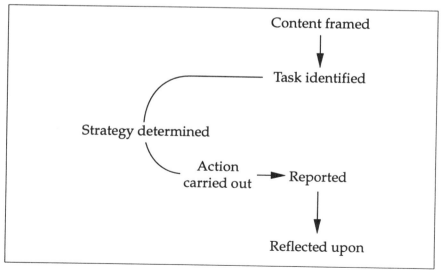

Figure 6.8 Research-like process in children: raising questions and investigating them

At a number of critical points, the whole class were gathered to be informed about what was to happen, or how to carry out a procedure, to raise or refine questions, to elicit a group consensus about how to proceed, to direct the setting of time limits and to reflect on various stages of the process. In the events where the teacher was not telling or directing, there was a characteristic pattern of deliberations, where either the teacher or the pupils initiated a deliberation which then went through more than three pupil turns. These sequences of dialogic argumentation seemed critical in the building of individual and common understandings in the classroom.

Shared Issues 3: The Problem of Oppositional Language

No matter which way one approaches argument, and three types of argument (didactic, socratic and dialogic) have been suggested, there is the notion, that, in order to progress, an argument must put forward an idea which is then refuted by another. In the didactic type, the pupils are without a voice but not without the means of thought, and to varying degrees the argument may be refuted in their minds. A similar situation occurs with socratic argument and this could be what leads to much of the confusion. It is in dialogic argument that the thesis can be openly, verbally refuted by an antithesis and some sort of resolution or synthesis found. It is this kind of argument which underpins collaborative, constructivist knowledge-building.

It has generally been assumed that conceptual change in individuals occurs when existing concepts are challenged (Posner *et al.*, 1982). Osborne and Freyberg (1985), for example, describe a method in which pupils are provided with carefully constructed challenges to their diagnosed existing understandings. Recent work on the speech of collaborative interaction in a primary classroom (Boulter, 1992) shows that when the children are allowed to raise their own concerns and questions within a negotiated framework their deliberations are numerous and involve a wide range of issues. These deliberations show meaning being shared in stretches of dialogical argumentation. In this, as in the other types of argument, there is an oppositional process at work. Consensual views are reached by the pupils through language that is fundamentally oppositional in character.

So far then we have offered no model of classroom interaction which is not based on the polarisation and conflict of positions. This could perhaps pass without comment except for a growing awareness that the language we use is 'man-made' (Spender, 1980) rather than natural or inclusive – and thus that it excludes certain (female) forms of experiencing. It is an uncomfortable thought that the language we use may be inadequate in form and process to express all that both men and women would want to say. Recognising dominant forms of language use – argument, for example – as patriarchal requires us to think about and value alternative or additional ways in which language might be employed. It has been suggested that an inclusive – rather than oppositional – language has more connection with personal experience (Belensky *et al.*, 1986). This connected language, which has been identified in the speech of women, operates through listening rather than striving to gain the right to initiate; through 'rapport' talk, involving telling what you are thinking, rather than 'report' talk (exhibiting knowledge and skill). It focuses on involvement and avoiding isolation rather than status and the avoidance of failure (Tannen, 1991).

Repeated surveys have shown that girls are dissuaded from the study of science by its objectivity and impersonality (Whyld, 1983; Harding, 1986). Some women scientists, like Barbara McClintock, whose work was characterised by a connected 'feeling for the organism', have challenged the prevailing stereotype, but their work has, as a consequence, taken a long time to be recognised (Fox Keller, 1985). Focusing on the oppositional nature of language by emphasising the importance of argument may not be the way to include these new emergent understandings which can enrich our common culture.

Conclusions

The connections between science education and argument have been sketched out and an attempt has been made to define three of the forms of argumentation in relation to classroom scenarios. Three issues have been drawn out which are summarised here as questions:

(1) Does focusing on the oppositional nature of language in argument exclude connected understanding and thus disadvantage women particularly in science?

The metaphorical nature of language means that it is analogical in character, and that the appreciation of similarities and differences is a fundamental activity. In argument, it is the focusing upon differences rather than the appreciation of a balance of both similarity and difference which we believe excludes connected thinking. Connected language should allow access into the discourse of science for girls and provide opportunities for girls to operate from the added strength of their connected selves. Many science teachers do not see the need or the means of doing this at present. The analysis of classroom discourse within a framework derived from the three classroom scenarios we have described, and in situations where access and participation in building scientific understandings in social settings is encouraged, might help to illuminate the way such argument can operate in real settings.

(2)   What is the relationship between conceptual change and argument in learning science?

If it is important that a balance is kept between similarities and differences during argumentation, then it is also important to consider the mechanics of conceptual change. It may be that in looking for the mechanism of conceptual change science educators have concentrated too much on challenge and that what is needed is a more thorough understanding of what happens during argumentation where individuals are also looking for similarities. The balance here between autonomous individuals and the interdependence of the social group is critical. Conceptual change is not a lonesome business, it is also social and affirming, and we need examples of this in practice.

(3)   How can we operate as teachers and learners in didactic, socratic or collaborative modes, and become flexible in operation and in our approach to science?

We suspect that within any event in the classroom there is a complex network of exchanges in the three modes and that the skilful teacher uses what she says at the boundaries between exchanges not only to frame and focus the content of what is spoken about but to indicate the procedures that she expects. There is a need to analyse the discourse of argumentation in the classroom and to find ways of explaining it that make the process clear and enable others to emulate it.

Although these questions have been raised by addressing the issues shared by argumentation and science education, they are questions vital to the development of schooling for the next century. It is already clear that such schooling will need to produce flexible and critical thinkers and learners who know how to build models which are appropriate and effective (ASE, 1994). In this endeavour, it will be important that language in science and across the curriculum becomes more inclusive. Teachers and learners alike will need to learn how to share the ownership of the discourse and content of classroom events and so become able to manage their own learning throughout their lives. Even beginning to answer these questions can take us towards a society where all are learners.

7 Raised and Erased Voices: What Special Cases Offer to Argument

JAMES MCGONIGAL

If you could hear me speaking what is written here, you would probably detect, behind a Scottish accent, the hesitancy of someone uneasily aware of approaching a crossroads where highways meet but the road sign is unclear. The main directions of argument to be puzzled over in this chapter are the continuities and differences between spoken and written argument, and the interplay of both personal and formal voices within the range of argumentation sanctioned within our educational system. And these crucial aspects of spoken and written modes and of personal and permitted voices meet for me now at a point where the words on the sign seem quite literally to be obscured: in the role of argument for school students with a variety of learning disabilities or special educational needs, particularly those struggling with specific language difficulties of a dyslexic nature.

I take argument in any case to be a form of struggle, of action and reaction leading to reflection. This process of argumentation, of trying to create through a sequence of reasoned statements some difference in our own or another's understanding, has been a feature of work in the area of learning disabilities for many years, focused most recently on questions of integration or equal opportunities within mainstream schooling. 'Dyslexia' is itself a term which is likely to cause the sort of lengthy and often bitter argument between professionals, parents and schools which it would be fruitless to enter here. Suffice it to say that for some individual children 'receptive aphasia', whether auditory or visual, defies their attempts to make words work for them as they do for peers, whether in reading or writing.

The frustration which this can cause to otherwise intelligent young people may be imagined, and can lead to some of the more self-defeating aspects of argument: the 'off-loading' or 'dumping' of frustrations and inchoate thoughts, or the self-display of argumentative sparring with adults or other children. Such forms of argument clearly fail to show verbal or intellectual gifts to best advantage, yet the alternative most frequently offered to these individuals in their final years of study in school is another form of argument as display, but so refined as to be beyond their reach. The formal essay or written discussion of a topic, which aims to reveal a command of the subject and to place individuals in some intellectual rank order among their contemporaries, in effect acts as a gate shutting these students off from further progress.

It is true that those who have special needs are entitled to additional assistance within many national or state assessment systems. In the Scottish system, for example, in which a final Standard Grade examination is taken at age 16 by the overwhelming majority of the school population, those who have 'a linguistic difficulty of a cognitive or specific nature' may request the services of a reader and/or a scribe for the examination in English, although their final certificate is endorsed to show that such assistance has been a necessary element in achieving their final grade. Alternative forms of assistance include extra time, enlarged print, tran-scriptions of answers – a range of devices negotiated by the school and the Examination Board, but most of them dependent upon the precise way in which the request is framed by the school, signalling a *specific* language difficulty and not a *general* one. In effect, this has meant that only those youngsters showing a marked discrepancy between the intellectual quality of their oral work in class and their written work (and fortunate enough to attend a school which actually recognises this) are entitled to such assistance. Other youngsters with 'mild' or 'moderate' disabilities of a more general kind are not entitled to extra help in terms of scribes or readers. And some children with specific language difficulties, who for reasons of pride or self-determination decline to accept this extra help with its ensuing endorsement, have had to struggle on in one-sided competition with their peers.

To such discrepancies of treatment between schools may be added further concerns about the innate discrepancy which arises from the very assistance offered. If a scribe or reader is involved, acting between the language of the task and the candidate's response to it, where does that leave the 'objectivity' of assessment criteria; and who exactly is doing the reading or writing for which the candidate gains his or her national certificate? This matters more in English and in other 'communication' subjects than it does, say, in the sciences, because the language is both the mode of assessment and the 'subject content' being assessed. English is already open enough to charges of subjectivity of assessment without such additional epistemological confusion.

Clearly some disentanglement is called for. A committee was set up in 1989 to consider the whole array of special needs issues within the Scottish national assessment system, and raised the radical notion of Independent courses in Standard Grade, designed by individual schools with the particular needs of their own pupils in mind and building upon the increased professionalism of learning support staff working in partnership with classroom teachers. This was a notion which uncovered for the bureaucratic mind deeps in which monsters swam: comparability, credibility and consistency of assessment being the most fearsome of these. In response, and to ease the existing concerns about scribes and modality in English already described, it was decided to develop two Independent courses in areas of English where some precedents already existed: in the special arrangements for candidates with specific language difficulties described above, and for those with hearing impairment.

Developing a Sense of Voice

For the last three years I have been involved with others in developing the first of those courses. The working group was itself a chorus of different voices and interests, sometimes competing or clashing, never in perfect harmony, but finally discovering coalitions of interest as we went along: a headteacher of a high school, two educational psychologists, two high school heads of English departments, a school inspector with national responsibility for special education, two officers from the Scottish Examination Board, and three staff involved in teacher education in the areas of English and supportive education. Each of us had, I suppose, particular children in mind: different individuals who had not only failed examinations but, more profoundly, in whom the examination system itself had been seen to fail.

Recalling the story of that group's progress now, I see it as a narrative shot through with argument. Each meeting in the early days seemed to start with a debate over terms: communication, disability, assessment, need. As Gunther Kress has suggested in his essay 'Texture and meaning' (Kress, 1989:12), narrative and argument can be seen as ways of handling difference in a culture, argument providing 'the means of bringing difference into existence' while narrative 'provides means of resolution of difference in an uncontentious mode'. This project proved an often contentious means of bringing difference (special need or difficulty) into view, each from our own perspective. The memories that spurred me were of children whom, as a teacher, I had failed to convince of the worth of their own writing, or of even starting to unravel the knot of their own syntax or spelling, despite evident sharpness orally; who would distort or deflect the force of an argument because they did not know how to spell what they had in mind to say; whose consequent banalities were an insult to their own intelligence.

But where were their voices in our deliberations? It seemed that they figured mostly in anecdotes of graphic failure and intermittent success. The latter depended upon an ability to make their voices heard through forms or genres which were already recognised within the educational system (group discussions, or classroom debates) and through others which they themselves were helping to devise: in multi-media presentations or talks on topics which they cared deeply enough about to research and demonstrate to their peers. Their ability to argue, it seemed, was dependent upon their finding a means to communicate which was recognised as valid by both school and community.

One answer to their problem, therefore, was to give their voices room and time. We decided to cut through the Gordian knot of dyslexic language by moving directly from writing to taped talk (renamed Communicating; as reading became Understanding) to achieve the same ends, using broadly the same criteria and texts as the national examination used for writing and reading. This last was vital if the new Independent course was to be credible, and also manageable within mainstream classrooms. What we envisaged was an approach which could operate as many teachers in the language arts or social subjects already tend to operate, with a variety of potential responses, some written and others spoken, to a given stimulus. This stimulus is often a text, but increasingly a media artefact or even a piece of pupil writing or talk may be used; and the element of differentiation arises from pupils' responses to it, as much as from alternative tasks that are broadly framed for different ability groupings.

Early in the group's discussions, it became clear that this new Independent course would be helpful not only to pupils with dyslexic difficulties but also to visually impaired pupils not confident in Braille; or to those in special schools and mainstream classrooms who had problems with the attention span or stamina that written examinations demand; or even to those with certain motor difficulties who sought to control for themselves their means of communication. Response in the classroom and examination room would involve listening to and composing on tape and learning the sorts of skills in giving and receiving messages that are increasingly useful in a world where, though the written word is still foregrounded, most of the busy background noise comes from effective users of the spoken mode.

Since much of that vocal dealing depends upon convincing others of the truth or worth of what we say, the skills of argument naturally enter the scene. They do so in a way that I would associate with Vygotsky (1986), in that the emphasis throughout is on language learned through negotiation with a given social context, which clearly registers and records the student's intended meaning. Moreover, it offers an almost immediate reflective reframing of this language as a mental construct, through the simple ability to replay and revise the voice on tape.

Study of literature is one traditional way of reframing human experience in English classes, but how could that be made accessible to non-readers? We decided to experiment with a return to its oral roots through existing broadcast resources, in particular a BBC schools radio programme which featured several short stories with a common hero – a picaresque Scottish schoolboy character. Each story combined a strong social theme with a broad and lively, often linguistic, humour; their author, Geddes Thomson, was himself a teacher of English who worked in an inner-city high school in Glasgow and had caught the energy and inventiveness of his characters' urban Scottish speech.

Three particular memories remain with me from trialling this material in schools. Firstly, there was the way in which those new Communicating and Understanding tasks proved actually more attractive to the pupils they were not aimed at! The pupil activities offered the option of a spoken or a traditional written response, but the 'dyslexic' target group in one school preferred to struggle on with the familiar written activities, while the others opted for the oral alternative. I do not think this was merely novelty value, though there may well have been something of that. (The very novelty which offered more confident writers a new challenge may equally have intimidated those who already felt themselves sufficiently 'challenged' by the orthography and time scale of the written task.) Listening to the tape, and the consequent interaction between the tape's voice (both as narrative and as a sort of 'talking task sheet') and their own voices, encouraged in most pupils an independence of response that seemed valuable in its own right and not merely a simplified task for slower learners. That was important if this course was to attain credibility within and beyond the school community.

I also learned that in the context of argumentative or discursive discourse silence can be as illuminating as voice. Since reading was to be replaced by listening in our new arrangements, we were at least dimly aware that listening must be a far more complex and interactive activity than some rather clumsy attempts to assess it in formal examinations have suggested. And yet it was only when observing young people whose intellectual functioning in learning situations depended upon listening, rather than on unreliable and lengthy decoding of print, that we could begin to appreciate what it entailed. My memory here is of a Chinese pupil whose English was not confident (she spent half the year with relatives in Hong Kong and the remainder in Scotland) who seemed to benefit particularly from being part of a group responding to one of the tape tasks. This was an imaginative response to the short story text, in which they were to record a telephone conversation with a grandparent, communicating something of the difficulties encountered by one of the characters on his first day at a new school.

Hearing other group members not only recording different responses but replaying and discussing these in terms of their content and register taught her much more about the forms and protocols of English in family situations than the original written task (the unlikely 'Write a letter to your grandmother … ') would have done. Here was a sort of oral redrafting, with the single sex group offering each other a supportive and quite sophisticated level of analysis, it seemed to me, while modelling for this particular pupil the lexis and grammar of a particular social situation. The Chinese girl did not record, but I have rarely observed anyone listen so actively.

A similarly active involvement was clear in a special school for 16-year-old students with moderate learning disabilities, where the use of an old telephone served to contextualise a reworked task which had turned a 'letter of complaint to your local City Council' … into a 'hot-line waiting for your comments on a local environmental issue'. As Medway (1981) has pointed out, it is important not only for our students to discuss matters which are of concern to them, but also to debate what it is worthwhile to discuss; reflection should not be limited to how the discussion went in terms of their individual or group performance. On this occasion the environmental topic clearly linked with other school and community activities in which these young people were involved. Both their genuine involvement in this task and the helpfulness of the formative comments to each speaker from the rest of the group took me by surprise, and gave hope for the relevance and reflectiveness which the new spoken course could offer. Again it was the sort of slow-motion action-replay of the talk that seemed to create a different sort of group attentiveness and a natural occasion for talking about their own language.

In each of those classrooms, the taped language seemed essentially different from what would have been achieved either through a written or a spoken response, whether group or individual. This had something to do with a single voice working over time to achieve particular effects.

Assessment as Listening and Response

All pupils handled the basic technology of tapes and recorders confidently, even when it came to testing them in ways that paralleled formal examinations in writing and comprehension. Our examination in Understanding demanded two or preferably three machines. One of these was for the taped version of the passage itself, recorded from a past examination paper but 'chunked' into five or six sections of larger-than-paragraph length for ease of reference back and forwards on the tape, the position of the sections being noted from the tape-counter on the first listening. Another machine was used to play a tape with the questions, specifically linked to particular sections in the passage to mimic the line references which are normally given (e.g. 'The answers to questions 10 and 11 are in Section 4 of the passage'). Either this second machine or a third machine, if available, was used by the candidates to record their answers on a third tape.

All of that is more complicated to explain than it actually appeared to be for those sitting the trial examinations. Using different machines keeps the tapes from getting muddled (though we colour coded and numbered them in any case), but more importantly keeps the tape-counter steady for accurate reference between questions and text. To provide an aural equivalent to the reading procedure of keeping one finger on the question while looking across at the passage and then checking back to ensure that the answer found is actually the correct one, each question was read out twice on tape. The listener could hear the question once and press Pause, then replay ('reread') the relevant section of the passage, and then release the Pause button to recheck the question being asked before finally recording the answer. This element of personal control over text and response worked well as a replacement for the intrinsically dependent relationship with reader or scribe.

The alternative to writing was a little more problematic. Our arrangements allowed candidates to use notes or a separate practice tape, or both, to rehearse and redraft their Communicating piece towards a final version in a mock examination. Now what happened with some dyslexic pupils was positive and interesting, particularly in their argumentative and reflective pieces: we observed apparently illegible notes being used as a sort of springboard into far more extensive or measured work than they could possibly have managed in writing. But in other cases candidates simply wrote out their response to the topic before reading it on to tape, and it was not always easy for markers to discern this from the taped evidence alone.

Of course, such pieces were often self-penalising since they were shorter, more stilted and lacking the markers of the sorts of spontaneity expected in spoken communication. Yet even impressive responses could pose problems. In a few cases, some pupils had simply repeated on tape a talk they had already given in class as part of their normal Talk assessment, in which solo talk to an audience as well as group discussion skills combine to give a final grade. The interrelationship between talk, 'communicating' and writing obviously needed to be teased apart for both pupils and teachers, and there are probably three ways in which this problem might be untangled. We can consider the pupil, or the teaching situation, or finally language itself, with the strategies of rhetoric which come naturally to mind in this context of spoken performance towards determined ends.

Firstly, it is helpful to remember the chief purpose of these new procedures, which came into existence because it seemed unreasonable and unreliable to assess dyslexic youngsters in the written mode in which they are predictably weakest. Rather like testing one-armed Tarzans in tree-swinging, that is a strategy in which everyone is heading for a fall. Assessment should seek to measure positively what candidates can achieve and the aim of the Independent course is to develop skills of articulateness, confidence and flexibility in spoken language which will be of greater use to such candidates in their future lives in society than further disheartening focus on their manifest failure in written language. Language skills are not being ignored here: rather, they are being explored and refined through the spoken rather than the written mode.

This would suggest that what we termed Communicating veers towards talk in its educational purposes, yet the classroom context in which much of the learning will take place points to a key difference. Talk in the classroom will always have a known and present audience whose reactions and attitudes will shape it in various ways: the vocabulary, accent and register revealed in any given task will be altered by peer-group and other social pressures. A key difference between Communicating and talk is that the former is composed for an absent audience, as writing tasks almost always are. Like writing, communicating on tape therefore demands an explicitness of detail to compensate for the lack of gesture or other paralinguistic features which carry a certain amount of information to the listener, and also an awareness of the need to signal much more clearly than in talk the stages of an argument or a narrative. In writing, titles and subtitles, paragraphing, punctuation and typography are all used for this purpose; so in Communicating, tone, stress, pause and emphasis should also be used much more consciously than they are in talk, where we are usually able to take our cue from the faces, comments or body language of our audience and signal changes of direction by subtle combinations of physical and vocal detail which interact or mesh with theirs.

It was interesting to note that, both under examination conditions and in the taped folio of work recorded over a period of time, it seemed more attention was being paid to formality or 'correctness' in the spoken discourse than would normally have been found in the classroom situation. The voicing of individual ideas on tape without interruption and with the option to rewind and record over false starts, or even to insert new sections within a spoken text, appeared to release some elements of structuring and also risk-taking which are features of the most effective spoken communications. In this way, these 'learning-disabled' students seemed to overcome some at least of the confusions which Gubb (1987: 163) encountered when young writers move from the dialogic context of group discussion of a topic to the monologic task of unifying various perceptions into extended formal prose and a single voice:

> Breakdowns occur in logic, grammar gets forgotten; changes of topic take place with disconcerting abruptness and passionately expressed views are reduced to trite one-line opinions ... Discussion suddenly seems to have little connection with discursive writing.

Insecurities with the coherence and cohesion of their own material, however, meant that some students declined to take risks. Those who opted to read a carefully prepared piece (in one or two cases, parental pressure to succeed seemed to have had a depressing influence) sounded awkwardly like the way some academics 'read a paper' at a conference. What we were hearing was in essence a written piece which took little account of the spontaneous quality of speech, which offers diversion to the listener precisely because it constantly tends to divert from its apparent purpose (into byways of anecdote, odd bits of information or 'for instances') before finding itself back on track again. Often as teachers we do this deliberately when students grow weary of our work ethic. In argument, too, this can be a useful procedure: commenting on the mathematical meaning of the term, Andrews *et al.* (1993: 13) reflect that

> any particular argument can be described in terms of its 'angles': sometimes the argument will run obliquely to previous points, and at

other times it will turn 180 degrees or proceed in a straight line for a number of points.

What is aimed for is, therefore, a stretch of spoken text which carries within it some of the markers of the written mode (explicitness, a certain formality, a sense of having been composed within the constraints of genre or register) but expressed through some of the conventions of the spoken (a seeming spontaneity, variety of tone, elements of accent and stress that lend a sense of personality or authenticity to the discourse). Teachers can help here by giving their pupils practice in the sorts of tasks and contexts that call forth such language. Not a letter to a newspaper complaining about a political or moral issue, then, but a radio phone-in or hot-line; not a short story, merely, but one to be put on tape for motorists to help them stay awake on motorways, or one to send 6-year-olds to sleep, or one for people in hospital; not a 'neutral' character description but a statement in defence or accusation which might be given in court ... and so on.

Rhetoric and Realities

Such tasks will demand adjustment of a tendency among many teachers of English to steer towards literary convention rather than social purpose. Common sense and observation suggest, however, that in the media language to which our pupils listen for much of the day, social purpose is paramount. There the context dictates much language that is 'written as if to be spoken' (radio or television news broadcasts, continuity links, or advertising voice-overs) and much that is 'spoken as if written' (commentary on a state occasion, for instance, or a serious news feature or charity appeal, or the sorts of language which in an intertextual way tend to play off a literary genre or socio-historical register, as in advertisements which employ the music, imagery and voice of 'heritage' or tradition to lend a seeming authenticity to a product).

All of that rhetoric of everyday life – its persuasive (and ultimately political) purposefulness – can come into play in an examined or 'denaturalised' way through the spoken course. Looking at it in language terms, we can note that whilst most teachers and their pupils by this stage have learned to focus on the power of the 'inner' aspects of context in shaping meaning in a text (namely user, purpose and audience), there is still more to be learned from focusing on the 'outer' aspects which shape the language choices which we make: whether the text is meant to be understood as written or spoken (or one of the more subtle mixed forms mentioned above); and how register and genre, once selected for an utterance, start to shape or bend it to their own formal ends. This sort of exploration is equally valid for developing self-aware young readers and writers, of course, as it is for those whose main sources of knowledge and control will emerge through the spoken mode.

It will be through some such contextual focus, formalised by discussion, storyboarding, mind-mapping, modelling or whatever, that pupils will begin to find their own way forward in the skills of spoken English. Communicating on tape gives them the opportunity to develop talk to the extent that it verges on writing, while still retaining the individually voiced response which differentiates it from that arena which for them is fraught with failure. The presence of the rewind button, with its potential to replay and reshape the spoken word, at the same time usefully moves us away from the dialogic continuum of talk and into the realm of rhetoric: in our society, much of the most effective communication occurs with a mixed audience, seen and unseen (points made both to the studio audience and for viewers at home) and in which the form and content of the message become intriguingly one.

The approach through rhetoric rather than writing, through communicating rather than talk, through a planned and polished effort rather than impromptu thoughts, moves us towards an interesting factor uncovered by Richard Andrews (1992) in his study of young writers: that they are much more willing to reorder the elements of argument than they are of narrative. Whether we lead our students through Aristotelian four-, five- or six-part orations, or whether they are exposed to the 'chunking' of texts on tape in the way described above, matters less than the potential of movement beyond the 'literary' paragraph plan towards conceptual mapping, flowcharts, storyboarding, prompt cues or a range of mnemonic devices which can carry the argument forward in ways which bear some resemblance to the classical and medieval *ars memoria*, and which actually might place dyslexic students at some advantage.

If that happens, it may well be because the tape in some way 'objectifies' the ideas, moving these students beyond a subjective sense of the inadequacy of writing to express what is deeply thought and felt. The taped text appears to offer utterance in its original sense of 'outerance', where the voice taking shape in the air both articulates and clarifies what was meant as it goes out from and returns to the speaker. The often (if partially) quoted phrase of Graham Wallas, an early Fabian campaigner with George Bernard Shaw, comes to mind: 'The little girl had the making of a poet in her who, being told to be sure of her meaning before she spoke, said: "How can I know what I think till I see what I say?" '

Or hear what I say, in this case. Certainly we found a tendency in the most unlikely candidates to write poetically, or to express and argue for deeply felt concerns about the nature of their own lives. And to do so at some length. They handled this reflective mode much better than they did narrative, in most cases. More importantly, there is a clear sense that the spoken approach offers young people the opportunity to move from fiction to commitment: the written task as imaginative response is changed in the utterance towards more 'politically' charged speech by a new focus on the voice that speaks. For them, an awkwardly composed letter is dismissible in a way that a 'live' phone call to a hot-line is not, where the power of the human voice to challenge and persuade is immediately evident. Interestingly, when reflecting on the difference between constructing narrative and argument, one of Richard Andrews' pupils took up this point: 'I think that voice has a lot to do with how good your argument is. You can use your voice like plasticine: you can mould it into the argument, bringing your voice high and letting it drop down' (Andrews, 1992: 124).

Questions of formality and standard English raise themselves naturally at this point, and the development of that literate, cohesive style which many adolescents find difficult to achieve, particularly those whose learning difficulties prevent them from taking pleasure in print. Bakhtin (1981) contrasts the centripetal, monologic, officially sanctioned forms of standard bureaucratic language (which may appear essential for the approach that is being advocated above) with the centrifugal heteroglossia of the dialogic imagination, issuing in the many forms and registers of spoken language, often with satiric intent. Teenage students can often seem incurably dialogic.

Yet moving towards a spoken form of standard English through taped work makes us reconsider that dichotomy. English as taught in schools may be more coercive as a discipline than the liberal credentials of many English teachers would have us believe. Performing well in English is perhaps too often a result of being inducted into a discourse which talks about texts within certain parameters, using terminology sanctioned by particular theories of reading (cf. Mitchell, 1992). The use of taped responses, however, opens all of that up for review, because this forces us as teachers to listen at *the pace of the speaker's thinking*, rather than racing ahead with our minds or our pens poised to detect deviation from the achieved consensus. Tapes thus enable us to listen patiently to what young people really think about the ideas we have 'discussed' with them. And when we comment on their work, our response too is voiced on the same tape for future replay. Or erasure?

The human voice has the power to move the hearts and minds not only of those who listen but also of those who speak. Once something is said, it might be argued that there is really no erasure. Tapes may be dubbed out, certainly, as print may be rubbed out, but an idea once expressed is very difficult to let die, particularly if heard coming to life in tones that are recognisably one's own. Play that again. Is it really what I wanted to say? Already that argument with first impressions has begun which is in reality, whether written or spoken, the life of the mind.

Note

1. Further information or materials about the examination in spoken English described here may be sought from the Scottish Curriculum Council, Gardyne Road, Dundee, Scotland, UK; or from the Examinations Officer in English, Scottish Examination Board, Ironmills Road, Dalkeith, Lothian, Scotland, UK; or from Dr Jim McGonigal, St Andrew's College, Duntocher Road, Bearsden, Glasgow G61 4QA, UK.

8 Extending Children's Voices: Argument and the Teaching of Philosophy

PATRICK J.M. COSTELLO

In the introduction to this volume, it has been suggested that the teaching of philosophy in schools may make an important contribution both to the theory and practice of argument. My aim here is to substantiate this thesis. The chapter is divided into three sections. In the first, I examine the relationship between 'argument' and 'philosophy'. Secondly, I suggest that introducing philosophy into schools provides teachers with an opportunity to 'extend children's voices'. Finally, in order to illustrate the view that young children are capable of engaging in philosophical debate and argument, I offer a dialogue in which I took part with a class of 10- and 11-year-old pupils.

Argument and Philosophy

The two-year project entitled *Improving the Quality of Argument, 5-16*, funded by the Esmée Fairbairn Charitable Trust, was informed and influenced by the different teaching and research interests of its two co-directors. Richard Andrews came to this project from a background of secondary education and English; my own previous experience had been in primary education and philosophy. In this part of the chapter, I propose to examine, in rather more depth than was possible within the confines of our final report (Andrews *et al.*, 1993), the relationship between argument and philosophy.

In recent years, calls for the teaching of philosophy in schools have become increasingly prominent (Lipman, 1988, 1991; Lipman *et al.*, 1980; Whalley, 1987). Elsewhere, I have advanced arguments for the introduction of such teaching (Costello, 1989a), examined recent developments in this field in Britain (Costello, 1994b) and discussed ways in which teachers might promote philosophical debate in the classroom (Costello, 1989b). Miller (1986) has suggested that in order to convince the sceptic of the value of such work, protagonists of philosophy in schools should provide substantial transcripts of pupils engaged in discussion. In response to this, I have offered a number of dialogues in which I participated with children aged from 8 to 11 years (Costello, 1988, 1993a, 1993b).

In seeking to elucidate the relationship between 'argument' and 'philosophy', it is necessary to offer stipulative definitions of both terms. In the Esmée Fairbairn final report (Andrews *et al.*, 1993: 16) it was suggested that ' ... we take argument to be *a process of argumentation, a connected series of statements intended to establish a position (whether in speech or in writing)*, sometimes taking the form of an interchange in discussion or debate, and usually presenting itself as a *sequence* or chain of reasoning.'

My stipulative definition of 'philosophy' suggests that it involves a thorough endeavour to develop, clarify, justify and apply one's thinking. The formulation and elucidation of arguments or theories is central to this task (Costello, 1989b). Here the focus is methodological and is intended to indicate a particular approach to the examination of *all* disciplines. Thus it is possible to speak of the philosophy of religion, science, mathematics, etc. where each denotes a critical scrutiny of the theoretical foundations, concepts and practices associated with individual subject areas. In addition, the teaching and learning of philosophy in schools involves introducing children to arguments and to ways of thinking which are central to its major constituent elements: logic, ethics, metaphysics, epistemology and so on (Abel, 1976; Almond, 1988).

On the basis of these definitions, I wish to suggest that the connection between 'philosophy' and 'argument' may be made at two levels, one of which focuses on the philosophical content of the subject matter being taught, while the second examines the means by which a person's performance within the discipline is to be assessed. As regards the former, 'a connected series of statements intended to establish a position', which is usually seen in the form of 'a sequence or chain of reasoning', may be considered 'philosophical' in so far as it relates to or is fundamentally concerned with the various branches of the subject outlined above.

The question of how teachers can assess progress made by children in acquiring the skills of argument is one to which teachers and researchers engaged in the Esmée Fairbairn project gave much thought. The model which was produced in our final report (Andrews *et al.*, 1993: 47–8), and which is based on the work of one of the teachers involved in the research,

John Adamson (Costello, 1994a: 83–4), also enables a link to be made between 'argument' and 'philosophy', since it offers teachers a check-list by which to determine a pupil's attainments in oral and written work of a philosophical nature (Appendix 8.1). Many of the criteria suggested will be particularly useful here as the study of philosophy is predicated upon one's ability to provide reasons, evaluate evidence, demonstrate a degree of logic in the development of an argument, and so on.

Extending Children's Voices

The notion of 'voice' as metaphor is a useful one. In the context of the title of this book, it was suggested by Sally Mitchell and refers, in my view, to the dual nature of argument as being essentially a tool that enables reasoned agreement or disagreement to take place. It also draws attention to the fact that arguments may be offered from many different standpoints and that this multiplicity of perspective may assist either in securing assent to or provoking disagreement with a proposition, point of view or set of beliefs.

In this chapter, however, the term 'voice' is used rather differently. It denotes the capacity, willingness and opportunity that children have to engage in various aspects of educational provision. For example, we might speak of a child's 'philosophical voice', by which is meant his/her ability and desire to participate in philosophical discussion, debate and argument, whether in speech or in writing. Alternatively, it could be suggested that a pupil has been unable to develop such a voice, not due to a lack of volition or capacity, but simply because the ethos of the school or classroom has impeded or prevented this outcome. As Corson (1993: 22) argues: 'Education is a field where the language rights … of children can be trampled on by the routine exercise even of legitimate power.'

How then might schools seek to 'extend children's voices' through the teaching of philosophy? In order to achieve this, certain prerequisites are necessary. Firstly, teachers need to be aware that the teaching of philosophical reasoning and argument has been and continues to be regarded in many quarters as having little or no importance in the education of young children. In other words, the philosophical 'voice' is conspicuous by its absence in many pupils (at least if evidence of their academic performance at school is the yardstick to which one is referring).

A realisation by teachers that children have not had and continue not to have adequate opportunities to examine philosophical ideas and topics is essential if progress in this area is to be made in the classroom. Attention may then focus on how the situation is to be improved. In seeking to offer a blueprint for success in schools, I suggest that the dispositions and abilities required of the teacher may be summarised as follows (see Lipman *et al.*, 1980: 98):

Teacher: LISTENS to what children say;
HEARS what children say;
EXTENDS what children say.

In the context of teaching philosophy, I would argue that 'listening', 'hearing' and 'extending' all involve a *willingness* on the part of the teacher to allow children to communicate their thoughts, to understand and to facilitate such thinking and to seek to improve it. Similarly, all posit a certain intellectual *capacity* on the part of teachers. This is evidenced by their ability to:

HEED what is being said in discussions and to treat children's thinking with respect;
DISTINGUISH philosophical reasoning from other forms of thinking and argument;
IMPROVE the quality of pupils' philosophical thinking, reasoning and argument.

As is evident from the emphasis on teachers' dispositions and abilities, there is a strong link between 'effective teaching' and 'effective philosophy teaching'. To the extent to which children feel that their views and arguments are being listened to, grappled with and valued, they are more likely to respond positively to the activities associated with such an ethos. Of course, the effective teaching of philosophy requires more than the desire or capacity to pay attention to children's utterances: some knowledge of the discipline and of what counts as operating successfully within it are also necessary.

To facilitate this, many proponents of children's philosophy offer training programmes to enable teachers to deepen their understanding of the subject and of how it might be introduced into schools. While agreeing in principle with such an approach, I have one reservation about it. Where a *specific* course of training is deemed to be an *essential* prerequisite for the successful implementation of an educational programme, this may lead to a reluctance on the part of teachers to engage in work associated with that programme since they may think, mistakenly, that there is a need to undertake lengthy study before any significant teaching can take place. Certainly some training and reflection is required and I have offered modules of 30 and 40 hours' duration, at Master's degree level, to facilitate this. However, while suggesting that teachers should seek to acquire a basic competence in philosophical content and method in order to develop children's ability to reason and to argue well, I always emphasise to course members that the questions which form the basis of philosophical discussions are central to *all* academic disciplines (for example, 'Why?'; 'What do you mean?'; 'How do you know?' etc.) as well as to effective teaching itself (see Costello, 1989b: 78).

Promoting Philosophical Argument in the Classroom

In order to illustrate how the idea of 'extending children's voices' through the teaching of philosophy might take place in the classroom, I offer the following dialogue which discusses issues raised by the exercise 'What Makes You *You*?' (see Appendix 8.2). Contributions made by pupils whom I have not been able to identify have been included without attribution. One of the aims of my commentary in the text is to make connections between the arguments children offer and those employed by professional philosophers.

PC:	'What makes you *you*?' is the question we are going to discuss, and the first thing Ian said was what?
Ian:	The personality.
PC:	The personality. What do you mean by that, Ian? Can you say a little bit more to me about that?
Ian:	What makes you *you* is there's a decision, and the decision you make on that, that's your personality. That's what you would say. That's what that person would say.
PC:	OK.
Ian:	That's their personality.
PC:	Excellent. Michael?
Michael:	Your soul.
PC:	What's a soul, Michael?
Michael:	The personality, you, what makes you *you*.
PC:	It's your soul. That's a very interesting thought. Any other thoughts? What were you going to say, Christopher?
Christ. Ss.:	I was going to say that myself.
PC:	You were going to say 'soul' as well?
Christ. Ss.:	Shall I tell you why?
PC:	Yes. I want to know why.
Christ. Ss.:	Because we were doing topic-work about Aidan and Miss G said 'What does ... '. Well, actually, it was St Cuthbert, but he saw the soul of St Aidan. So Miss G

asked us what the soul was and we eventually came up with that your soul is what makes you *you*.

(*Comment*) This view competes with that offered by Clarence Durrow, in his article 'The myth of the soul' (1972: 291–9).

PC:	Oh super. So I've … come upon a subject that you've already touched on before. Did Miss G ask you what the soul looks like?
Chorus:	Yes.
Terry:	Yes, but you can't see it.
PC:	Terry?
Terry:	You can't see it.
PC:	Well, I can't see my liver either, can I, Eve? But I have a good idea what my liver looks like.
——	It's invisible.
PC:	It's invisible.
	[*Laughter*]
PC:	What do you think, Helen?
Helen:	It's a ghost-like figure that you can't touch.
PC:	A ghost-like figure that you can't touch. Christopher?
Christ. Ss.:	Nobody actually knows what it looks like because nobody has seen one … Well, Cuthbert saw one, but he didn't … He thinks he saw one. But he didn't actually explain what it was. Well, he did, but …
	[*Laughter*]
PC:	But what? I've lost that bit.
——	There's lots of different stories. There's some stories … Some books say he saw this and some books say he saw something else. So, you don't actually know what he saw.
PC:	So, let me ask you this: if we don't know what the soul looks like and if Cuthbert thinks he saw one, but we're not sure whether he did, how do we know that what makes you *you* is your soul? How do we know that? What's our … what am I looking for?
——	Explanation.
PC:	Explanation or … ?
——	Argument.
PC:	Argument or … ?
——	Reason.
PC:	Reason or … ?
——	Proof.

PC: What's our proof that, in fact, we have a soul? What's
                 our proof? Because you just said to me 'What makes you
                 you is the soul.' And I'm saying to you: 'Well, no one has
                 seen that.' Have you seen your soul, Sarah?
                 [*Sarah shakes her head*]
PC: Not at all? Not even once? No?
                 [*Sarah shakes her head*]
PC: Have you seen your soul, Louise?
Louise: No.
PC: No? Have you seen your soul, Scott?
Scott: No, because no one knows what it looks like.
PC: Well, if no one knows what it looks like, how do we
                 know we have a soul, Christopher?
Christ. Ss.:   I don't know, but I think I've heard of 'soul' meaning ...
PC: Meaning?
Christ. Ss.:   Like you were sort of on your own.
Ian: That's 'solo'.
                 [*Laughter*]
PC: Well let's leave this idea of a soul for a moment. What
                 other answers might we give to this question: 'What
                 makes you *you*?', Christopher?
Christ. Ss.:   How tall you are, the colour of your eyes, how big your
                 ears are, how big your nose is.

(*Comment*) Christopher subscribes to the philosophical view that the
problem of personal identity can be resolved by referring to an individual's
bodily features.

————   How big your mouth is.
PC: OK, Jenny?
Jenny: Heritage.
PC: Heritage. Say something about that to me, Jenny.
Jenny: It makes you look how your mother and father look.

(*Comment*) Reuben Abel (1976: 188) asks: 'Is ancestry part of the person?
The genes you inherit from your parents, and which were fixed at the
moment of your conception, will normally be transmitted unchanged to
your descendants.'

PC: OK, Christopher?
Christ. Ss.:   Well, I think it could be your brain, because your brain
                 makes you do things, and your brain makes your
                 decisions.

PC:	All right. Any other thoughts on what makes you *you*? Ben?
Ben:	Your bones, because if you didn't have any bones, you'd be floppy.
PC:	Your bones. Yes. And some people ... say: 'I've got large bones,' and some people say: 'I've got small bones.' OK. Let me ask you this, then. Let us say you decided this evening: 'Oh well, I've had enough wearing the same old clothes that I always wear. On Saturday, I'm going to go into town and I'm going to buy myself some new clothes.' And you go into town and you spend a fortune buying some new clothes. But the thing about these new clothes is they are not at all like any other clothes that you previously liked. Let's say your favourite colour used to be blue; you decide: 'Everything I buy is going to be black.' Let's say your favourite fabric was silk; you say to yourself: 'No more silk for me – leather.' And you put your new clothes on and you're walking in the city centre, and you're feeling very happy with yourself. And then you say to yourself: 'I know. I am going to have a new hair-do. Lots of people compliment me on my ginger hair, but I'm going to have a change. I'm going to go blonde. Lots of people have complimented me on my curly hair. I'm going to have a change and I'm going to have it all straightened out. I don't want to be blonde any more. I'm going to go dark. Now, imagine that you went into town and you bought a lot of new clothes, you went into the hairdresser's and you got a new hair-do, a new hair-style. Would you be the same person?

(*Comment*) In discussing personal identity, John Hospers (1989: 410) asks: ' "Under what conditions is X the same self, or the same person as before?" That is, what mental or physical changes can occur in Mr X without his ceasing to be Mr X?'

——	Yeah.
——	No, you wouldn't have any money left.
	[*Laughter*]
PC:	That would be one difference. You would have no money left, but would you be the same person, do you think, Jenny?
Jenny:	Inside you would but outside you wouldn't.
PC:	Can you say a little bit more to me about that?

Jenny:	Well, say you were a very nice person.
PC:	Yes.
Jenny:	You'd still be a very nice person, but you've just had a new hair-do and got new clothes.

(*Comment*) Jenny suggests that the notion of 'personal identity' incorporates both mental and physical aspects.

PC:	So, you are a different person on the outside, for you. What do you say, Christopher?
Christ. Ss.:	Well, if … you took everything off and cut all your hair off, if you did it with your new image and your old image, you'd still look the same.
PC:	Except for the hair …
Ian:	You wouldn't have any hair, would you?
PC:	Let's say I go on a diet. I say to myself: 'No more sweets for me.'
——	No more 'Mars' bars.
PC:	I like sweets, so it's very unlikely I'm going to do that. But let's say I do, and come in to you in a month's time and I say: 'I've lost two stones. I feel like a new person.' Am I?
——	No, you're not.
PC:	Am I a new person, Abigail?
Abigail:	No, because you can't change what you are inside.
PC:	What can't you change then? Give me some examples. That's a very good comment. Give me some examples of what you can't change. Because you've said I can change my hairstyle, I can change my figure, I can change my clothes. What can't I change, Abigail?
Abigail:	You can't change your personality.
PC:	Can you not?
Ian:	You could because you could stop doing what you used to do and do other things.
PC:	Can you give me an example of that?
Ian:	Well, say you never ever took white sugar, you always have brown sugar in your tea or whatever.
PC:	OK.
Ian:	And you hated coffee.
PC:	Yes.
Ian:	Then you started having coffee and never have tea, or always have white sugar …
PC:	Yes.

Ian: ... that would be changing your personality, in a way.
PC: OK Carl?
Carl: I think what makes you *you* is your philosophy of the world. The decisions you make.

(*Comment*) Carl argues that a person's mental functions are central to his or her personal identity.

PC: OK. So, it's your personal philosophy of the world that makes you *you*. Well, let's say, talking about Abigail's point that you can't change what's inside, let's say I'm a liar, and let's say I'm a thief, and let's say I'm a bully. And, consequently, I'm not very popular, as you can imagine. But one day I go home and I say to myself: 'From now on I'm not going to be like that any more. I'm never going to tell any more lies. I'm never going to steal things that do not belong to me, take things that do not belong to me, and I'm not going to bully anyone any more.' Have I not changed inside and therefore become a different person, Carla?

Carla: In a way it is inside, those feelings of kindness, instead of being just like a bully.
PC: So, have I become a different person, Carla?
Carla: Not entirely a different person.
PC: OK.
Carla: Because on the outside you have changed, though on the inside you've probably changed.

(*Comment*) Carla distinguishes between one's overt behaviour and one's disposition to act in a particular way, which may be motivated by a number of different considerations. As Shakespeare's Richard III (Act III, Scene 1) notes wryly: 'Nor more can you distinguish of a man / Than of his outward show, which, God he knows, / Seldom or never jumpeth with the heart'.

PC: OK.
Christ. Ss.: You're not an entirely different person unless you're born again ... Because you're always you, aren't you?

(*Comment*) Christopher suggests that bodily activity is constitutive of personal identity. As Anthony O'Hear (1985: 244) notes, this view concurs with that adopted both in law and in everyday life.

PC: OK. I'll come back to that point. A very good point. Christopher?
Christ. Ss.: Well, I couldn't say to myself: 'I want to be like Paul R' ... And anyway, even if you stopped being a bully and

was really nice, you've changed what you do but you haven't changed how you speak and what your eye-colour is, and things like that. So, you've just sort of changed a bit of you.

PC: Let's say I said to myself: 'Not only am I going to change my hairstyle and my clothes, but I'm also going to change my personality. I am going to behave differently towards people from now on.' So I've made some outward changes and some inward changes. Am I now a totally different person, Christopher?

Christ. Ss.: No, because ... It's hard to explain really but you are not a new person because you're still you. You're still you aren't you?

PC: Right. Well, let me push you a little bit more. Imagine that I'm poorly ... my heart isn't working very well ... Let's say I need a new heart. And the surgeon at the Royal Infirmary rings me up and says: 'Mr. Costello, we have a new heart for you. I am going to perform the operation tomorrow morning.' Tomorrow evening I wake up, open my eyes, look around me, see familiar sights. I feel quite well. On the other hand, I've got someone else's heart inside me, haven't I? So does that mean, Terry, that I'm a different person?

(*Comment*) The relationship between organ transplantation and personal identity is discussed in Lamb (1985: 89–90).

Terry: You're yourself ... You're the same person, except you've got a different heart.

PC: But I might have Mr Smith's heart. I've got a part of Mr Smith inside me. Doesn't that mean I'm a different person?

Terry: No.

PC: Jill?

Jill: You're still the same.

PC: OK.

Abigail: Well, you can't change your brain.

(*Comment*) The notion of brain transplantation has, in fact, been the subject of much philosophical discussion. See, for example, Shoemaker (1963); O'Hear (1985: 246–53).

PC:	Go on. You can't change your brain. I'm interested in that line. Right, have a think about that and I'll come back to you. Helen?
Helen:	Well, even if you have got Mr Smith's heart, all your heart does is pump blood round your body. So, in a way, you can't change your personality from that.

(*Comment*) Unlike a number of patients who have received transplanted hearts, Helen does not believe that the recipient of such an organ is likely to acquire certain personality-traits of the donor. See Lamb (1985: 89–90).

PC:	OK. Carl?
Carl:	Your attitude makes you different. Like yesterday, when we were doing those votes, not everybody got the same answer. People had different views on what was good and what was bad.
PC:	That's right ... Christopher?
Christ. Ss.:	Well, Michael Jackson is still the same Michael Jackson except he looks a lot different. But he's still Michael Jackson.
PC:	Even though he's had a lot of ... ?
Ruth:	Plastic surgery.
PC:	Plastic surgery. Christopher?
Christ. Ss.:	Even if you did have your heart changed, you'd still have your skin the same, so you'd still be the same person. And you couldn't really change all of you. You couldn't get all the rest of somebody else's body because your body would be somebody else. [*Laughter*]
PC:	Right, let me give you this example. Joanna goes out to afternoon break and she's playing. She falls over on the yard and bangs her head on the concrete, and is knocked unconscious. When she wakes up, she can't remember who she is, what her name is. She can't remember any of you. She doesn't know who Miss G is. She doesn't know who I am and, what's more, she cannot even remember anything about her past life. Now, Roddy, is she the same person?

(*Comment*) Memory has also been advanced as a criterion of personal identity. See Abel (1976: 191–2); Hospers (1989: 413–5); O'Hear (1985: 243–53).

Roddy:	Yes.

PC:	So, if I said: 'What's your name?' She says: 'I don't know.' How many brothers and sisters have you got?
——	She wouldn't be able to speak.
Joanna:	None.
PC:	None. Any sisters?
Joanna:	One.
PC:	Right, let's say, I'll ask her: 'How many sisters have you got?' And she says 'I don't know.' And say her [mother] comes to pick her up in the evening [and she says:] 'Come on now, Joanna, it's time to go home.' [Joanna says:] 'I don't know you, who are you?'
	[Laughter]
PC:	Is she still the same person? Because now ... something [has] happened to the brain. You were saying to me before: 'If something happens to the body ... if I get a new heart, I'm still the same person.' But now her attitudes are going to change. Let's say she previously liked vanilla ice-cream and I offered her some. She says: 'No, I can't stand that, I'll have some of that red stuff. What's that?', I say, 'Oh, strawberry, oh yes.' Whereas previously she'd really disliked strawberry. So, Carl, her attitudes have changed as a result of this fall. Is she not now a different person, Christopher?
Christ. Ss.:	No, because all that's happened is she's been knocked unconscious and she can't remember anything. The rest of her is still the same. It's just that the brain is not working that well.
	[Laughter]
PC:	Jenny?
Jenny:	Well, in about 30 or 40 years' time they will be able to change your whole body.
PC:	So, what point are you making there?
Jenny:	So, you won't have to be the same person.
PC:	OK. Listen to this example. Roddy also decided he is going to go out and play on the yard this afternoon, and, would you believe it, he falls over, like Joanna, and bangs his head on the concrete? Now, his condition is a little bit different. When he wakes up, this is what he says: 'My name is Thomas.'
	[Laughter]
PC:	How many brothers have you got, Roddy?

Roddy:	Two.
PC:	Two brothers; and how many sisters?
Roddy:	None.
PC:	None. Two brothers. 'My name is Thomas,' he says, 'and I have four brothers.'
———	And a sister.
———	And two cats.
PC:	And three sisters.
———	And a dog.
PC:	And, of course, Christopher, [who] is a very sensible boy, says: 'You must be joking. Your name is Roddy. You sit next to me in class. This afternoon we were discussing philosophy with Mr Costello.' He says: 'Who? Oh, I don't remember any of that. Anyway, I thought philosophy was something that you did at university. It can't be true [that] I've been learning philosophy all term with Mr Costello.' Now he believes his name is Thomas. He thinks he's got four brothers and three sisters. Johanna, hasn't he surely now become a different person?
Joanna:	No.
PC:	No? Why not? ... He names the brothers for me: Adam, Bill, Charlie and Dave. 'You should meet them. They're such nice fellows,' he says. Where do you live, Roddy?
Roddy:	65, High Street.
PC:	65, High Street. He says: 'I live in 108, New Street, and what's more, Jenny, you can come round for tea tonight.' Now, surely at this point, we would want to say, Ben ... that Roddy has become a different person?
Roddy:	No.
PC:	Ruth?
Ruth:	If he couldn't remember anything, he wouldn't know that Jenny's name was Jenny.
PC:	No. That's true.
Christ. Ss.:	He could say: 'I'll invite Gertrude round to my house.'
PC:	Yes, he could ... Now, one more experiment. Let me see who I'm going to get to be in this experiment. Michael, stand up, and Katie, stand up. Now, let's say someone performed an experiment on these two ... And this is what happened as the result of the experiment. Katie's memories and attitudes, and, as you might say, Carl, philosophy of life, all transferred to Michael. Michael's

	attitudes and values and his philosophy of life transferred to Katie.
——	That happened in 'Laurel and Hardy'.
PC:	Yes it did happen in 'Laurel and Hardy', I remember that. Yes, now, what's your favourite colour?
Michael:	Blue.
PC:	That's your favourite colour now. And what's yours?
Katie:	Pink.
PC:	Yours is pink. And what's your favourite chocolate bar?
Michael:	'Dairy Milk'.
PC:	'Dairy Milk'. What's yours?
Katie:	'Kit-Kat'.
PC:	'Kit-Kat'. So, yours is 'Kit-Kat' and yours is 'Dairy Milk'. Now, if that had happened, and, say, someone was capable of swopping these persons' memories and attitudes and values and so forth. Would it not be now the case, that, although this person, to all of you, looks like Katie, she is really Michael because she thinks like Michael. She acts like Michael ... Now if that was the case, I know it's an hypothesis, it's not really factual. But if that could take place, would they not now be different people ... Chrit.?
Chrit.:	The brains would be different, but they'd still be the same ... They'd still look the same but they'd have different ways of thinking and different brains.
PC:	So, would they be the same person? This is what I want to know.
Terry:	They won't have different brains. The brains won't move like that.
——	Well the thoughts won't either.
PC:	Well, let's say we could have an experiment that would transfer these thoughts. Let's just say it was possible. Christopher, would they not now be different people?
Christ. Ss.:	Well, I'd say: 'Yes', because, well, they've both been changed round, so Katie would be Michael and Michael would be Katie.
PC:	You think that. What do you think, Jenny?
Jenny:	Their DNA won't have changed.

(*Comment*) Jenny's argument also recognises the importance of the physical aspect in determining a person's individuation. However, in being concerned with the basic biochemical structure which causes such individuation, she focuses on the absolute determinant of external characteristics.

PC:	What's DNA?
Jenny:	It's the genetics inside your body.
PC:	Excellent. And what difference would that make, Jenny?
Jenny:	They'd still look the same.
PC:	They'd still look the same. So, even though we had to get used to the fact that Katie's favourite chocolate bar was 'Kit-Kat' now, and that her favourite colour was blue, when we look at her we'd still say: 'Well, that's Katie. That doesn't look at all like Michael ... And vice versa. OK. ... One last question needs very careful thought. If a witch came along or a warlock – what is a warlock?
——	Is it just like a little man?
——	A creature in the shape of a man?
PC:	Perhaps. Eve?
Eve:	A male witch.
PC:	A male witch. You see them in fantasy stories. If one of them came along, a warlock or a witch, and turned you into a frog, would you be the same person?

(*Comment*) At this stage, the presumption is that the frog still displays the thought patterns of a human being. John Hospers (1989: 410–11) discusses a similar example concerning a man who turns into a monkey. In addition, Franz Kafka's story *The Metamorphosis* (in Glatzer, 1988), focuses on someone who changes into a beetle while retaining his original personality traits.

Chorus:	Yeah.
PC:	Carl?
Carl:	Yeah, it's just like when you changed your hairstyle and your clothes. You just changed into a frog.
——	Yeah, it don't matter. You've just turned into a frog.
PC:	But you jump like a frog, don't you, Carl?
Carl:	That's because your muscles have changed.
PC:	But you're still the same person?
Mark:	You're the same person. It's just that you've shrunk, changed the colour of your skin, lost all your hair and ...
PC:	What else?
Mark:	... don't wear any fancy clothes.
PC:	Now, after all of those changes, Mark, you tell me that you're still the same person?

Mark:	Yeah.
PC:	What do you think, Jenny?
Jenny:	Your thoughts haven't changed.
PC:	Your thoughts haven't changed. Let's say that not only did this witch turn you into a frog, but she also gave you the thought patterns of a frog.
———	Oh no!
PC:	Whatever they might be. Chrit.?
Chrit.:	I think you are completely different, then.
———	I don't.
PC:	What if she has given you the thought patterns of a frog, but left you physically exactly as you are – so you are thinking like a frog but you look like yourselves? Chrit.?
Chrit.:	I don't think you're different then.
PC:	So, you need physical change and mental change. Jenny?
Jenny:	If she gives you the thought of a frog and you're still as you are, you haven't actually changed – just your insides.
PC:	OK. Paul? …
Paul:	Right, well just say, like if you … take everything out of my body and put it into, say, Dean's body? …
PC:	Yes.
Paul:	… and take all his things, and put it into mine. We'll be completely different people, but we'll be under the same name.
PC:	OK.
Scott:	Mr Costello.
PC:	Yes, Scott.
Scott:	When you've changed your personality into a frog, but you're still human, all it does, it makes your brain think that that's a frog. But you're still the same person.
PC:	Last comment from Jenny.
Jenny:	Well, to change the whole of you, you'd have to get your DNA out, and work out all the patterns and what they mean, and then stick it back in in a different way.

In conclusion, I suggest that the teaching and learning of argument is an important aspect of all academic disciplines. However, as the above dialogue demonstrates, this endeavour should not be confined to established curriculum areas such as English, history and science. To improve the quality of children's philosophical reasoning and argument is essential if they are to emerge from compulsory schooling as reflective citizens who are willing and able to play a full part in helping to shape the society to which they belong (Costello, 1994c). In this regard, extending pupils' voices in the classroom is crucial to their development as reasoning, morally mature and intellectually independent persons.

Appendix 8.1: Assessing Progress in Argument

Processes of argument

The pupil is able to:
(1) express a point clearly
(2) take a point of view, express an opinion
(3) make a personal value statement
(4) express a preference
(5) give an example
(6) give several examples
(7) give appropriate examples
(8) make a comparison
(9) draw a contrast
(10) use an analogy
(11) use supposition
(12) use persuasive language
(13) give a reason
(14) give a variety of reasons
(15) give appropriate reasons
(16) quote evidence
(17) weigh up evidence
(18) refer to own experience to support arguments
(19) appeal to authority (of various kinds)
(20) stick to the point, be relevant
(21) show a degree of logic in the development of the argument
(22) repeat an argument in another form
(23) take into account others' points of view

Specific to oral argument

(24) listen and respond to others' points of view
(25) sum up the progress of a discussion or argument
(26) speak at length, linking several points together
(27) avoid diversion
(28) speak with authority, and without hectoring or aggression

Specific to written argument

(29) vary the structure of written argument
(30) write in various forms (e.g. letter, dialogue, essay)
(31) use appropriate connectives (e.g. although, nevertheless, on the other hand)

(32)   introduce and conclude well (if necessary)
(33)   write in a lively, readable way
(34)   be sensitive to the purpose of the argument, and to the audience

Appendix 8.2:   What Makes You *You*?[1]

- Would you be the same person if you changed your hairstyle/mode of dress?[2]
- If you were given a new heart, would you be the same person?
- If someone is a liar/thief and then changes for the better, is he/she still the same person?
- If I decided to go on a diet and a month later I said: 'I've lost two stones, I feel like a new person,' am I?
- Robert falls over on the school yard and bangs his head on the concrete. When he wakes up, he is unable to remember who he is, or anything about his past life. Is he the same person?
- If Robert wakes up and says his name is Thomas and that he has three sisters (whereas Robert has none) and goes to St Paul's School (whereas Robert goes to St Philip's School), is he the same person?
- If someone performed an experiment on you and on your best friend, which resulted in you receiving your friend's memories, attitudes, likes and dislikes and vice versa, would you be the same person?

Notes

1. This exercise is based on ideas found in Abel (1976, Chapter 17) and examines the philosophical problem of personal identity.
2. Abel (1976: 186–7).

9 Conflict and Conformity: The Place of Argument in Learning a Discourse

SALLY MITCHELL

> At any moment we are using language we must say or write the right thing in the right way while playing the right social role and (appearing) to hold the right values, beliefs and attitudes. Thus what is important is not language and surely not grammar, but *saying-(writing)-doing-being-valuing-believing-combinations*. These combinations I call 'Discourses' ... Discourses are ways of being in the world; they are forms of life which integrate words, acts, values, beliefs, attitudes and social identities as well as gestures, glances, body positions and clothes.
> (Gee, 1989: 6–7)

James Gee's description of discourses is a useful starting point for this chapter, which looks at the nature and function of argument in learning situations, in particular the learning of academic disciplines in post-compulsory education.[1] The inclusiveness of the description captures the substantiality of lived situations in which language plays a part and in which meaning is richly embedded in context. Whilst I find Gee's description highly suggestive, in my own understanding I have adapted it to think of discourses not only as 'ways of being in the world' but as themselves constituting 'worlds'. These worlds are not discrete or coherent but are in flux, actively constituted and reconstituted over time and in the spaces they occupy and create. Moreover, we generally inhabit more than one discourse or world and our conversations and behaviours are not pure but hybrid enactments. At different times we are at various stages of transition between worlds – this is particularly the case when we are engaged in processes of learning within an education system.

In this chapter, I want to suggest that the occurrence of argument is integral to transitionary processes and that it operates not only between worlds but also within them. Willard (1989: 11) comments that the point of studying argument is 'to explain how groups sustain intellectual stability yet are able to change'. Argument is both a means by which discourses come to be established and shared and a process through which those discourses are constituted as dynamic, subject to modification and challenge. Through argument, stability is achieved by the establishing of position; change, by an identical process of exploiting difference. Within argumentative processes, as a result, are potentials for conflict and disintegration as well as construction and consensus.

Change and stability – in tension – are key components in defending old and learning new discourses. Argument does not, however, simply enliven discourses; it also – as Gee's highly peopled description suggests – produces individuals. Yet individuals and discourses are not set apart; rather, as Rom Harré (1983:65) writes, there is 'a thoroughgoing reciprocity between the social and the personal'. It is through Harré's notion of 'personal identity projects' that I want to explore both the dual impulses of change and stability and the relation of the individual to the social world. In setting out his theory, Harré (1983: 65) writes:

> I am not suggesting that persons and their talk exist prior to social reality and engender it as an effect. People and their modes of talk are made by and for social orders, and social orders are people in conversation.

Harré proposes a model (Figure 9.1) for the successful completion of personal identity projects within the social world. The model consists of two axes – the public/private and the individual/collective – which when they intersect create four quadrants. In personal identity formation the quadrants are traversed from the public/collective in a clockwise direction by four types of operation: Appropriation, Transformation, Publication and Conventionalisation.

We can think of the operations as a learning cycle in which the student appropriates knowledge and skills, internalises and adapts them, creates products or performances by which these processes are made public (assessed) and is then rewarded – or otherwise – by some kind of agreed public recognition (a certificate; entrance to a higher course, etc.). The model pictures as dynamic and interconnected the relations between public consensus and private difference, the given way of being and the development of distinctive identity. It suggests that the given and the new are not opposed and separate modes of existence but are constructed and developed through each other, the individual attaining distinctive identity through both appropriation from and recognition by the given. The given, in turn, is constantly renewed by the conventionalisation of what the private/individual publicly offers. Argument, we could say, is what motors the cycle; a process of thinking which enables the individual to engage with the collective, to appropriate and transform it. Through publication, what has been transformed is stabilised. In the British educational tradition, the dual functions of argument are differently emphasised in the spoken and written modes; where speech is valued as an open and transformative process, writing is the site of closure; the assignment which marks the end of a period of study. Thus publication and conventionalisation tend to take place on the basis of written products rather than interactive spoken processes. This chapter looks at the important function of argument in speech but suggests its limitations in the completion of personal identity projects, where the stabilising public function is culturally assigned to another mode: that of writing.

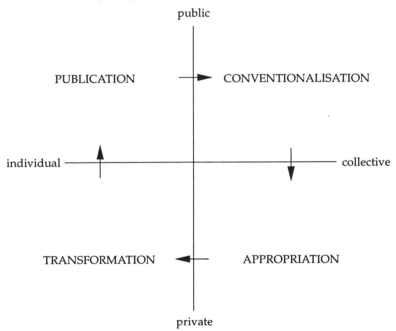

Figure 9.1

Harré's model is a useful heuristic for understanding the place of the individual within a cultural identity and the role of argument in learning, but it should not be interpreted too simply. Its limits lie in the diagrammatic representation of the public/collective and individual/private quadrants as singular and unified (rather than as themselves constituted by multiple, often competing discourses). Education is not about appropriating and transforming discourse into the blank and unformulated private world of the individual; it involves taking on additional discourses to those into which the individual was first socialised. These transitionary processes can be sites of conflict in which discourses compete for acceptance and, because discourses are more or less powerful within certain social, educational and institutional contexts, certain of them predominate above others. Individuals for whom the conflict is too great are likely not to succeed or remain long within those institutions; they will certainly not get beyond being, say, *students of sociology* to being *sociologists*. So the cycle represented by Harré's model cannot be thought of as smooth, continuous or univocal; nor as fully carried through in perhaps any but the most rare educational 'journeys'. Instead the personal identity project contains within it potential for disorientation and disruption – and for argument in its most passionate and conflictive form.

Argument as Opposition

Let me take my first example. It comes from a sociology class in which the students (17–18 years old) have been introduced to Ivan Illich's (1977) theory of Iatrogenesis. This sociological theory, which contends that medicine and its institutions can have a detrimental effect upon health and well-being is an instance of a new discourse. In the discussion from which the extract is taken, this discourse is in conflict with another, 'older', more commonsensical way of believing and valuing. The conflict is enacted as a clash between two students; Andrew, who seems able to operate comfortably with the new idea (to appropriate it), and Susan, who is unable to reconcile it with the way she thinks about and values the health service.

Susan:	All right, things like heart disease and stuff and – you need treatment. You can't just get over it, sat at home in bed. Like AIDS and stuff.
Andrew:	There again you get over it anyway – I mean if you've got ...
Susan:	No you're not. You're not ...
Andrew:	If you've got a bad heart, you're not going to ...
Susan:	What about leukaemia, chemotherapy and all that?
Andrew:	You still die though don't you? It don't usually ...
Susan:	Yeah, but you want to live longer, you want to live as long as you can ...

Andrew:	... cure you. Eh, you're living longer, but you're in like pain. It's costing more money as well isn't it?
Susan:	Rubbish. No sorry Andrew I don't agree.
Andrew:	Why?
Susan:	Because I wouldn't want to die and I don't think you would and if it comes to the choice where you'd have to *(breath)* got a chance o' living, would you treat me? You'd have it. You would have it! *(very emphatic; crescendo)*
Andrew:	Depends on – how you were living. Depends how you were living.
Susan:	You would have it. *(softer)*
Andrew:	If you were living w' no hair and in total pain all the time, then what's the point?
Lynda:	When you're going to die anyway.
Susan:	Yeah! *(shouts)*. But I'm on about heart disease and stuff. If you have a heart attack and you get taken to hospital, you want the ...
Andrew:	Yeah but. Yeah, yeah, all right. *(conciliatory)*
Susan:	... treatment to get over it.
Andrew:	Yeah, but you see, you're going back to the symptoms aren't you? They're only looking at the symptoms aren't they? Doctors, they're not looking at the causes, so once you've got it yeah, fair enough, you need the doctors, but ... it's getting it in the first place.
Susan:	Yeah – but you've ... that's the argument. *(tapping paper)*
Andrew:	You're eating fatty foods and that, just thinking, 'Oh, if I do get it ... '
Susan:	*(exasperated)* Don't you want hospitals or sommat?

For Susan the real-life situation and common sense view override the academic argument. She cannot keep the two discourses apart, nor can she synthesise them. Andrew, in contrast, is able dispassionately to draw a distinction between the quality of life and life at whatever cost (and, indeed, actual cost). Whilst he talks in terms of 'it depends ... ' and uses abstract and classificatory language, Susan's argument is rooted in absolute conviction and takes the form of a personal attack.

What sorts of worlds are in conflict here? Common sense, says Clifford Geertz (1993: 76) is a system in which the basis of meaning – because taken for granted – is not articulated; it operates on the 'unspoken premise'. If this is the system by which Susan is operating then the clash seems to be generated by contact with one which is precisely its opposite. The sociological thinking instanced here turns common sense on its head by scrutinising its 'unspoken premises'; the belief in a health service, for instance, which allows us 'safely' to neglect our health. The clash between these two systems can be interpreted in at least two ways. In the first, violence is done to Susan's closely held beliefs and values by the cold academic analysis she is asked to take on if she is to succeed within the discourse and the education system. The overall context in which she speaks renders her argument, however forcefully expressed, the least powerful, the least likely to be heard. It is significant that it finds expression in speech (the vehicle of learning, not of assessment in the British system) rather than in writing and that her voice is raised not in the whole class, teacher-led situation, but in a small group. The small group situation has long been used in teaching as a site for 'free expression' and the negotiation of underlying assumptions (see Berrill, 1991).

The alternative interpretation sees the sociological discourse as liberating. As a consequence of its reluctance to resolve or exploit the inconsistencies and contradictions in life – what Geertz (1993: 90) calls its 'immethodicalness' – common sense is a conservative system. Susan's *ad populum* argument culminating in her challenge to Andrew – 'Don't you want hospitals or sommat?' – seeks to suppress protest and dissent by the obviousness of its case. If common sense performs the ideological function of safeguarding what is natural and proper, then sociology – and other, what Gee would call 'Secondary Discourses' – might offer new and freeing ways of looking at the world. Whilst acknowledging that these discourses are not equally available to everyone, Gee makes the observation:

> Primary Discourses, no matter whose they are, can never really be liberating literacies ... 'Liberation' ('power') ... resides in acquiring at least one more Discourse in terms of which our own primary Discourse can be analyzed and critiqued. (Gee, 1989: 10)

A mature undergraduate student I interviewed put this rather more concretely:

Mary: For me, sociology, I did a little bit of it last year and I felt that all my life I must have been living in a kind of box really, because I suddenly had my eyes opened to things. I found that fascinating and I wanted to learn more. All the sort of misconceptions I'd had about things in society, you know. I'd always felt a failure myself at school because I'd left at 16 and I felt that I'd failed the system and I suddenly felt gosh, you know, there's a possibility here that maybe the system failed me, you know and it was really interesting to explore things like that and it opened up a whole new world for me to explore things like that ... I think for me it was to stop seeing myself as a wife, a mother and to start seeing myself as an individual, as more than just these two or these very few roles that I was playing, as somewhere, you know, inside that I was with this individual whose life had been shaped by factors outside and I mean at the point that I think I started thinking sociologically, I started to see myself as more than just, as a person ...

For Mary, though the movement into disciplinary discourse has required – as for Susan – a reciprocal movement away from personal conviction, it has also come to constitute new belief; the sociological discourse appropriated and transformed in the personal identity project.

But if taking on disciplinary perspectives can be liberating, it can equally be enculturation into new orthodoxy. In the final year undergraduate class in sociology – from which my next examples are taken – the distinctive features of disciplinary argument become more apparent, but so too does the extent to which its discourse is itself conservative and totalising; it frames what can be said and excludes or seeks to subsume other discourses and by implication, other possibilities for the development of personal identity. Billig (1991: 43) describes an opinion as a 'dual expression' – a statement which both indicates something personal and distinctive about ourselves and simultaneously locates us within a larger controversy. Our opinions, that is, arise not out of the blue nor as something we are born with, but from what is current, what is available for us to think; from, in fact, the available discourses. As Foucault (1972: 64) said: 'One cannot think of anything at any time; it is not easy to say something new.'

A similar interdependence of same and other, the given and the new, underlies a dialogic view of language (as it does the personal identity project). Bakhtin (1981: 281) writes:

> ... actual meaning is understood against the background of other concrete utterances on the same theme, a background made up of contradictory opinions, points of view and value judgements – that is precisely that background that, as we see, complicates the path of any word towards its object. Only now this rather contradictory environment is present to the speaker not in the object, but rather in the consciousness of the listener, as his apperceptive background pregnant with response and objections.

For Bakhtin, every use of language carries with it a history of usage in different contexts and itself constitutes a new context. In addition he sees meaning as activated not by the speaker but by the listener since it is she, in responding, who determines how the utterance is understood. This stress on the creation of meaning not in utterance (origination) but in response (orientation) makes knowing mutable and contingent rather than given and fixed. It also suggests difference as a vital element in communication; making sense is achieved through otherness, both in the actual dynamic of conversation or dialogue and also internally, within language. Bakhtin uses the language of ownership to address this notion of identity:

> The word in language is half someone else's. It becomes 'one's own' only when the speaker populates it with his own intention, his own accent, when he appropriates the word, adapting it to his own semantic and expressive intention. Prior to this moment of appropriation, the word does not exist in a neutral and impersonal language (it is not, after all, out of a dictionary that a speaker gets his words!), but rather it exists in other people's mouths, in other people's concrete contexts, serving other people's intentions: it is from there that one must take the word, and make it one's own. (Bakhtin, 1981: 293–4)

For Susan, this description might have a particular resonance: the words of the discourse are alien, they do not feel right; moreover adapting them to her 'own semantic and expressive intention' feels like a betrayal or distortion of that intention. Argument as opposition is the result. For Andrew, by contrast, argument fulfils a different function; he uses it to appropriate Illich's theory and then extends it by making a connection between the way both individuals and the government use the health service as an excuse for neglect:

Andrew: So it's an excuse for, like, the government not intervening in causes of ill health, isn't it?
Susan: Oh it's not the government!

Argument as Appropriation and Transformation

The examples below – from a course on 'The Sociology of Murder' – show how far this process of making the 'word' one's own can progress by the third year of undergraduate study at university. There appears to be consensus within the seminar group about shared disciplinary identity, despite the fact that the tutor remains the leader and has an overview of the entire course which the students only acquire as they experience it. Argument now operates less on opposition than on degree of difference; less as clash, more as decorum.

To begin the course the tutor presented a common sense theory of murder: murderers are mad and bad. He could no longer rely on the students to supply this view, since, for them, sociology now represented common sense. Nonetheless the mad and bad position remained strategically and rhetorically important; it constructed the sociological perspective on murder as other, as representing an alternative. The course was designed to follow the argumentative strategies employed by the tutor in his own doctoral research; it was in this sense a thesis writ-large, retaining its textual shape but rendered fluid and mutable by its negotiation through spoken dialogue. Figure 9.2 represents the 'novelty-oriented' shape of the argument. The common sense starting point is followed by discussion of various sociological accounts – both what they say and what they omit to say. As these are progressively examined and critiqued, a space for the author to make his original contribution is constructed (see Kaufer & Geisler, 1989, 1991). This contribution is very different from the common sense view and different by increasingly small degrees from existing positions within sociological discourse. The diagram suggests how small the novel contribution can – and generally will – be. The argumentative method both legitimises and delimits the original thinking.

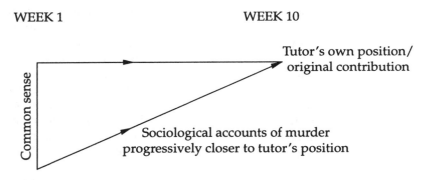

Figure 9.2

Figure 9.2 also pictures the shape of the course; at this macro-level the students were not learning to be novel for themselves, but were learning the process by which novelty might be produced. The tutor commented:

> I like to think that I'm dragging them after me, but I like to kind of structure things so that they come to it step by step ... You implicitly structure the thing as a stage by stage thing.

The seminar from which the examples are taken was the second on the course and the teacher saw its function as 'opening up the field'. A text on criminal homicide and the subculture of violence (Wolfgang, 1967) was used as 'a tool for getting somewhere else'. The first example – in which the group is discussing the association of violence with masculinity –

demonstrates the leading role the tutor takes in modelling the discourse; in demonstrating, that is, a sociological way of thinking. The transcript is not easy to follow. The sentences are often hesitant and incomplete; they rely for their completion on the understanding and response of others present: what Bakhtin (1981: 282) would call the 'activating principle'. This is discourse which, in Gee's terms, is very far from 'grammar'; it is a way of doing which serves the communicative purposes of this particular world. The transcribed words make up only part of these purposes; vocal indications are also included as are those apparently extraneous features of Gee's definition: 'gestures, glances, body positions and [even] clothes.'

Tutor: So in a sense then you could actually try and broaden Wolfgang's argument out to say that well okay it may occur within these communities, but really the engagement with violence – the engagement in violence is partially conditioned not simply by subcultural values, but by kind of broader constructs of kind of masculinity and femininity, yeah? In other words the engagement can be if you like a status thing, can't it? Yes? It can be like a positive affirmation of masculinity – that's what I'm getting at. And that's why you often get this kind of asymmetrical treatment of kind of genders within homicide, in that, a man who commits murder, shall we say, is seen as engaging in violence which is a kind of subcomponent of aggression which in itself is a subcomponent of masculinity. Yeah? So in a sense the male engagement in violence – and by extension, homicide – is actually a kind of a confirmation or an affirmation of masculinity, yeah? So in other words a man committing murder could be seen to be over-conforming to those kinds of constructions of masculinity, the masculine stereotypes. A woman who commits murder – and we'll see this later in the course – is more likely to be understood in terms of a radical departure from conventional ideas of femininity – the woman as nurturer and so forth. [*pause*]

Liz: Do you think then that premeditated murder by a man shows that, cos' I would think that says he's not very masculine. When it's premeditated it seems quite a – it's a sort of weaker thing to do. But doing an act of violence and for it then to result in murder.

Tutor: Yeah, that's right. I mean there's two points there. I think, Wolfgang argues that most of these murders are the result of violence which has fatal consequences which is not the premeditated kind. He then talks about what he terms middle class homicides, which as he would have it, is the classic kind of premeditated act – or undertaking of malice aforethought and has all the components of the classic British murder, if you like, or the classic murder. I'm, I'm not sure [*pause*] whether you can see as you say the premeditated murder in terms of that same kind of affirmation.

The tutor talks for sustained periods – there's an expectation that he will lead the thinking and that he is in control of the stimulus text, both in terms of knowing its content and of knowing how to criticise it, to locate its weaknesses. Yet as his argument unfolds, it is punctuated by requests for the students' compliance. At signalled moments (the first pause) the students may test their understandings. Liz's contribution here does not simply echo what has been said but extends it. Similarly the tutor's reply is both an acceptance and reformulation, though more public and authoritative than hers. The process is both disciplinary and pedagogical; the argument is both already formulated (in the tutor's understanding) and dialogic, open to mediation and change.

To a considerable degree the teacher's agenda marks the parameters of what can be said and the speech is generated not freely but within the discourse which both controls and makes it possible. The most evident instance of this is the way the group uses classifications such as race, class, age, and – here – gender. The use of these classifications provides a progression for the seminar as a whole as the implications of applying them to homicide is considered in turn or in combination. The classifications perform a normative, stereotypical function. Workable because they arise from what is common, rather than unique, they are a conservative restraint on the argument, limiting the proliferation of meaning. A clash between discourses is not, at this stage at least, apparent. The speakers rarely refer to their own experience as a source of knowledge; they talk, for instance, about possible scenarios between husband and wife in a working class setting, but do not attribute their suppositions to any first- or second-hand experience. The discourse is premised on neutrality and equality; the speakers are disinterested theorists who have no stake in the phenomena they are discussing.

Nonetheless, although the seminar is a collaborative occasion, the roles are not shared. The teacher's overall tendency is to move away from agreement with the text, towards difference; the students have a less radical orientation. The next example comes towards the end of the seminar when the teacher introduces new information that one-fifth of murder victims had originally intervened to stop violence. He invites the students to consider how this fits with Wolfgang's subculture of violence thesis, 'where violence is almost ... a linear process entered into by two parties who have some kind of consensus'. His own tendency is to suggest that this new evidence undermines Wolfgang. Notice how he reformulates his view as a question:

Tutor:	I think, if you take the bare bones of Wolfgang's argument it seems to be that people inhabit this subculture and there is this kind of localised consensus that this recourse to violence is a socially valid means of acting, yeah? Now presumably the people on the sidelines who then engage with these kind of consensual violent parties, they're actually, are they acting in accordance with a kind of counternorm of violence, are they departing from those kind of localised norms aren't they? Do you see what I mean?
Liz:	But are they using violence to stop the violence?
Tutor:	Uhm?
Liz:	I mean how do they stop the violence? By just saying 'Excuse me, could you stop?' or do they go in with their fists and ...
Tutor:	Well, I mean, I don't know.
Liz:	... 'cos if they went in with their fists, then they're also descending into violence as well no matter why. Doesn't really matter does it, they're still ... ?
Tutor:	Yeah that's right, but I mean in having I mean I suppose this argument leads you down to psychological motives, but in intervening in the fight in the first place, you know to try and with the idea that 'This is a bad thing and I have to try and stop it even if I have to use violence myself', it's still, it's not acting in accordance with what Wolfgang implies – is that there's this kind of localised consensus towards violence.
Anna:	Maybe it is, maybe it's like um er I can't remember where I read it, I was reading about violence amongst teenagers, and this was teenage girls in you know like borstals.

	There is a certain level where the violence is allowed to go to and maybe that also applies in this case where some kind of physical aggression is allowed but murder is obviously beyond it, and if the intervener thinks the violence is going too far, then he's justified by the rules of the culture in actually limiting it.
Tutor:	(*thoughtful*) Mmm, uhm.
Liz:	Could it be though that you've not necessarily got any proof that the person went in to stop the violence, but they may disagree with why – the sort of cause of the violence, but they may be in full agreement with the actual violence, they may not mind the violence – it's just that they might not think it's valid for that particular case.
Tutor:	Yeah, that's a good point.

The students, rather than accept the criticism of Wolfgang, seem to prefer to assume the text's coherence and employ tentative hypothetical explanations, which would support him. The tutor's first impulse, by contrast, is to disconfirm the text's claims to knowledge. To say that the students are primarily 'obedient' whilst the tutor is 'suspicious' is, however, to overlook the subtlety of their thinking.[2] If they do not seek a position of radical difference from Wolfgang, they are nonetheless thinking in terms of difference, but at a closer level, questioning the gradations of violence and motivation within the act itself, and introducing new factors and definitional boundaries. Whereas the tutor was content to take the intervention in violence at face value, the students want to know more about what is involved. In a sense the dialogue in which they are participating demands of them that they differentiate themselves from the tutor; in talk there is no participation without difference. In important ways, then, the students are aligned with neither the tutor nor Wolfgang's text, but take these as starting points from which to open hypothetical enquiry. Theirs is a more fluid position than the tutor's, since in many ways his argument is already closed down. The tension seems to be a productive one: challenged on the one hand to reject Wolfgang and reluctant on the other to do so, the students come up with subtle interpretations and extensions which are new. And since the tutor is actively rather than purely instrumentally engaged – in a process of discovery, rather than reiteration – the dialogue with others can also lead him to new meanings.

The above example shows the students to be well advanced in their disciplinary apprenticeship, to be talking within rather than against or about the discourse of sociology. Consensus, not conflict, has become the basis for argument of a detached yet exploratory kind. At the end of the series of seminars, however, when the novelty of the tutor's thinking was revealed, this consensus was disrupted. Considering the motivations of serial killers, the teacher insisted that everything is socially determined, that the actions of serial killers can be explained purely by social factors, that psychology is simply a subset of sociology – it has beneficial uses, but little value in explaining how things actually are. This was too much for many of the students. They held on to another earlier set of beliefs and relations (perhaps necessary for survival in the 'real world') which says that individuals are responsible for their own actions, that to be an individual is in fact possible, that some part of an individual – the residue of a true self perhaps – is not determined by social factors. At the point where they were asked to accept that a serial killer is an extreme manifestation of social – not psychological – characteristics, the common-sensical resurfaced as a rival discourse and challenged the attempt of the sociological to account for all difference within its own (invisible) parameters.

One of the students, Liz, gave her interpretation of what happened: the non-equivalence of, on the one hand, following a strong line of argument and, on the other, of making a leap of faith which would allow that argument to come to fruition purely on the basis of its disciplinary directionality:

SM: Do you think that people will end up just holding his [the tutor's] view [on the explanation for serial killers]?

Liz: No, I don't. I think today we just saw that people just can't. I mean because it is quite, he can't back it up with enough evidence, because it's very much a theory and like what a lot of people said about serial killers how, I found that very difficult to understand how, the way some do it and some don't. It's very sort of tenuous the idea that right at the end … You build up to it and it's all going along very nicely, but the very last thing it's like you just have to take it on trust really. I don't think every one will agree. I think people might understand it along the way, but at the very last if you're more, think more in a psychological way – because I only tend to believe in that I know it's sociology, I sort of believe in sociology, it must be right probably … Yeah, I think in a way as well in that particular case you could even say that the reason you doubt it is because this thing about you don't want to believe that it could be part of society, so even the doubting can be sociological.

Liz's explanation is full of ambivalence, but at the same time her sense of belonging to the discipline of sociology allows her to give the tutor the benefit of her doubt. The logic of his particular argument is less important to her than is allegiance to the ways of being and thinking that the discourse in general offers. This becomes all encompassing – she is even able to interpret the failure (her own and others') to believe as itself a sociologically explicable phenomenon. Belief at one level subsumes the crisis of belief at another.

Argument as Publication

Conventionalisation, in the full sense of acceptance into the public world (how this is defined, delimited, is of course another problem), takes place for very few students – most of us remain people who, in Gee's terms, know *about* a subject rather than know *in* a subject. Fewer of us still have our knowledge published in a subject: transformation is rarely of such precision (in terms of orientation to the discourse), nor of such 'originality' that it can lead to this. The transition from knowing *about* to knowing *in* is an attenuated one and is complicated (as I suggested earlier) by the non-equivalence in most British academic institutions at least, between the spoken and written modes of expression. Here the written, not the spoken word, is seen as the measure of belonging, the means by which one is judged to have passed institutional and intellectual hurdles. So it is not simply the word in language but the word in *written* language that students of a discourse need to appropriate and make their own.

Taking Liz as an example makes this point. Consider both the full contributions she makes to the group discussion and the way she analyses and feels about her own status as a sociologist. Then compare this with the grade awarded to her written assignment: 60%, an average grade, certainly not sufficient to qualify her to continue her apprenticeship in the discipline through funded post-graduate study. In her writing, Liz does not give her sociological thinking the appropriate textual shape (see Figure 9.2); her claims are large and forceful, not shown strategically to emerge from the texts of others; she believes too much and wants to say something too big for the tightly controlled conventions to allow. She states her position from the outset and makes her points with passion. Belief in sociological explanations *expressed in such a way* does not though gain entry to the way of being (writing) that sociology – at least within academic contexts – is.

So Liz's identity project is, after all, incomplete. Although she has taken the discourse of sociology into her private and individual space, made it a part of her belief system, she has not made the further transition away from the open, dialogic mode of speech to the highly controlled convention of the written essay. Almost paradoxically, given the trajectory we have been tracing, there is no place in the sociological for the personal: belonging entails the subordination of believing to the impersonal logic of teleological written argument. The leap of faith she makes when she expresses her allegiance to sociology is not sufficient to a system which demands that its adherents mould themselves to its own textual image. Notice that the definition of discourse with which I began this chapter referred to the need to 'say or write the right thing in the right way' whilst only '(*appearing*) to hold the right values, beliefs and attitudes' (my italics). These last – values, beliefs, attitudes – are perhaps less crucial than forms and roles, and the 'combinations' to which Gee refers are perhaps less integrated than we might at first assume. You cannot believe like a sociologist – and indeed talk like one – and still write as yourself. Gee (1989: 9) says of discourse: 'You are either in it or you're not': when it comes to conventionalisation – the point of acceptance or rejection – there is no room for argument.

Notes

1. This chapter is based on a three-year study funded by the Leverhulme Trust: *The Teaching and Learning of Argument in Sixth Forms and Higher Education* (see Mitchell, 1994).
2. These are terms used by Ricoeur (1970: 27) to describe the positive and negative modes of interpretation; the first characterised by a 'willingness to listen' and a 'vow of obedience'; the second by a 'willingness to suspect' and a 'vow of rigour'.

10 Signalling Valuation Through Argumentative Discourse

MAUREEN A. MATHISON

When we think of written argument we often think of it as an attempt to persuade readers to believe particular claims over other competing claims. In constructing arguments, writers advance claims and support them with convincing evidence, a strategy that makes a text compelling. But in thinking about argument, we must also think about its counterpart, critique. Argument implies critique. Just as *writers* argue for particular claims, *readers* must determine where they stand in relation to them. Readers interpret, analyse, and evaluate writers' lines of reasoning to reflect upon arguments and determine their persuasiveness. Critique is important, then, because it allows readers to question and make decisions about which specific claims they value in a text and how they position themselves in relation to them.

In a disciplinary community, the claims suggested by a text can be treated in two ways. First, they can be reproduced. This occurs when readers support the position advanced in a text. In this way, the established way of thinking about the issue is not challenged and remains intact. Second, claims can be transformed. When claims are transformed, readers wish to say something different from what is presented in the text and they propose alternative or novel ways of thinking about the issue. In either case, whether readers support (reproduce) or challenge (transform) established claims, they must operate within the framework of the disciplinary community for whom the information is relevant. For example, when critiquing texts in sociology, readers must demonstrate how a stance taken will suggest a text's applicability to the interests of the community. Is it theoretically useful? Is it methodologically sound? Will it further discussion of the issue? And so on. As readers make their critique relevant to the community *they become writers of arguments* as they construct texts that persuade others of the validity of their critique (Brockriede, 1974; Carlson, 1994). Combined, then, argument and critique work in tandem to transform or rebut knowledge claims, a process that generates the potential for new arguments.

Writers can signal a stance toward a text in various ways. For example, some writers may choose to withhold judgement as they describe claims. They may be more interested in mapping out the main points of a text. Other writers may choose to describe the text and select particular claims about which to comment. The comments may be negative, challenging claims, or they may be positive, supporting claims. Other writers may construct mixed configurations in which negative and positive comments are threaded throughout. The configuration of claims and comments in a critique may suggest a particular stance toward the source article. According to Rosenfield (1968), the selection of claims and their comments influences the function of a critique. Thus, the textual patterns writers construct signal how they have approached the task, for example, as a supporter of information or as an agent of change.

While critique is a common practice in disciplinary communities, it may be problematic for students, who often believe that they must learn the material in a text rather than evaluate it. Asking them to dismantle and critique a text may be inconsistent with their views on knowledge. McCormick (1990) points out three ideologically grounded views that students may bring to their schooling: (1) a need for closure, in which working hypotheses are unacceptable; (2) a need for objectivity, in which personal ideas are edited out; and (3) an avoidance of contradiction, in which competing accounts are glossed over and ignored. These views may impede students' ability to critically read academic texts in order to construct written positions of their own, a task valued in the disciplines. Little research has been conducted, however, that examines how students take critical stances toward claims. How will they construct their written arguments when they are explicitly asked to critique a text? And, just as important, how will professors respond to students' efforts?

In this chapter, I examine critique from the perspective of students and professors in the context of a college or tertiary level sociology course. My goal is twofold. First, I describe how students signalled valuation of the article to which they were responding through their treatment of its claims. And second, I examine why particular critiques may have been judged to be of better quality by professors in the discipline.

Studying Critique

To examine the practice of critique in an academic context, I asked 32 students in a sociology of religion course to allow me to analyse texts they had written for a class assignment. The course in which they were enrolled was open to students in all levels and programmes throughout the university. The instructor designed the course to 'introduce students to the ways sociologists think about and understand religion'. Discussion of content in the classroom was closely tied to how sociologists might think, reason, and argue about issues.

Toward the end of the term, the teacher asked students to read an article and to write a critique of it. She explained that their responses would serve as the basis of class discussion. Instructions for the assignment were given verbally in class:

> For next Thursday you are to hand in a critique of the Greil article, 'On the Margins of the Sacred'. It is good we didn't discuss it because I want your fresh responses to it. So, in fact, we won't discuss it in class until you've written about it. I want two pages, typed (with margins), in which you respond to this paper and its ideas.

The text assigned was a lengthy theoretical article that challenged standard definitions of religion with an alternative definition of religion: quasi-religion (Greil & Rudy, 1990). Quasi-religions call the traditional Judeo-Christian approach to sociological religious theory into question and offer an alternative view of what counts as religion. The authors claim that current approaches to religion assume that in order for someone to be religious, she or he must believe in a transcendent world. They claim that a proper definition of religion should be subjectivist, based on what an individual believes is religious. This novel definition departs from currently held definitions of religion in the field and thus, the critique assignment served to make students think through the concept and determine its value as an approach to understanding religion.

To determine how students signalled their valuation of these ideas through various text features, I first had to make diagrams of their texts. This involved mapping out what I call the 'topics' and 'comments' in each of their critiques before moving on to examine their treatment of them. A topic refers to the thematic focus of a statement that students selected from the article to include in their texts and a comment refers to the evaluative commentary a student made regarding the topic. Take, for example, the sentence: 'It will be immediately obvious that it is impossible to define quasi-religion without first coming to an understanding about what we mean by religions' (Greil & Rudy, 1990: 219). Broken into a topic-comment pattern, we have:

Topic: Quasi-religion-definition.
Comment: Is contingent upon a definition of religion.

Once the topics and comments were determined, I analysed each individual comment in a student's critique for its treatment. This consisted of the type of evaluative commentary the student made about the topic and the source of support for that particular comment.

Students made three types of evaluative commentary. The first type was positive. A comment was considered positive if it suggested support of a topic:

First, of all, the authors make a very good critical statement about the substantive and functionalists [sic] in sociology.

The second type of comment was negative. A comment was considered negative if it suggested lack of support of a topic:

If the authors would have taken more time with clearer definitions, more in-depth study with statements that could have been considered fact, this article would have been much stronger and more credible.

The last type of comment students made about topics was suspended. A comment was considered suspended if it did not suggest any judgement of a topic. Usually, suspended comments were a reporting of information:

Greil and Rudy explain that quasi-religions are neither sacred nor secular.

I also mapped out how students configured their comments (positive, negative, and suspended) in order to better understand how students approached the task. Two patterns emerged. In the first pattern, students provided suspended comments about topics from the article in the first part of their critique before moving on to provide negative or positive comments. This configuration suggested a critique in which students summarised or interpreted the article before providing an evaluation of it or particular aspects of it. Students employing this pattern first summarised and then critiqued. In the second pattern, students launched into their evaluation from the beginning, interweaving topics and evaluative comments throughout. This configuration suggested a critique in which students brought up one topic for commentary and responded, then brought up a second topic for commentary and responded, and so on. Students using this pattern thus integrated topics and comments throughout their texts as they critiqued.

Finally, I analysed the types of support students used to substantiate their comments. There were two types, disciplinary support and personal support. When students made use of material from the article, class discussions, related readings, or other background information in sociology, to support a comment, the support was considered disciplinary:

> Most likely [the American Folk definition is losing its hold] because while people still have the same needs that caused them to turn to religion in the first place – need to have answers to the unanswerable, sense of order in the world, sense of community, help in dealing with human dilemmas – many of these needs have grown due to changes in society.

When students made use of material from their personal experience, background or opinion, the source of support was considered personal:

> A friend of my father's is an alcoholic.

In this particular investigation, I was interested in the relationship of these text features and the professors' ratings of students' critiques. For example, were texts that were heavy in one type of commentary judged to be of better quality than texts that were heavy in other types of commentary? Sometimes students are expected to reproduce knowledge, showing they have read an article and understood it, while at other times students are expected to transform knowledge, challenging information and considering rival interpretations. Also, were texts that substantiated their evaluative commentary with one type of support over another more persuasive? One of the goals of teaching sociology is to help students link the personal with the sociological. I had witnessed this in various sociology courses I had attended and heard it from sociology professors when interviewing them about their teaching. But in the case of critique, how would students be perceived if they brought their personal knowledge to the task? And finally, did topic-comment patterns of configuration influence the degree to which students were perceived as exhibiting a critical disposition? Did a particular form suggest the type of thinking more indicative of critique?

Features That Contributed to High Quality Ratings

To answer these questions, I gave the students' critiques to four sociology professors who rated them holistically, applying the criteria they believed appropriate for a critique task in sociology. The scores potentially ranged from 4 (a low rating of 1 from each professor) to 20 (a high rating of 5 from each professor). I also interviewed the professors afterwards to discuss the criteria they had applied when rating the students' critiques. In this way, I could compare what professors said constituted a quality critique with the features of the students' texts.

I found that students who received higher quality scores from the professors constructed critiques that included more negative commentary that was supported by disciplinary source of support, and signalled valuation by integrating topics and comments throughout their texts. Professors may have evaluated texts with these features more highly because they demonstrated an effort on the part of students to think through the issue and to make their critiques relevant to sociologists. Negative comments may have been viewed in a positive light because it would appear that students were thinking more deeply about the issue than if they simply reported information from the article or agreed with it. One professor said he thought it showed students 'grappled' with the article. By substantiating negative comments with disciplinary support, students were able to show how their insights and challenges to the article were of consequence to the study of the sociology of religion, or at least related to the material they had been studying over the past months. Moreover, the critiques that suggested that students had struggled with the ideas in the article and had shown how these struggles were related to sociology were more likely to integrate topics and comments.

Further qualitative analyses of the texts showed that the overall patterns signalled different kinds of text transformations and thus unique internal dynamics, which may have influenced the quality ratings. Texts are said to have an 'internal dynamic' that distinguishes the types of rhetorical action they signal (Campbell & Jamieson, 1977). According to Miller (1984: 152), 'Human action, whether symbolic or otherwise, is interpretable only against a context of situation and through the attributing of motives.' Texts that used one pattern rather than another were interpreted as signalling a different rhetorical action (motive), given the task of writing a critique (context of situation). There appeared to be four unique internal dynamics suggested in the texts, with two dynamics more likely to correspond with the pattern in which topics and evaluative comments were separated, and two with the pattern in which they were integrated. These were:

Summary and response

Eight students constructed critiques that signalled summary and response. The average score for this type of text was 8.4. When students supplied suspended comments before moving on to supply evaluative comments, they often emphasised a reporting of topics rather than an evaluation of them. They spent much of their writing space summarising the source article before commenting. When they did comment, many of the students provided personal responses.

Natalie's critique is similar to many of the students whose texts suggested this dynamic. She begins by mapping out the main points to the article:

> The essay 'On the Margins of the Sacred' is a very interesting idea based on the concept of quasi-religions. This essay is split into basically two halves, the definition and the authors' interpretation of the proper use of this term and examples of what they believe to be 'appropriately classified' as quasi-religions.

Much of her critique describes the article, paraphrasing various parts of it, for example:

> The main focus of this essay is based on the American folk definition of religion, which is that religion 'to most Americans ... refers to beliefs and practices focusing on a transcendent deity, standing above nature, controlling but not controlled by natural law' (p. 220).

In the last half of her critique, Natalie provides evaluative commentary, which is her own personal response to the material:

> The authors showed a great amount of insight into their topic of choice, quasi-religions. I feel that I learned a great deal about what these organizations stood for, believed in, and why they would choose to be the way that they were ...

She concludes saying that:

> [t]heir essay went along with most of my beliefs about religion and I could identify with what these groups stood for through my own individual experience.

Interpretation and response

Some of the students constructed texts that seemed to interpret the source article rather than to summarise it, before moving on to provide commentary. While the configuration of topics and comments was similar to the summary and response texts, students tended to use the task to make sense of the article. Ten students' texts fell into this category. The average score for these texts was 10.5, slightly higher than the summary and response texts.

An example of a text that seemed to suggest an interpretation is that of Mark. He begins his critique by quoting the authors' definition of quasi-religion. Then he states:

What this basically means is that people in the groups find a common point of view or source of a problem on which to draw, join together, and work together to find a solution to their problems.

Mark continues elaborating on the authors' main point, which is that traditional religions do not fulfil spiritual needs in contemporary society. For example, he says:

Perhaps as society becomes increasingly complex, people simply need more flexibility in their lives. While many religions have specific rules which dictate to the masses, quasi-religions have much less defined paths.

Finally, Mark concludes by explaining why these organizations have become important:

By leaving the individuals open to their own paths of finding an answer to their problems or to find inner strength, the individuals guide themselves through the problems using aspects of the religion that suits [sic] their needs.

Analysis of parts

When a text suggested an analysis of parts, students had constructed their critiques bringing one topic up for commentary, followed by a different topic, and so on. Seven students wrote texts whose configuration suggested this dynamic. Professors scored these texts higher than the two previous types, with an average score of 12.4. If we look at one student's text, we may understand why these texts have been awarded higher scores.

Lauren provides a brief description of the study before launching into her commentary. She introduces a first topic:

First of all, the authors make a very good critical statement about the substantives and functionalists [sic] in sociology.

This is followed by discussion of a second, unrelated topic:

The authors go on to give examples of [and provide statements about] quasi-religious organizations … [However] these statements are not backed up with proof.

Lauren then introduces a third topic and so on. She concludes by saying that the idea the authors present is very interesting but their treatment of it needs improving. Lauren's critique, then, is a string of unrelated topics interwoven with evaluative comments that point out strengths or weaknesses of the article.

Argument

The fourth internal dynamic that students' texts suggested was that of the argument. Here, a writer sets up the major premise of their critique in the first segment of the discourse and elaborates upon it throughout the text, providing reasons for their commentary. Seven students wrote such texts. Their average score was 14.7.

Kathryn wrote an argument that was generally supportive of the article but critical of its weaknesses. She began her critique by demonstrating her support of the authors. This was followed by her discussion of two points that she felt deserved more attention:

> First, I see a need to differentiate between the quasi-religions which are organised around a specific problem and those which are not. And, secondly, I question if quasi-religions, which tend to be therapeutic-oriented, are useful for adults only, or can they be functional for children and their socialisation needs as well.

The remainder of her critique elaborates these two points in detail. For example, Kathryn shows how she reasons about these ideas. In the case of the first point, she explains how some of these organizations may be therapeutically oriented rather than religious, and some people may quit a group once a particular personal problem is solved:

> The need for therapeutic services arise because an individual has experienced a loss of meaning in their life and is searching for a belief system which will relieve themselves of feelings of loss and confusion. But it is important to note that what has caused this loss of meaning is closely linked with the type of quasi-religion one chooses ... Once they have successfully dealt with their problem, their affiliation with the group will diminish.

This would be quite different from people who join to 'formulate a new belief system.' Kathryn believes it is important that the authors differentiate between these two types of groups. In the case of the second point, Kathryn draws upon her sociology knowledge to discuss religion as an integral part of socialisation. She wonders if quasi-religions, which are more therapeutic, can be of any benefit to children, who have limited experience:

> Can a child, then, benefit from a quasi-religion when he or she has not yet recognised his or her individuality, or has not yet experienced a crisis?

These four internal dynamics of configuration described here signalled how students approached the task. Students who wrote *summary and response* and *interpretation and response* texts were more likely to include a large proportion of comments that supported the claims advanced by the authors than students who wrote texts signalling the other two configurations. The rhetorical action of their texts signalled more of a recitation of information than an evaluation of it. Students who wrote *analysis of parts* and *arguments* often disagreed with the authors, offering novel ways of approaching the issue or providing insights that might further thinking about it. The rhetorical action of their texts signalled more of an evaluation of information than a recitation of it.

Insight Into Quality Performance

The internal dynamics described here help distinguish what it meant for students to take a stance. Students summarised, interpreted, analysed, and argued. Each of these rhetorical acts signalled a different configuration of information and were rated accordingly. When I asked the professors what constitutes a quality critique, all of them responded similarly in that they mentioned four features.

First, students had to show an understanding of the article they were critiquing. To do this, professors seemed to expect a brief summary of the main points of the article. One professor commented, 'They need to be able to distinguish the main forest from some of the beautiful trees that may have been planted there.' A high quality critique then would be one that showed some conventionalised understanding of the text.

The second feature professors said they valued was students' ability to go beyond summarising and evaluate the source text. This was done by pointing out its strengths or its weaknesses, or a combination of both. Professors valued texts that clearly signalled evaluative commentary, particularly in the introduction of the text. This gave professors a way of anticipating a particular type of text and how it was going to be developed. Other types of discourse markers were important in students' texts. Professors commented favourably when students included language that indicated evaluation. It made it easier for them to discern what positions students were taking. These included explicit statements such as 'I agree' or more subtle cues such as subordinators (e.g. but, however).

The third feature the professors commented on was evidence. When students made a claim, the professors wanted them to substantiate it. When students failed to, they were criticised by the professors. For example, one student was criticised harshly for making a strong negative evaluative statement without sufficient evidence: 'I don't see how you're in a position in a discussion like this to simply say you disagree unless you quickly follow that by some substantiation of your disagreement.' Another professor called it 'evaluative posturing'. Three of the professors said the evidence should be disciplinary based. But one said that he expected disciplinary based support for general points. If students wanted to apply experience from their own lives on smaller points, that was fine because the goal of sociology is to get students to step back and think about their own lives in relation to sociological issues. This position is similar to that of other sociology professors. In conducting interviews with sociology professors, Williamson (1988) found that one of the goals of the study of sociology is for students to connect their own individual experience with larger sociological issues, to see that the individual life is part of a larger social pattern.

Finally, professors appeared to want students to place the article in a broader context. This meant they had to demonstrate some knowledge of the article's value to the sociological enterprise. In this way, the source article could be made relevant to the community of sociologists. When asked if this would involve having an extensive background in sociology, the teacher of the course responded:

> To some extent I would say that's true ... that you do need some background to be able to figure out where something stands in the schema, the idea system. But on the other hand, by the time they had to write this, they had dealt with substantive and functional definitions of religion and they had at least grasped those concepts ... And they had at least some amount of understanding of the different ways sociologists of religion define religion.

Students were expected, at least from the teacher's perspective, to fit the article into a larger scheme of knowledge. For other professors, this scheme of knowledge could vary. One professor had a 'strong version' of context, which was similar to the teacher's and a 'weak version,' which did not hold students accountable to disciplinary knowledge but to 'mak[ing] sense of things.'

The criteria the professors mentioned as a group seem to suggest a shared concept of what it means to critique, at least on a general level. This shared concept appears to be compatible with how scholars in a disciplinary community might transform knowledge through the insights and evaluations they make regarding claims. A scholar working on the text of another might summarize it to acquaint the reader with the article, point out ways in which the claims might be valuable to the disciplinary community or are in need of revision. The scholar would draw upon work that has been completed in the area to support such observations, and so on.

Signalling Valuation

We see, then, that a quality critique has a particular rhetorical space, an interpretative orientation between a writer and a reader that is made possible through the use of textual cues; the writer provides textual cues for a reader and the reader uses those cues to construct meaning. In this case, rhetorical space was defined by the textual patterns suggested by the students' critiques. Students signalled critical stances through the configurations of topics and comments they created and professors interpreted the configurations, with some texts being viewed as more critical than others. Students whose critiques included particular topic-comment evaluative combinations in their texts were judged to construct a rhetorical space that signalled:

a knowledge of the source article content;
an evaluative disposition;
a disciplinary source of support for evaluative claims; .
an ability to place the source article within a larger context.

There seemed to be a continuum of quality that corresponded with the type of internal dynamic a text suggested and the features listed above. Critiques that signalled a summary and response were at the lower quality end of this continuum, exhibiting fewer of these features while critiques that signalled an argument were at the higher quality end, exhibiting more of them.

The students' performance indicates that their conception of critique did not match up with that of the professors. More than half of the students' texts signalled configurations of topics and comments that were more likely to reproduce rather than transform knowledge. In addition, many of these students, when they did provide evaluative commentary, substantiated it with their personal opinions or by drawing on personal experience. Their critiques appeared to be focused more on their own concerns rather than those of the discipline.

These findings point to a need to develop a pedagogy that facilitates the use of generic features of critique, not as a formula, but as a means to understand its purpose — its rhetorical action. Students are not expected to learn the discourse of a discipline only for the sake of form because form is entwined with content. Coe (1987: 16) explains that, 'There is no meaning without form: information is formed matter (which becomes meaningful in relation to contexts).' In teaching students to understand the relationship of discourse and purpose, teachers can provide them with the intellectual tools to develop the writing skills necessary to transform or rebut claims and perform rhetorical action related to critiquing. Some of the intellectual tools in the students' critiques that were regarded highly by the professors included: (1) looking for the main points of the argument; (2) determining the meaning and assumptions of the argument; (3) judging the strengths and weaknesses of the various claims in the argument; and (4) engaging in argument as a critic, persuading others of the validity of a critique by providing lines of reasoning.

A pedagogy that incorporates rhetorical action into its practices differs from other approaches of teaching writing that tend to emphasize the writer (process) or the text (product). A rhetorical action approach addresses both writer and text, emphasising the appropriateness of the writer's efforts at producing discourse for particular social situations. Emphasising the role of the writer in a community of discourse would provide a backdrop against which what is written is interpreted, analysed, and evaluated by others. In this manner, students can develop their own stances toward disciplinary information and at the same time, demonstrate the relevance of their position to other members in a disciplinary community so that they, too, may make decisions and construct their own arguments to further thinking about issues.

Acknowledgements

The study reported was conducted with the support of a grant from the Office of Educational Research and Improvement, US Department of Education and the Center for the Study of Writing and Literacy, University of California, Berkeley and Carnegie Mellon University, Pittsburgh, PA. The writing of the article was supported by a Charles Phelps Taft Postdoctoral Fellowship, University of Cincinnati, Cincinnati, OH.

11 Thinking Through Controversy: Evaluating Written Arguments

CHARLES A. HILL

Teaching students to analyse and evaluate arguments is one of the most complex and demanding tasks that teachers face. Yet the ability to evaluate arguments effectively is one of the most important skills that our students can develop. Learning to analyse and evaluate arguments can help students further their understanding of a variety of academic fields by helping them understand and negotiate the various controversies within these disciplines (Beyer, 1985; Brookfield, 1987; Siegel, 1988, 1989). Perhaps more importantly, developing the appropriate reasoning skills may help students to evaluate the kinds of claims and arguments that they will encounter outside school – the arguments of politicians, advertisers, and various other interested parties who will try to convince them what to believe.

After centuries of philosophical inquiry, we have a variety of models for how we *should* evaluate arguments. However, argument pedagogy cannot consist of merely exposing students to ideal models of reasoning. Rather, these models must be reconciled with our knowledge of how people actually *do* evaluate arguments when asked to do so. In short, without some sense of how students tend to analyse and evaluate arguments on their own – before any formal instruction in argument evaluation – we cannot begin to design the types of educational interventions that can help them further develop their argument evaluation abilities.

In this chapter, I will survey some of the research that has already examined the ways in which people evaluate arguments. I will then discuss my own study, in which I observed college students and their instructors evaluating written arguments in an essay format. This study focused on the question, 'What *criteria* do students and their instructors use to evaluate written arguments?'

Recent Research in Argument Evaluation

For many years, the process of evaluating arguments was considered to be a rather straightforward matter of applying the appropriate logical principles. In the 1960s, however, many logicians were beginning to recognise that the principles of formal logic, in themselves, were not very useful for the analysis and evaluation of the kinds of extended arguments that people are likely to encounter in their daily lives. These scholars then began the work of trying to find useful and practical ways to apply logical principles to the evaluation of 'everyday' arguments – i.e. the kinds of arguments one finds in political speeches and in newspaper editorials. Thus was born the field now known as *informal logic* (Johnson & Blair, 1985; Kahane, 1992).

But informal logic has also been criticised, mostly because it begins with logical principles, and assumes that these principles should be and can be applied to the arguments that people naturally encounter (Secor, 1987). One of the problems with this approach is that, in order to apply these principles to extended arguments, it is first necessary to *reconstruct* the argumentative texts that are being analysed – in other words, to recast them in forms that make the logical principles underneath more explicit. Reconstructing an argument is a complex procedure, and somewhat subjective; different readers often end up with different reconstructions of the same argument. Ultimately, such a procedure is impractical because it fails to reflect the kinds of constraints under which people normally must make decisions about the arguments they encounter. Outside the class-room, people do not often have the time and inclination to rewrite an argument in order to evaluate it.

In order to develop a sound pedagogy for evaluating arguments, we need to know more about how people tend to evaluate arguments when they are *not* attempting to follow the dictates of a logic textbook. We should not give up the practice of constructing 'ideal' models for argument evaluation, and the work of informal logicians is valuable in this regard. However, in order to change people's reasoning behaviours, we need to know more about those behaviours as they naturally occur. We need to address questions such as the following: What criteria do people 'naturally' use to evaluate arguments? How do they evaluate different *types* of arguments? What are the cognitive, educational, and social factors that influence the criteria that people use? Only recently have researchers developed the methodologies needed to study such questions in any detail.

Though the research into argumentative reasoning is still somewhat sparse, some consistent findings can be found in the literature. For instance, studies in syllogistic reasoning have consistently found that people tend to base their evaluations of arguments on the truth value of individual premises within an argument rather than on the validity of the inferential links between premises. (See Johnson-Laird and Byrne, 1991, for a review of the research on syllogistic reasoning.) Consider the following argument:

Premise: All whales are mammals.
Premise: All whales are warm blooded.
Conclusion: All mammals are warm blooded.

The research in syllogistic reasoning suggests that most readers would immediately judge this argument as valid, as soon as they recognised that the conclusion and both of the premises are true. Johnson-Laird and Byrne (1991) suggest, though, that most readers would analyse the argument further by trying to think of all the scenarios in which both of the premises could be true. If, in any one of these scenarios, it is possible for the conclusion to be untrue, then the argument is judged invalid. When faced with this example, then, a reader might construct the following scenarios (which Johnson-Laird and Byrne call 'mental models'):

(1) All mammals are whales and all whales are mammals, and they are all warm blooded.
(2) Whales are a subset of mammals, and all mammals are warm blooded.
(3) Whales are a subset of warm blooded animals, which constitute a subset of mammals.

Since (3) describes a situation in which both of the premises are true while the conclusion is false, the reader would reject the argument as invalid. However, if the reader stopped after constructing the first two models – that is, failed to think of all the scenarios that could account for the premises – then the reader may mistakenly judge the argument as being a valid one.

Voss and his colleagues have found that personal values will also influence a person's evaluation of a given argument (e.g. Voss *et al.*, 1989; Voss & Means, 1991; Voss *et al.*, 1993). When offered two sound arguments, readers will consider one stronger if it activates a value that is seen as more important. For example, their participants rated the argument, 'All states should have a 55 mile-per-hour speed limit because a 55 mph speed limit reduces traffic fatalities' as stronger than the argument, 'All states should have a 55 mile-per-hour speed limit because a 55 mph speed limit reduces gasoline consumption', presumably because the participants considered loss of human life to be a more important consideration than gasoline consumption.

Personal beliefs and knowledge can also play a large role in how people evaluate arguments. For instance, many of the arguments in the public arena deal with large demographic variables, and these arguments are sometimes the most difficult to evaluate by most citizens, who have little knowledge of the appropriate statistical facts by which to judge the argumentative claims. In the United States, debates about issues such as health care and gun control often rely heavily on a bewildering array of statistics. Social psychologists have found that individuals tend to judge the plausibility of such statistics based on the relevant examples that they can quickly retrieve from memory (Matlin, 1983: 300; Nisbett & Ross, 1980). For instance, a written argument that rests on the assertion that violent crime is on the rise across the country will be judged as strong by a reader who has recently been robbed or who has seen many recent news reports of violent crimes, while another reader who has not seen such reports or who has not experienced violent crime first-hand may be more critical of the argument – even though neither reader has access to the relevant statistics that would (presumably) tell whether violent crime is *really* on the rise nationwide.

Finally, the research has consistently found that people's evaluations of arguments are biased by their attitude toward the claim (e.g. Evans, 1989; Kuhn, 1991; Voss *et al.*, 1989; Voss *et al.*, 1993; Waly & Cook, 1965). Specifically, people will be much more charitable toward arguments that support a position they believe in than they will be toward arguments supporting a position that they oppose.

It seems, then, that a complex mixture of personal knowledge, beliefs, attitudes and values work together to determine how people will evaluate any given argument (Voss & Means, 1991). It is also clear that people do not, in general, apply the rules of formal logic when asked to evaluate arguments. The criteria people use to evaluate arguments – even when they are being highly rational – do not reflect the dictates of the formal logical systems created by philosophers and mathematicians. As Johnson-Laird and Byrne (1991: 215) conclude, 'No formal logic exists in the heads of anyone other than logicians. The principles of thought are not based on formal rules of inference'.

Evaluating Argumentative Essays: A Descriptive Study

For the most part, the psychological research discussed above has examined readers' reactions to syllogisms or to simple arguments consisting of a claim and a single premise (such as the following two):

- The United States should build more nuclear power plants because doing so would result in lower energy prices.
- Genetic engineering should be encouraged because it may lead to new treatments for deadly diseases.

In contrast, my own research has examined individuals' responses to the types of arguments that we try to teach our students to analyse and evaluate – that is, extended written arguments on a single topic. This research was designed to determine whether the process of looking at arguments embedded within an extended essay or article is much different from the process of looking at a series of simple arguments in isolation. For instance, I wondered whether readers might take cues from the surrounding text that would influence the ways in which they evaluate the arguments embedded within the text. More specifically, I thought that the elaborated nature of the arguments in an essay format might mitigate the bias of the readers' prior attitudes toward the issue being discussed. I also hypothesised that readers would rely less on their prior beliefs and be more willing to accept the authority of the writer when reading an argumentative essay than when reading simple arguments in isolation. In general, then, my purpose was to extend the research discussed above by examining the argument-evaluation processes of students reading complete argumentative essays, rather than syllogisms or isolated single-premise arguments.

In order to look at the process of evaluating extended arguments, I asked 20 first-year university students to read and evaluate two argumentative essays. One of these essays argued that drugs such as marijuana, cocaine and heroin should be legalised, and the other argued against legalising these drugs. Both of the essays were of the style, length, and format that a reader might encounter on the editorial page of a typical American newspaper. Each essay contained the following types of argumentative appeals: testimony from experts, statistics, analogy, and emotional language.

I also hypothesised that the process of evaluating arguments might be influenced by academic training and experience. In order to explore these influences on argument evaluation processes, I also asked 10 university instructors to evaluate the same essays – instructors with extensive experience in the evaluation of argumentative essays.[1] Almost all of the previous research in argument evaluation had used students as participants – I wondered if these instructors would tend to use logical criteria more than the previous research would indicate.

I asked the students and instructors to comment on the arguments in the essays while reading, and I analysed their comments to see what criteria they were using to evaluate the arguments. In general, I found that the students and instructors applied a wide range of criteria to their evaluations of the arguments, and that there were systematic differences between the criteria used by the two groups.

Criteria Used to Evaluate Written Arguments

Over one-quarter of the instructors' comments indicated that they were trying to apply some sort of *generalisable criteria* when evaluating the arguments. In other words, they used criteria that would presumably apply to any argument, regardless of content. Statements made in this category included:

- Comments about the presence or absence of 'support' or 'evidence'.
- Comments stating that certain statements in the essay were contradictory with other statements in the same essay.
- Comments about objectivity – stating that the writer had made statements that put his or her objectivity into question.
- Any other comments questioning the rationality of the argument or in which the words 'validity', 'soundness', or 'logic' were explicitly mentioned.

The students mentioned such general criteria only about half as often as the instructors did.

I should point out that I did not attempt to determine the 'accuracy' of either group's diagnoses. For instance, in one case, an instructor claimed that a particular argument was 'not logical', but it was unclear what logical criterion the instructor was attempting to apply. The point here is not that the instructors' thinking was 'more logical', but that they at least *attempted* to apply generalisable criteria more often. In other words, they saw the task of evaluating arguments as one in which general criteria of 'logic' or 'support' should be applied.

Rather than focus on 'logic' or 'support', several of the students made comments about how a general reading audience might react to the argument being offered, while the instructors made almost no comments along these lines. For instance, one paragraph of the anti-legalisation essay focused on the monetary cost of drugs to society, arguing that legalising drugs would cost US taxpayers billions of dollars to tackle social problems tied to increased use of these drugs. One student responded to this paragraph by saying: 'This is a very good paragraph, strengthens it a lot, I feel. Whenever you pull at somebody's purse strings, reach into their wallet, it makes them stand up and notice.' Most of the comments about audience reactions were made by two students, who tended to rely on this criterion a great deal. Even though the instructions for the evaluation task specifically asked for the readers' own reactions to the arguments – not to judge how other people might react to them – these students relied almost exclusively on rhetorical considerations for evaluating the arguments. They did not seem to consider the possibility that a distinction exists between an argument's persuasiveness and its soundness. In other words, their judgements of an argument's strength seemed to rest solely on the probability that the argument would be persuasive to a general audience.

The evaluations made by both students and instructors were often influenced by the particular type of appeal that was being used in the argument. For instance, the anti-legalisation essay included two specific examples or anecdotes. (The instructors in the study called them 'anecdotes', but the students tended to label them 'examples'.) The first anecdote was the story of a 16-year-old girl, related in the second paragraph:

> Drugs are terrible, and it was a horrible, vicious cycle I lived in [when I was on drugs] – drugs took me over. I can remember one time when I was high I needed a fix so bad, I had sex with a man around 55 years or older. For a few days' worth of drugs, it was worth it at the time. I was once pregnant, but because of the drugs, I had the baby when it was five months into my pregnancy – the baby's arm was at its leg and its ear was at its cheek – the baby died. Drugs ruined my life, and I regret it so much.

Seven of the 10 instructors thought that this paragraph weakened the argument because they doubted its credibility or because it was 'an overdramatized example'. But 16 of the 20 students thought that including an anecdote such as this was a strong strategy: 'The second paragraph strengthens the argument a lot because it gives an example of someone who was on drugs and it is a concrete example of what happened to them specifically.' The second anecdote – in the sixth paragraph of the anti-legalization essay – told about the time the author was held up by a drug addict:

> I've been held up by an addict, a nine-inch butcher knife held to my throat. Because of a legal technicality, the bastard did not serve one day in jail. Naturally, I want to see him punished. I want not the legalisation

of drugs, but laws that would allow offenders to receive mandatory sentences – life imprisonment without the possibility of parole for drug-related killings and for the sale of drugs to children.

Again, eight out of the 10 instructors thought that this anecdote, like the first one, weakened the argument. The students, however, were almost evenly split on their ratings of this paragraph. In general, they seemed to think that it was a powerful story, but that it weakened the argument because it revealed the author's personal bias toward the issue.

Overall, the students felt that including personal anecdotes could be a powerful and appropriate strategy. However, several students indicated that using anecdotes can backfire if they are anecdotes *about the author*, because they can reveal the author's bias. The instructors, on the other hand, generally rejected the use of anecdotes as an inappropriate emotional appeal or as providing just 'one example' from which it would be inappropriate to generalise.

Sometimes the essays used emotional language, appealing to abstract emotional values, in order get their claims across. For instance, the concluding paragraph of the anti-legalisation essay relied heavily on the terminology of war:

> It is time to escalate the war on drugs, not to capitulate by legalising these substances. We must fight this enemy until we conquer it, not raise the white flag of surrender. We must continue to fight to curtail drug trafficking and end this threat to our national security and well-being. It is time to act assertively, rather than to fall victim to despair or to be victimised by utopian proposals.

Only the instructors ever explicitly mentioned the way that language was used in the arguments. When they did mention the use of language, it was to point out that such tactics are meant to elicit an emotional rather than a reasoned response:

> For a conclusion, he hasn't concluded by saying anything factual. It's a conclusion that uses all of these words, you know, 'the white flag of surrender', 'curtail', 'threat to our national security', 'act assertively', 'fall victim', 'victimised by utopian proposals'. These are all words that are going to bring out the reader's emotional response instead of a factual response or something that you can see concretely, and this is an appeal to the emotions.

The use of such language did evoke an emotional response in one of the instructors, but it was doubtless not the type of response that the writer of the essay intended:

Now see, this is that bullshit again, of no development of this initial idea ... it's just name-calling ... because it wasn't developed and he moves instead into this short, underdeveloped rhetorical jargon – I'm annoyed and irritated with the entire argument.

Both students and instructors had a variety of reactions to the ways in which the writers of the essays used statistics. Sometimes students seemed to feel that including statistics – any statistics – automatically makes an argument stronger: 'It's a good paragraph, has a lot of statistics.' More often, though, the students and instructors commented on the way in which the particular statistics were used. They thought that the statistics, in order to be effective, needed to be clear and not too 'dry': 'The numbers in this paragraph were much more recognisable and understandable and they make a better point. They are not as tedious or taxing.' Finally, some readers, like this instructor, merely registered dismay at their inability to deal with the large numbers of statistics that were sometimes embedded into the arguments: 'Maybe it's just me, I can't figure these, this weakens it. These numbers are driving me nuts.'

For both groups, the reader's evaluation of a particular argument was often influenced by whether he or she agreed with an assertion that was made in the text. Sometimes a reader would simply evaluate an argument based solely on his or her agreement or disagreement with the argument's assertions. For instance, readers would often state that a particular argument was strong because 'I agree with what they're saying' or 'what they're saying there is true'. Conversely, readers sometimes stated that a particular argument was weak because 'I don't agree with that' or 'I don't think that's true'. On many other occasions, though, the reader would go beyond the text to offer additional information from his or her own experience, beliefs, or prior knowledge, or to make an inference based on these experiences. In other words, these comments did not point to universal criteria that any argument should meet, but to a perceived consonance or dissonance between the particular argument being read and the reader's own beliefs about the facts of the matter. For each group of readers – instructors as well as students – the largest number of comments fell into this category – referring to the credibility of the assertion rather than to any logical aspect of the argument.

For example, one paragraph of the pro-legalisation essay argued that legalising drugs would lead to a large decrease in street crime by making drugs cheap and plentiful:

If drugs were legalised, pushers would be put out of business. There would be no purpose in creating addicts who would be driven by desperate compulsion to steal and kill for the money necessary to maintain their habit. The wave of street crimes in broad daylight would diminish to a trickle.

This argument is based largely on the assumption that most of the street crime occurring in the United States today is the result of the illegal drug trade. However, several of the readers took issue with this assumption, arguing that there are other causes, besides illegal drugs, behind much of the street crime that currently takes place:

> This paragraph says that – this assumes that the only reason why people mug or rob is that they need the money for drugs. But I don't agree with that. Because there might be some people that are just kleptos, that just want to steal, and not need the money.

In various ways, then, many of the comments made by both students and instructors focused on the truth values in the essays, rather than on the internal logical soundness of the arguments or on the amount or type of support that was offered. If these observations are indicative of the ways in which most people evaluate arguments, then they suggest that the way in which any reader will respond to a particular argument will depend in large part on the knowledge and beliefs that the reader already holds.

Implications for Teaching

At first glance, the instructors were being more 'logical' than the students in this study. The instructors mentioned general criteria such as 'logic' and 'support' more often, and they downplayed emotional appeals and personal anecdotes. However, we need to keep in mind that some of the students seemed to be evaluating the arguments in terms of their rhetorical effects; in other words, they were more concerned with the arguments' persuasive effectiveness than with some general ideal notion of rational argument. From these students' perspective, it may have made sense to rate personal anecdotes and emotional appeals highly, rather than relying on general criteria of logic and support.

In retrospect, it is not surprising that some students relied on rhetorical, rather than logical, criteria. Students in my own classrooms have often seemed confused by the conflict between abstract, logical notions of 'rational' argument and what they know to be rhetorically effective. It is easy to understand why they are not motivated to learn to apply the more abstract, 'general' rules of the textbooks in lieu of what their own experience tells them is effective. As teachers, we need to make clear to students that the rational and rhetorical models for argument evaluation come from different scholarly traditions, with different agendas. We also need to be clear about why it is useful to apply general criteria of logic and support, and how these criteria tie into notions of rhetorical effectiveness. At the same time, as scholars and researchers, we need to continue to try to reconcile the logical and the rhetorical aspects of argumentation, so that we are not continually faced with the task of teaching argument from two (often contradictory) viewpoints. Surely personal anecdotes do not provide the same type of information as statistics do, but they do provide *some* information – information that perhaps should not be ignored when making decisions on controversial social issues.

The most striking finding in this study was that both groups – students and instructors – relied heavily on their own beliefs when evaluating the arguments. Our prior beliefs play a necessary and inevitable role in our evaluations of arguments, and we should not ignore this role (as pedagogies based in formal logic, and sometimes even informal logic, tend to do). We might respond by saying that students simply need more relevant knowledge about the issues that they are being asked to reason about. However, changing these reasoning strategies is not merely a matter of exposing students to more 'objective' information. Rather, we need to stress to our students that prior beliefs in themselves should not drive our reactions to arguments just because we are used to or comfortable with these beliefs; rather, our beliefs and assumptions need to be opened up for critical review along with the arguments that challenge them.

Controversial issues and arguments themselves provide, not just a setting for applying known information, but also an opportunity to obtain additional relevant information. But argumentative settings are often not as educational or enlightening as they could be, largely because we tend to absorb and retain new information only when it is consonant with our own beliefs and values, and reject information when it conflicts with these beliefs and values (cf. Cederblom, 1989; Kuhn, 1991). Too often, the task of dealing with controversy becomes one of maintaining our assumptions rather than one of examining and challenging them. And this is true of educated and experienced argumentative reasoners just as it is true of our youngest students.

We should continue to develop instructional methods that might make students more reflective about their own beliefs, ultimately more willing to be as critical about their own beliefs and opinions as they are about arguments that challenge them. Indeed, getting students to open up their *own* beliefs for critical reflection may be the central problem in the teaching of argumentation skills, and the most important contribution that a curriculum based in argumentation can make to our students' intellectual development.

Notes

1. In universities in the United States, all entering students are required to take a course designed to enhance their writing skills. In this course, they are exposed to the types of writing tasks that they will likely encounter during their university education, and they are given practice in the types of general cognitive skills – analysis, argument, interpretation – that will be expected of them. While the instructors who teach these courses are not usually trained extensively in logic and argument analysis, part of their job is to teach students some general principles of effective argumentation and to evaluate the argumentative essays that their students write. The instructors who I asked to read the argumentative essays had all had several years' experience teaching this course.

12 Negotiating Competing Voices to Construct Claims and Evidence: Urban American Teenagers Rivalling Anti-Drug Literature[1]

ELENORE LONG, LINDA FLOWER,
DAVID FLEMING AND PATRICIA WOJAHN

What happens when an intellectual strategy, strongly associated with scientific and philosophical argument, moves out of academic discourse to become a strategy that inner-city teenagers use to talk and write about the highly charged topic of drugs? This chapter addresses this question by looking at the logic of 10 teenagers (14 to 16 years old) participating in a summer literacy programme at the Community Literacy Center (CLC). Located in the inner-city of Pittsburgh, Pennsylvania, USA, the CLC is a collaboration between the Community House (with an 80-year history as a settlement house in a culturally diverse neighbourhood) and the National Center for the Study of Writing and Literacy at Carnegie Mellon University. Independent of state schools, the CLC designs and co-ordinates literacy projects in which inner-city teenagers investigate and write about issues affecting their lives. The writers in this project signed up to produce a public document that would better address how to talk to friends about drugs than the existing anti-drug literature. To consider and to develop alternative arguments, the writers learned an intellectual strategy called 'rival-hypothesis thinking'. Unlike rival-hypothesis thinking in school, where demonstrating mastery of the strategy might be the goal of a composition course (Higgins *et al.*, 1992), at the CLC, the highest priority was for the writers to take literate action (Flower, 1994). That is, the writers' collective goal was to create a purposeful and effective document that would participate in a community conversation about youth and drugs.[2]

Given this goal, the writers' learning experience at the CLC existed at the intersection of academic discourse, self-expression, and community action (Peck, 1991). The logic of the writers' inventive adaptation of the rival-hypothesis strategy suggests that they constructed claims and evidence in response to the competing voices that informed the rhetorical context in which they wrote. Some of the most salient voices were the imagined voices of tough, street-wise youth, who would be impervious to arguments against drugs, and the real voices of adult mentors who encouraged both rival-hypothesis thinking and reference to external sources of evidence. In particular, this chapter suggests that for these teenaged writers, the respective status of arguments based on probability and those based on possibility had to be negotiated among multiple competing voices.

To set in relief a description of these teenaged writers negotiating among a wide range of rhetorical alternatives, this chapter first turns to an overview of a rhetorical tradition which has positioned arguments based on probability and possibility as polar opposites. Throughout classical and contemporary rhetorical traditions, arguments based on possibility – that is, those based on particular cases, stories, and immediate experience – have typically been held in low esteem. Aristotle, who upheld probabilistic reasoning as that which persuades reasonable and educated auditors, gave damning praise to the power of stories and maxims to persuade 'the vulgar ... mob':

> [T]he uneducated are more persuasive than the educated before a crowd ... for [the educated] reason with axioms [*koina*] and universals, [the uneducated] on the basis of what [particulars] they know and instances near their experience. (1982/330 B.C.E.: 1395b)

Much more recently and describing scientific discourse, Lyotard (1984: 27) has argued that in modern scientific discourse narrative statements are out of place, not only because they cannot be held up for interrogation but also because they 'belong to a different mentality', one which is considered 'savage, primitive, underdeveloped, backward, alienated'. The hallmark of traditional theories of argumentation is the contention that the reasonable mind is persuaded by arguments based on what is factually or probably true, rather than that which is merely possible. Implicitly, such prescriptions of 'the reasonable' have given privilege to notions of autonomous, decontextualised texts (Olson, 1977), to p-values and other statistical measures whose significance is considered self-evident (Moore & McCabe, 1989: 309), and to the notion of a competent judgement that links all humanity – at least all 'reasonable' humanity (Perelman, 1981: 18).

As the language of Aristotle and Lyotard makes clear, argumentative models based on the probable and on the possible are often treated as polar opposites (e.g. appealing to the educated vs. the uneducated, to the civilised vs. the savage). What this chapter suggests, however, is that in contextualised rhetorical situations like that of the Community Literacy Centre, use of one model neither logically nor reasonably disqualifies use of the other. Instead, rhetors in such a context persuade by constructing arguments from a whole range of options, some that appeal to probability and others that appeal to possibility. Considering these options for constructing claims and evidence, a rhetor makes choices while negotiating a wide range of constraints, goals, and pressures.

The teenaged writers in this study were asked to construct arguments that would be more persuasive than the existing public documents against drug use. The existing literature, at least in the United States, is often out of touch with the discourse of the street (Hayes & Schriver, forthcoming). For instance, a brochure called *Snappy Answers*, published by the National Clearinghouse for Alcohol and Drug Information, recommends to young readers that if someone offers them drugs, they should reply, 'No thanks, I'm too special' or 'Nope, I've got to walk my pet piranha'. To start imagining alternatives to this and other brochures, the writers learned the rival-hypothesis strategy. Within scientific, philosophical, and academic discourse, rival-hypothesis thinking is typically used not only to consider additional evidence that challenges one's claims, but also to anticipate questions and objections that subsequent readers may pose to the presented argument (Flower *et al.*, forthcoming). Within the CLC, rival-hypothesis thinking was quickly renamed 'rivalling'. Literacy leaders and mentors introduced rivalling with the aim of helping the writers both to integrate outside scientific information into their arguments and to consider alternative responses and counter arguments to the positions they posed in their texts. When considering rival responses to the list of pithy comments in *Snappy Answers*, for instance, the writers contended that the suggestions were not only naive but even dangerous, that they could make a person (especially a young man) look foolish if he didn't get beat up first for appearing haughty and impertinent – or, in the teenagers' words, for 'having an attitude'.

Daily one-on-one mentoring sessions and group discussions were designed to support and scaffold the writers' rivalling. Mentors served as one-to-one collaborative supporters (Flower *et al.*, 1994) as the writers developed plans for their 'how to talk about drugs' texts. Working in pairs, the mentors asked the writers such questions as, 'What's your point?', 'How might your reader respond?' and 'How are you going to deal with that in your text?' Similarly, during group discussions, literacy leaders asked writers to take rival positions to one another, and they sometimes questioned writers whether their plans were realistic enough to be persuasive.

In adapting the rivalling strategy to build their own claims and evidence, the writers' thinking reveals a range of argumentative options. Some of these practices are typically valued in schools, some on the street, and some seemed to be invented literate experiments that show an intermingling of norms, strategies, and goals. In constructing claims and evidence, writers were responding to the force of various currents: the comments and questions of literacy leaders, mentors, and peers that merged and collided with the internalised voices of teachers past and present; the expectations of other teenaged readers interpreting their texts; the shaping power of available models; the discourse of drugs; and – what often goes unseen – the writer's own goals, interests, and interpretations.

The Status of Facts and Probabilities

With the academic presumption that effective argument should deal with what is factually or probably true, there is a movement from particulars to generalities, from single events in time to predications and explanations based on aggregates of particulars. The 'purest' form of this probability model is the scientific method of induction. But even outside the laboratory, what is often prized in privileged literacies is what is reliably true, what is generally the case, what is likely to be present in contexts other than the one at hand. Narration and example may be used in this kind of discourse but only as indicative of the data as a whole.

At the CLC, this logical, probabilistic, scientific model of argumentative reasoning had some currency. The literacy leaders for the project, for instance, compiled a drug library for the project consisting of scientific information on the effects of drugs. They invited a nurse who specialised in the detoxication and recovery of alcoholics and a police officer whose round of duty was a nearby area of the inner-city. These guests were asked to inform the writers of the facts regarding drug abuse and drug offences. As mentioned earlier, the literacy leaders and mentors also encouraged the writers to talk about drugs 'realistically' and to incorporate medical information, including statistics. For instance, while presenting to the group a plan for her contribution to the newspaper, Shaunise[3], a 15-year-old sent to live with an aunt in Pittsburgh because of some unspecified trouble in another city, described the scenario she wanted to depict in a comic strip:

Shaunise: A whole bunch of situations, with steroids, heroin, cocaine, marijuana, beer. Everything like that with your best friends, strangers, somebody on your team, your mom, your dad, everything like that ... Like for the heroine, you could have a lot of kids whose parents are strung out on cocaine. Have a situation like that.

A mentor tried to push Shaunise to consider ways of incorporating what the mentor considered to be real responses to such a scenario:

Linda/mentor: Is there some way you can get in sort of rival responses? Is there a way to make these show somebody the kinds of responses they might really make to a friend, say, and complicated enough to be realistic?

One week later, mentors and a literacy leader further questioned the effectiveness of Shaunise's proposed ending in which the two main characters die from drug overdose after the mother leaves some of her own drugs on a table:

Linda/mentor: Yeah, what I'm wondering is if there is a way you can work in those rivals so you get your story believable.

**Lorraine/
literacy leader:** Could you work that into the story?

Linda: Yeah, I think that would be good because you get closer to being realistic, that someone like you would believe.

Shaunise: The point of the story is that you can say anything, but you take too much of any drug and you're going to die.

Linda: Yeah?

Shaunise: Eventually, you will die.

Joyce/mentor: I think you have to be real careful and say it depends on how often you take it ... because if they know people like I know people who have been using coke, marijuana, and a few other things for years and years. They might just say like I'm saying now, I know people who used drugs for years and they didn't die.

In part, such prompts were intended to help writers move away from the moralising and simplifying that is typical of much anti-drug literature. During a staff meeting midway through the project, some mentors mentioned that they had hoped to see rivalling and collaborative planning move the writers away from arguments based on myths and slogans, to deal with drug abuse in a more critical way. In attending to this concern, mentors gave voice to a related academic schema, one that emphasises the important role played by facts and probabilities in argumentation.

The writers, too, often seemed aware of the persuasive power of facts, statistics, and probabilities. For example, as Raymond planned his text with his mentor, he demonstrated a telling familiarity with the power of statistical language:

Raymond:	And I could put here since he is injecting it into his legs, I could say the consequences, that 9 out of 10 that you're going to lose them.
Elenore:	Did you, is 9 out of 10 an actual fact?
Raymond:	Well, no. I'm just predicting that because all of these people are losing their legs because it blocks off the circulation and all that.

In their written texts as well, a few of the writers chose to include arguments based on statistics and facts. One writer made fairly extensive use of outside source information provided in the drug library, citing a study of drug use among high school seniors as well as detailed descriptions of physiological effects of cocaine use. Another writer demonstrated in her text an awareness of the potential value of using outside sources. She wrote, 'I got the medical information in this article from an experienced detox nurse.' In a sense, then, these moves represent the conventional strategies of academic argument: persuade by appealing to probabilities, to statistical evidence, to informed experience. With such moves, the rhetor breaks away from the immediate context at hand to a deliberative space that is abstract and objective.

In general, however, the writers in this project demonstrated a low estimation of the transactive power of facts and probabilities. In their planning and writing, they implicitly acknowledged the difficulty of persuading people – particularly people on drugs – with hard, factual evidence. In planning his scenario, for instance, Shennod considered including a situation in which a boy would use factual, medical information to try to convince his mother not to use drugs. He eventually abandoned this approach: 'She probably wouldn't believe [it] – she'd say, "How do you know?" ' On a number of occasions, mentors referred the writers to the drug library for information that would perhaps support arguments in their texts; yet, with one exception, the writers did not make use of this information. One student, for example, was encouraged to use published information on steroids. But, like many of the other writers, she rejected scientific resources for her argument, relying instead on information she gathered from a guest speaker, what she remembered of famous athletes' testimonies regarding their drug addictions, and her own notions of the health-related consequences of drug use.

In sum, we saw little discussion or use of statistics or facts in writers' plans and texts. The writers seemed acutely aware of the general difficulty of persuading people in this context to change their behaviour by using factual or probabilistic arguments. As Romanda said about an imagined drug user, 'He just don't wanna listen to nobody, 'cause he thinks he's the main man. Nobody else can tell him anything, 'cause he's always right. That's what he thinks.' Though this attitude on the part of an interlocutor would make much academic argument a waste of time, there is no doubt that real-world rhetors often encounter it.

The Status of Performances and Possibilities

If students for the most part avoided the school-sanctioned logic of probabilities, what then was the source of their persuasive power? In many cases, they moved to arguments based on possibilities, sometimes extreme ones. Such an argumentative strategy was often instantiated in performance rather than text. For example, the writers' arguments often took the form of invented scenarios based on a series of imagined events. Sometimes these were 'what if ... ?' stories: '*What if* your body starts to break down and [your boyfriend] takes you to the hospital and finds out that you was tested for the use of steroids?'; '*What if* you bought a house and there was a bush, and it was marijuana, but you didn't know it?'

When using such argumentative conventions, it is not so important whether the evidence is truthful. For example, in a planning session, Mariah proposed the following strategy for keeping a friend off drugs: 'I'd tell her, that, if she seems real outside, you know, I'd lie or something ... I'd just, you know, say things that would make her think, make her think what would happen.' As possibilities, Mariah listed 'going mental', getting raped, and getting kidnapped. Similarly, Raymond did not hesitate when he explained to the group that some of his examples were fabricated: 'I gave some of my examples of about when my friend was in the hospital – I made that up, right?'

To make their claims and evidence more persuasive, students often imagined extreme situations, many of which served the purpose of scaring drug users. In many of these instances, the action of presenting the situation itself serves as evidence for the case. Below are some of the moves the writers suggested:

- try to scare them out of it (Mariah);
- take the drug user on a tour of the local jail (Kevin);
- have the user watch the documentary *Scared Straight* or listen to a rap song by some former criminals about prison life (Kevin);
- tell the user that marijuana can slow down your thinking and reflexes, thus making it more likely that you'll be raped or kidnapped (Mariah);
- argue that 'Even if you take it at all, you're going to die' (Shaunise);
- argue that 'One time is all it takes … One time to get hooked; one time to die' (Steve);
- tell the user that he'll 'get real skinny or die in two years or something like that' (Shennod);
- give an example of 'somebody … in your neighbourhood that's real skinny or almost dying, and say that's gonna be you' (Shennod);
- argue that drugs give you skin ulcers but cover up even more serious side effects (Raymond).

As the above list indicates, the writers often constructed arguments that were based on particular examples and extreme possibilities. We heard the guest speakers make these kinds of arguments as well. The police officer, for instance, told of a grandmother losing her home because her grandson had been secretly selling drugs on the premises. And the detoxication nurse described a young woman who contracted AIDS after having sex with a dog as part of a challenge to get drug money. These types of arguments were deemed to have a persuasive power far stronger than those using statistical probabilities or formal medical information.

The writers' explorations of context and appropriateness also frequently seemed to result in sensitivity towards the tone of argument. For example, early in the programme, the group debated the appropriateness of 'talking smart' (being flippant) to an older kid selling drugs. Some of the young women demonstrated their quick insults, arguing that it would be best in such a situation to 'have an attitude' (put on an air of contempt). Shennod, however, argued that such a tone would be dangerous for males and could incite a fight. In these kinds of argumentative situations, performative strategies become key persuasive options, intimately tied to a logic of possibilities and extremes. For the young women, performing 'with an attitude' was judged to be a strong argumentative claim.

Perhaps nowhere was the writers' choice of performative strategies and conventions more obvious than in their selection of genres for their final texts. Though the group chose a newspaper format for their final publication, the discursive practices they brought together gave rise to genres that fit neither a conventional newspaper format nor the standard academic essay. Instead, the pieces were generally in a performative or dialogical realm, instantiations of the multi-modal argumentative world that these writers constructed. Of the seven texts in the newspaper, one is in the form of a traditional school essay. But each of the others works to capture the performative and interactive dynamics of rivalling:

- an advice column with letters and responses to letters;
- a fictional interview with a friend on drugs;
- a fictional dialogue between the author and his cousin;
- a comic strip about a drug user and his friends;
- a play about two friends, one of whom is a drug user; and
- a story about two friends having a conversation about drugs.

Rather than relatively sterile essays about drugs using school-sanctioned claims and evidence, these students relied on interactive, performative literate acts to build their arguments and to achieve their rhetorical goals.

These writers were not simply rejecting academic literacy in favour of what Peck (1991) has called community literacy; nor were the mentors trying to do the exact opposite. Instead, the writers drew from a broad range of available argumentative options. For example, although the literacy leaders and mentors did place somewhat heavy emphasis on academic style rivalling, they also provided information for writers that seemed to support directly their own literate acts. Along with the drug library, they provided a novel, an interview with a former drug addict, and a song about a user 'coming down' from the influence of a drug – all as other kinds of evidence that the writers could incorporate into their arguments against drug use.

In collaboration with their mentors, in group discussions, and in the texts they wrote, the writers showed an awareness of the range of argumentative options available to them for persuading their intended audience. They explained why one choice would best suit teenaged readers, would be easiest to handle, or would be preferable given their own rhetorical goals. Repeatedly, in working to negotiate such choices, they constructed claims and evidence that came largely from imaginative representations of the world around them, and they used an argumentative style that was performative and dialogical.

Negotiating the Force of Various Currents

An analysis of the CLC writers' rivalling sessions, group discussions, and planning episodes suggests that for many, their negotiations included attending to numerous constraints and alternatives. Figure 12.1 is a graphic representation of some of the many currents that the writers worked to negotiate.

Many of these currents – or voices – are implicit in the earlier discussion of the writers' arguments. To explicate several more, this chapter will now consider three quite distinct voices: a call for ethos, a cautionary voice that concedes the difficulty of rivalling, and the assertive voice of personal goals.

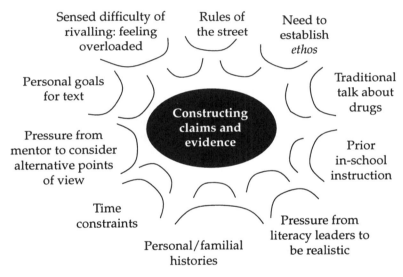

Figure 12.1 Some of the many currents that the writers tried to negotiate

Ethos

In their performative acts, writers made explicit attempts to establish their credibility in the acts themselves. Kevin, for instance, spoke with his mentor about building *ethos* by serving as a 'barber/guru' for his less self-confident friends. He explained that while cutting his friends' hair, he could assume a stance that permitted him to talk about drugs as a type of slavery and about other options rather than violence to settle disputes. Tee maintained in her text that she wasn't 'the *type of person* [emphasis added] who makes stuff up'.

Difficulty of rivalling

Raymond mentioned several times to his mentor the extra burden that rivalling presented for him as he tried to write his play: 'It's hard to write about John [a central character] because he's always asking all these questions [i.e. rivalling] about, ah, "Give me some examples" and "How you'd help me?" and all that. And it's hard for me to get all that together in my head.'

Personal goals

Chiante was adamant that his text should have a final resolution. Despite the insistence from another teenaged reader and mentor that his final scene could only happen 'in the town of merry fairy tales' or a soap opera, he held to his personal goal of a happy ending. For Chiante, the happy ending was non-negotiable. Why this way of dealing with the threat of drugs was so necessary for him is not always clear. But Chiante was not alone among the writers in his intense desire to envision an end both to the problem and to the sequence of rivals. The logic of Chiante and the other teenagers suggests that they are involved in intense and strategic negotiations as they work to construct claims and evidence. Within a sea of goals, invitations, options, pressures, and expectations regarding claims and evidence, writers attend to – and sometimes resist – the force of the various currents.

Conclusion

O'Banion (1992: 277), in *Reorienting Rhetoric: The Dialectic of List and Story*, has argued that we live '[i]n an age so enamoured with List' – that is, the logico-scientific reasoning made visible in graphs, charts, linear reasoning – that we have lost sight of 'the importance of Story [narrative, examples, maxims] and … its role in rhetorical theory and practice'. Contemporary thought has wrong-headedly assumed, he continues, 'that foreground is possible without background, that truth is possible without meaning, that conceptualization is possible without imagination, that the rational is possible without the narrational'. The literate activity of the teenage writers at the CLC underscores the notion that List and Story – probability and possibility – need not be understood as distinct modes of reasoning or ways of knowing. Rather, appeals to probability and possibility are among a range of argumentative options available to a writer in a particular rhetorical situation.

O'Banion calls for an infusion of List and Story, a 'continuing dialogue on what it is to be fully human and fully responsible in a world where Story and rhetoric are inescapable'. The literate activity of the writers at the CLC illustrates some of the dynamism that is integral to this continuing dialogue. Underlying the claims and evidence the writers constructed is a logic suggesting that in the face of an indeterminate rhetorical context, constructing claims and evidence becomes an act of negotiating the multiple – often conflicting – expectations, opportunities, goals, and constraints that the rhetorical situation offers. For the writers in this study, claims and evidence had to be actively constructed for the situation at hand and in response both to the strategic repertoires they brought with them to the CLC and to the goals and constraints that emerged there.

Notes

1. The project reported herein was supported in part by the Mellon Literacy in Science Center (MLSC) and by the Office of Educational Research and Improvement/Department of Education (OPERI/ED) for the National Center for the Study of Writing and Literacy. However, the opinions expressed do not necessarily reflect the position or policy of either the MLSC the OERI/ED, and no official endorsement should be inferred. The project is part of a larger study (Flower et al., 1993).
2. Community Conversations are events at which writers present their work and invite community members – including district representatives, school board members, peers, and teachers – to enter into a discussion of issues relevant to the particular literacy projects.
3. As published writers, all but two of the teenaged writers gave us permission to use their names; exceptions are the young women referred to here as Shaunise and Mariah.

13 The Burning Issue Paper: A Different Way to Teach the Writing of Argument

AUDREY BERNER AND WILLIAM BOSWELL

Introduction

The Burning Issue assignment is an integral part of the Effective Written Communication (EWC) course we teach at McGill University. We have been using this assignment for a number of years because we believe it provides the basis for many important elements of written argument. Also, it draws on the knowledge and expertise of the individual student and makes each student aware of the fact that, in order to be effective, any piece of writing requires commitment from the writer. One of our students states what he learned from the assignment in the following way:

> The most rewarding experience I had with this course was with the Burning Issue ... It helped me overcome a lot of inner fears and insecurities and I gained a lot of strength from producing this assignment. I felt I had succeeded in my writing because I believed in what I was writing and therefore felt a passion for it that I think came across to the readers.

Effective Written Communication, which started in 1980, currently serves over 2,000 students a year from a variety of faculties in the university, mainly Management, Engineering, Social Work and Education. Because McGill's student population is becoming increasingly international, it is not uncommon for any one of our classes to have students representing more than a dozen ethnic or cultural groups. Our goal is to help students become aware that they can be writers as long as they struggle to express themselves in writing. EWC bases this philosophy on the theoretical work of such people as Peter Elbow (1973), James Britton (1975) and James Moffett (1968).

Classes are conducted as writing workshops in which students share their ideas and work collaboratively to become more effective writers. We instructors try to create a responsive learning community in which students are valued as individuals who have worthwhile things to say and as experts in their own areas. We encourage them to bring their own life experiences into their writing and we try to provide a supportive environment for them to take risks if they wish.

Our philosophy is in line with that of Donald Graves (1981) who writes about the importance of students 'owning' their writing as opposed to 'renting' it from the teacher. We therefore expect our students to be responsible for their own learning and become committed to their writing. As instructors, we act as participants, guides, partners and evaluators of the writing process as well as the finished text. We help students discover and trust their own resources, help them develop strategies to improve their writing, provide them with a wide range of audiences and genuine purposes for writing, and respond to their writing as fellow writers, interested readers and compassionate editors.

The title of the text that has been developed specifically for EWC is *Writing for Ourselves/Writing for Others* (Dias *et al.*, 1993). As it suggests, an important part of the course is what James Britton (1975) calls 'expressive' writing. We expect our students to 'practise' writing on a regular basis by freewriting every day. Students may write anything they wish, including fiction and poetry, but they must freewrite without editing or revising their work. When we collect these journals, we read whatever the students select for us to read and we respond as peers, as co-respondents. We never correct anything in the journals, but simply encourage the communication. The students become more comfortable writers; freed of the urge to write perfect first drafts, they learn to take risks with their writing. We also encourage the students to write expressively as they prepare to undertake more formal writing assignments. Sometimes, as we show later, they even draw on material they have already written in these journals.

In keeping with our belief that students should become responsible for their own learning, we stress the importance of their also becoming self-aware writers. The writers of our text tell students:

> We have stressed the link between your development as a writer and your growing awareness of your writing processes ... As soon as you stop monitoring your progress through a piece of writing, it is quite likely that you have ceased to care about it. (Dias *et al.*, 1993: 229)

Therefore, in addition to journals, the EWC course depends heavily on writers' logs. In the logs, students write about the steps of the process they are following as they create the drafts of each assignment. Here the students discover which processes work for them and which ones do not. They explore their own ideas, experiment with styles and record everything. For example, on 19 November, David, struggling with a paper, talked about his frustrations with the first draft. He began again on 22 November: 'I restarted my paper today. I couldn't bear to look at what I'd written, so I wrote from the beginning again. Same result.' On 26 November he talked to the teacher and realised 'I had jumped into the writing process too quickly without really thinking on who I was writing to, what my venue would be, etc.' He announced on 26 November that 'I finally got it' and completed a first draft in one-and-a-half hours. In effect, he had used his log to discover that he must find a focus before writing.

In addition to the log requirement, we also expect the students to assume responsibility for evaluating their own writing. They receive feedback from us and from their peers, but ultimately, they are the ones who must decide about the effectiveness of their own work. With every formal assignment the students must submit not only a log, but also a self-evaluation in which they explain how successful they feel they have been in accomplishing the task they have set for themselves. In most cases, their remarks are perceptive, convincing us that the students truly own their own writing.

The Burning Issue

Students in EWC are required to complete four formal assignments during the course. While instructors tend to use their own favourites, we all try to do a 'how to' paper, an argument, a letter or application with résumé and a piece written in collaboration with others.

In the argument, our students are required to take a stand on a particular topic and, in some cases, convince their readers to adopt their point of view or to take some form of action. Many of us call the argument 'The Burning Issue' paper because we recommend that the students write on a subject of real importance to them; it must 'burn' them in other words. As Dixon (1975) explained in *Growth Through English*, students write better for real reasons rather than being forced to do 'dummy runs'. To begin with, they must believe in the topic and be committed to the writing throughout. Thus the paper must grow out of their concerns and not be imposed by the teacher. In addition, the students must choose real readers for their writing; if they wish to express dissatisfaction about the conditions of the roads in their local community, for example, they should write to their town council. Finally, the students should assume that they will send their writing to the readers they are addressing. In fact, some of them have sent their letters or have had their articles published.

Specifically, the two of us tell our students that their Burning Issue papers should fulfil the following requirements:

(1) The topic should demonstrate OWNERSHIP; that is, that the writer has the resources and is in the best position to determine how to present, explore and resolve that problem on paper.

(2) The appropriate READERS should be challenged, yet not over-whelmed.

(3) The FORMAT should allow for creative solutions.

(4) The LENGTH should demand and support a sustained argument.

(5) The paper should provide for a CONSEQUENCE: that someone can act as result, something can happen, or solutions appear.

(6) The writer should MONITOR the progress of the writing (through the writer's log).

(7) The student should spend enough TIME on the paper to allow for experimentation and development of the strategies advocated by EWC.

(8) The paper should make productive use of the STRATEGIES taught in EWC.

(9) The paper should allow us sufficient scope for a full and proper ASSESSMENT.

(10) The paper should provide the kinds of evidence we can point to as signs of the student's having achieved the objectives of EWC.

The first five criteria allow students to develop an argument that has a real purpose. The remaining criteria encourage students to use the techniques developed in EWC.

We introduce the Burning Issue assignment approximately six weeks before it is due. We do this because we believe that to be effective, the paper requires a great deal of preliminary thinking, exploratory writing, and discussion with others. We suggest that the students write about possible topics in their journals or talk about them in their groups in class or with friends. In some instances, students may already have used their journals to write about matters which concern them; they are encouraged to draw on such material if it is appropriate. The following excerpt from Alistair's journal shows how he searches for possible topics:

> I hate hangovers. I hate my laziness. I hate narrow minded people. I hate writing letters. I hate potholes. I hate the thought of myself or anyone I know catching a horrible disease. I hate AIDS/Cancer/drug addiction/the thought that people are born disabled and that they

aren't given the chance to excel. I hate racism. I really really really hate racism. I hate the thought of first and second class citizens. I hate neo-nazis (I hate their ignorance). I hate the KKK. I really can't understand what motivates them ...

Yes, I can feel it. I think I have decided on the thing in the world that I hate most. It is narrow minded, ignorant people. I hate people who honestly believe that as a race or religion they are the best and all others are inferior. I hate the stuff I read on bathroom walls.

We find that initially the students tend to choose topics that are too broad; the environment, abortion, difficulties with their first year of university, and violence in society are typical examples. The next step, therefore, is to help them while they go through the process of focusing – first in choosing a specific aspect of the topic they want to write about, and second in choosing an appropriate form in which to present their arguments. Again, writing in their journals, brainstorming, and/or discussing various choices with others helps to clarify their thinking. We provide guide questions such as the following:

- What is the specific purpose of your argument?
- How can the piece you propose to write achieve this purpose?
- What form will best persuade your reader(s) to your way of thinking, or to take certain action?
- How are you going to treat the issue in a fresh and different way?

The following serves as an illustration of the thinking that takes place before the students write their paper. Two engineering students expressed serious concern about environmental damage and chose to write their paper together. While they were in the process of focusing their topic and choosing an appropriate form, they considered a variety of possible approaches, such as:

(1) A letter to a local member of parliament in which they demanded to know what steps the government was taking to ensure that the environment was being protected for future generations.

(2) A column in a student newspaper in which they tried to persuade fellow students to become active in environmental protection.

(3) A narrative describing a worst case scenario which could be the result of failure to protect the environment.

(4) An open letter to the leaders of industry challenging them to alter their present policies which were harming the environment.

The two students eventually decided to prepare a report addressed to the Dean of Engineering which included an outline of a course which they had designed for engineering students. They argued that their faculty had a social responsibility; not only should it teach prospective students, but it should also concern itself with the implications of what it was teaching. 'Engineers play a significant role in environmental matters,' their covering letter to the Dean stated, 'since it is we who design the processes and systems that pollute. As such, we feel that our engineering programme does not adequately deal with the environment.' They therefore recommended that the course they had designed, or one like it, be integrated into the engineering curriculum.

Other topics we have seen in our classes over the years include:

(1) A letter to a faculty dean describing what the writer felt were weaknesses in current evaluation practices and offering alternatives.
(2) A letter to a suburban newspaper addressed to the parents of 'little league' hockey players. In it, the writer attempted to persuade his readers to avoid encouraging their children to win at all costs. Such behaviour, he argued, led to violence in sports.
(3) An article addressed to the youth of the Middle East. The writer argued that only through mutual understanding and dialogue could hostilities in the area cease.

All of these, it will be noted, deal with topics that are of concern to the writers. They also have very specific purposes and clearly defined readers. We have found that papers that lack such focus often turn out to be unsuccessful.

Once the students have focused their ideas, they are ready to write their first drafts. We stress that their writing must not sound like traditional five paragraph school essays. As we described earlier, during the composing, revising and editing of their pieces, the students depend a great deal on feedback from others, either in class or outside. They might ask, for example, whether their pieces succeed in convincing their readers and, if not, what changes or improvements they could make. It is also possible for the writers to discover for themselves that what they had originally planned does not seem to accomplish their purposes. As one student put it: 'I don't feel comfortable with the issue I chose – there's no outrage in me or anything.'

Finally, the papers come to us for assessment; we do not correct them and try not to sound judgemental. Instead we try to react as real readers might to what the writers have said. For example, a response to the paper written by the two engineering students might be, 'If I were the Dean, I would want to know more about … ' The students may make further changes and resubmit their papers if they wish. Many do, and often show significant improvement. In providing the final feedback, we try to avoid giving direct instruction about what must be done, because we believe that the most valuable aspect of this assignment, as with the others in EWC, is what the student writers discover for themselves.

The writers' logs assume a particular importance in connection with the Burning Issue. One creative student, in fact, referred to them as Burning Logs! The following selections provide an illustration of the logs we receive:

Emilio: Sunday 10 March

I have to make up my mind. Open letter or short story. An open letter has the following advantages: it can directly address the burning issue in a way that is very convincing if it is well written. Almost any audience can read it, however only the target audience will understand it; and the open letter is relatively easy to write when asking rhetorical questions that are on the minds of the target audience.

A short story has the following advantages: It can indirectly (or directly) address the burning issue in a way that can be thought provoking ... any audience may read the story and get *some* understanding of the conflict and although relatively difficult to write, the short story may also convince the readers ...

I think I can do this burning issue paper best in a short story format, because I believe this is how it can have it's [sic] greatest effect.

I hope I'm not setting myself up for a big mistake.

Alexa: 10 Nov:

I think I'm in over my head.

12 Nov:

I really thought this task would be impossible. I still hadn't found a focus. Then I started getting ideas. One came in the middle of the night, then a great one hit me after a snooze in the bus. From the beginning I really wanted to write this piece. Now I know I can, and its going to take a lot of hard work and writing.

28 Nov:

Thank God I have a sister. After writing about four pages I went downstairs to let her critique what I had written. She wanted more examples because she said she is often oblivious to what is happening ... Anyway, she sat down with me for over an hour making me really think and come up with concrete ideas ... she was such a big help and I now fully realise the importance of having someone revise my writing.

The importance of the logs for us as teachers is to provide evidence of process, including the extent to which the student writers seem to be developing an awareness of what constitutes effective written argument.

Conclusion

Ever since we began using the Burning Issue assignment in our classes, we have discovered that students create powerful and exciting writing. We feel that the samples below illustrate strong individual voices and commitment.

Motti: Israel is where I 'received' my first stone, fired my first rubber bullet and learned to use a 'billy' for the first time, seeing the horrible things it does to its victims. This is where I saw for the first time bleeding women running scared, looking for their men and children, crying for help; the air was heavy with a strange mix of sweat, spices, noise and blood. It all happened about four years ago (late 1980s) in a regular morning patrol in the casbah of Shechem and it was my first face to face encounter with the 'intafada'. Since then, I have seen enough misery and pain, enough beaten men, weeping women, and enough confused, young Israeli soldiers left without answers to realise that a drastic change must be brought about.

Karina: You may ask how one's decision whether to eat meat or not could possibly have any impact on such an overwhelming area? Every person who switches to a non-meat eating diet spares one hectare of trees each year. Over a seventy year lifetime, this would result in saving 700,000 m^2 of forest ... Still not convinced that one person can make a difference? Let's imagine that the City of Ottawa stopped eating red meat. Given a population of approximately 300,000, one generation of Ottawa residents would save 21 billion square meters of trees.

Yannick: During our time at McGill we may have learned about integrals or political systems but I cannot say that my university education has made me a better citizen of this country. We are here, I feel, to get an education not only to prepare us for careers, but also to be able to function well in society. While we may be very successful in our field of study, we lack the social skills required to fulfil our responsibilities as members of society. It is no wonder that in their quest for higher profits, businesses have been regarded as being disrespectful towards people, cultures and the natural environment. Most of these company and community leaders have been educated at universities such as McGill. Because of the leadership position which they hold, their lack of concern or awareness of social issues affects our standard of living. We must try and improve our education system to include greater awareness of those around us, so that our future decisions as community leaders will have a positive impact, thereby reflecting our understanding of the community we live in ...

You, the teachers and administrators at McGill, have a resource of 20,000 students. Your purpose should be to educate us to the best of your ability to help us integrate into society and make this country stronger. It would just take some leadership from some of you to get this 20,000 strong population started on a good cause. A centre run by students could be created on campus for those in need ...

Nabila: I am the girl who is sitting in the second row of your class. As I listen to your lecture, I come across something I don't understand. I wonder if I should ask. Just then, two students, one male and one female, raise their hands to ask a question – I hope it is the same thing I don't understand. You pick the male student first. His question impresses you and so you go into a detailed and lively explanation. You forget about the girl who had her hand raised and continue on with the lecture. A couple of minutes later, I come across something else I don't understand. Again I wonder if I should ask. In my mind I phrase the question properly so that I won't sound dumb and then I raise my hand. It seems like an eternity before you call on me. I finally ask my question and soon feel really stupid for doing so. Your tone seems somewhat different when answering me and it makes me feel as though I am being a nuisance. I don't understand your brief explanation, but I act as though I do. I look down at my paper. I let you continue with the lecture and I wonder who I can ask the next time I don't understand something.

An important feature of the Burning Issue assignment is that it reflects the writing done in the real world, unlike schools and universities where writers are often required to write from a position of weakness to someone who knows more than they do (the teacher). As one student wrote at the end of the course:

I enjoyed writing on matters which were important to me ... Throughout high school I was given writing tasks and told what to write ... I realise why I didn't enjoy writing.

In our EWC assignments we try to ensure that our student writers are the experts, writing to inform or persuade those who are less knowledgeable. Despite the on-going evolution of EWC, we have retained the Burning Issue assignment in its current form because it works so well in establishing a clear purpose and specific readership for written argument. It provides a vehicle for effective presentation, logical development of ideas, and the possibility of a response from the intended reader(s). For all these reasons, we believe it is a different and effective way to teach the writing of argument.

14 Argumentative Writing and the Extension of Literacy

PAT AND MIKE O'ROURKE

Our aim in this chapter is twofold, both theoretical and practical. Theoretically, we hope to place the question of argumentative writing in schools in a wider setting, which we call 'the extension of literacy'. Practically, we will look at an example of classroom work which seems to show some success in fostering a greater competence in this form of writing. We hope that the theoretical framework will both explain and justify the practical approach and its outcomes.

We will deal first with the place of argument in a wider educational framework. In Britain at the moment, the vital pedagogical problem of the extension of literacy is in danger of being submerged in distracting ideological battles. Instead of asking: how do we teach our students to read and produce more complex texts, the argument (led from above) has centred around which texts should be read. But the problem of literacy, once the stages of initial literacy have been passed, remains to be examined. By concentrating on lists of prescribed authors and recommended texts, we are encouraged to by-pass the essential question: what do we mean by development in English reading and writing?

This question had already been raised by Henry Widdowson in a short article written in 1972. He begins by asking why reading and writing, in their initial stages, are so much more difficult for the child to acquire than speaking and listening. His answer is that we must look beyond technical difficulties to the very nature of the communication involved:

> ... for the child learning to read and write is not merely a matter of learning to operate a different medium: it involves learning a new mode of communicating. Up to the point at which the child receives

formal instruction in how to read, his experience of language has been in the mode of face-to-face interaction: his concept of language is one of reciprocal exchange. Reading, therefore, represents a different form of communication altogether ... the child is called upon to change his concept of language and to adapt himself to non-reciprocal communication. (Widdowson, 1972: 209)

An even more challenging task awaits the young writer, who must 'learn to use language in a void, to communicate with an absent addressee' (p.209). Writing is more difficult for other reasons as well: its relationship with the other modes is asymmetrical: 'it depends on other language abilities but no other language abilities are dependent on it'; but above all 'the demands made upon our ability to write are, in fact, relatively few' (p.206–8).

Widdowson (p.208) explains:

The majority of people seldom write anything at all: their writing is generally restricted to the filling in of official forms of one sort or another and the occasional letter to relatives. The vast proportion of written language is produced by professional people and serves institutional needs. Its principal function is to maintain social structure and to give it a stability which it would not otherwise have.

New working conditions and practices have altered this situation in the 20 or so years since Widdowson wrote his article. As Trim (1989: 45) points out:

the so-called second industrial revolution ... places much higher demands on the ordinary individual's communicative skills than has been the case at any time in the past. Indeed, a failure to develop adequate communicative skills now produces, and even exacerbates, a very real social deprivation.

The need for computer literacy, for example, actually increases the pressure on our students to develop their reading and writing skills. Nonetheless the point remains a valid and important one: the vast majority of writing produced in society is produced by the few for the many – it is institutional writing.

What is the implication of this for the teaching of English and in particular for our understanding of development in writing? Widdowson adduces and then criticises a common objection to his description of the problem:

Of course ... the teacher cannot teach children how to write like lawyers and businessmen and textbook-writers, but he can teach them

how to express themselves in writing, and this is the important thing.
(p.209)

The implication behind such thinking is that there is 'a great natural store of language in children ready for release' (p.210). Widdowson produces a twofold objection to this view. Firstly he suggests that the non-reciprocal nature of the written mode may be by-passed in certain kinds of free expressive writing. Far from learning to communicate with an absent addressee, the child is largely addressing him or herself: 'the child avoids the problem of non-reciprocal communication by assuming both the roles of producer and receiver' (p.210). Secondly, he criticises the view that a facility in personal expressive writing will lead naturally to a facility in other forms of writing without these forms needing to be taught explicitly.

Nowadays English teachers are much more aware of the need to introduce their students to a wide range of text types, both in reading and writing. Yet, in our view, some of the fundamental questions raised so suggestively by Widdowson in this article remain unanswered. Let us re-word the questions so as to bring them into line with current preoccupations and debates: the British National Curriculum in English refers constantly to the need for a range of text types to be introduced, in both reading and writing. How do texts in this range vary in the demands which they make on young learners? How can we describe, analyse and then help to effect the transition between personal and institutional forms of discourse? Is there a 'natural' progression from skill in 'personal' writing to skill in more 'impersonal' forms; or in the movement from what Linda Flower (1979) calls 'writer-based' to 'reader-based' prose – that is, towards a planned form of writing that consistently acknowledges the needs of the reader? Or does this transition need to be specifically analysed and taught? We would like to add our own question here: how far does the acquisition of an 'institutional competence' entail loss for the young writer – or for any writer – loss of written discourse as an outlet for personal views and experiences?

We will begin to address these questions by proposing another reformulation: let us replace the dichotomy 'personal/impersonal' or 'personal/institutional' or 'formal/informal' with the notion of the continuum from 'unplanned' to 'planned' discourse. This terminology is proposed by Elinor Ochs (1983: 133) who defines the two ends of the continuum as follows:

> *Unplanned discourse* is discourse that lacks forethought and organizational preparation.

Planned discourse is discourse that has been thought out and organized (designed) prior to its expression.

Most of the discourse we encounter or need to produce in everyday life falls somewhere between the two extreme ends of this continuum. The important point for our purposes here is that unplanned discourse is primary. It draws upon features of language 'learned in the early stages of first language acquisition.' (Ellis, 1985: 86) Planned language use, on the other hand, 'draws on knowledge that is acquired or learned later in life' or 'upon knowledge transmitted through formal education' (Ochs, 1983: 131). This means that by looking at the nature of unplanned and planned discourses we may be able to attempt an answer to our questions about the range of texts, the nature of their difficulty and the process of making the transition to more institutional varieties of writing.

Before continuing, we must here enter a brief caveat. A vast amount of research has now been conducted in the field of first language acquisition, taking us from the pre-verbal stages to the 'steady state' of spontaneous and unplanned speech. Very little has been said, however, about the next stage: the transition from unplanned to planned discourses. This means that, far from providing answers, we can only begin to suggest fruitful lines of thought and research. Our suggestion will be, however, that the teaching of argumentative writing can play a vital role in the process.

We will now look briefly at some of the features of relatively unplanned and planned discourses. Ochs' analysis of unplanned discourses is based on spoken texts, but her categories illuminate the area of written discourse as well. The first feature identified by Ochs is the much greater reliance, in unplanned discourse, on the context. The context is used to link referents to their predications and to link propositions to each other, on a principle of 'nextness'. As she puts it (p.145):

Our observations of discourse indicate that context is an alternative to syntax and that planned and unplanned discourse differ in their utilization of the two alternatives.

Planned discourses tend to make connections overt by the use of syntax. Compare:

I'm exhausted. I've just been running.
I'm exhausted because *I've just been running.*

In the first example the causal link is left implicit. We infer it from the nearness of the propositions. In the second example the link is made overt through the use of a subordinator.

The second feature of unplanned discourse is its greater reliance on morphosyntactic structures acquired in the early stages of language development. There is a preference, for example, for coordinating conjunctions where planned discourses will use a higher proportion of subordinating conjunctions. There is a reluctance to use relative clauses and hence a preference for constructions such as: *There was this woman. Her back was turned.* And so on.

The third feature of relatively unplanned discourse is the phenomenon of *afterthought*. Speakers or writers change their minds or add essential but omitted information at the end of a discourse.

The fourth feature is a tendency to rely on the repetition of the same or similar lexical items and formats. Again, this is characteristic of early language. In writing we could compare this with students who begin a number of consecutive sentences with 'I think ... ' or 'Then he ... ' or 'People say ... ' Planned discourses show a much more self-conscious variation in form.[1]

It is not our intention to suggest, by this use of Ochs' continuum, a linear model of language development. She herself repudiates, at the opening of her article, the 'stepwise' notion of language acquisition. In fact, the unplanned/planned continuum itself takes its origins in a very different view. The stepwise image of language development posits a linear journey towards an adult goal. At each stage the child produces 'an imperfect version of the adult code' (1983: 129), which is then replaced by a better version and so on until the target of an adult linguistic competence is reached. On the contrary, Ochs suggests that what we find in the unplanned/planned continuum is evidence that early and late communicative patterns co-exist with each other throughout our lives. Depending on the communicative situation and its demands, we will call upon a range of linguistic potentialities from early and later stages of our linguistic development:

> A major condition affecting adult reliance on early communicative patterns is the extent to which the communication has been planned prior to its delivery. We find that adult speech behaviour takes on many of the characteristics of child language, where the communication is spontaneous and relatively unpredictable. For example, spontaneous dialogues and multiparty conversations among adults evidence greater reliance on developmentally early communicative strategies. Similarly, stream-of-consciousness writing, casual letter-writing, and so on display this reliance. On the other hand, more planned communicative behaviour makes greater use of more com-

plex structures and of strategies developed later in the child's life. Formal expository writing, for example, or presidential addresses to the nation display this kind of speech behaviour. (p.131)

If this is so, then it follows, firstly that planned discourses, far from naturally following on from skill in less planned forms, will in fact not arise unless the student is placed in a situation which makes the necessary demands. In conditions of spontaneous speech or free writing, the earlier structures and patterns will be produced because they will rightly be felt by the speaker or writer to be both appropriate and sufficient. Secondly, since planned discourses draw upon 'knowledge that is acquired or learned later in life' (Ochs, 1983: 131) it would seem likely that the situation alone is not sufficient. The need for some form of deliberate pedagogical intervention seems to be indicated.

Our suggestion, then, is that the problems presented to learners by more complex texts, and the nature of the transition involved in becoming a confident producer of such texts, can be approached through the model of the unplanned/planned continuum. We will now turn to the role of argumentative writing in this teaching and learning process.

The question of the role of argumentative writing is sometimes dismissed as a pseudo-problem. What is the 'opinion essay' after all? What relevance has it for our students, and who, in the world after school, will ever ask them to write one – unless they should chance to become the editor of *The Times*? These questions are perfectly valid, but our suggestion is that argumentative writing, precisely because it is not an authentic institutional genre, has a key pedagogical role to play in the classroom. Argumentative writing combines the expression of personal opinion and feeling with the norms of more impersonal forms of discourse. That is to say, it presents us with a useful and creative tension between the need for students to explore and define their own ideas, on the one hand, and on the other, the need to communicate those ideas to others in a reasonable and persuasive manner. Because of this it can be used by the teacher to form a heuristic bridge between unplanned and planned uses of discourse. Seen as an end in itself, 'opinion work' may indeed seem rather anachronistic; seen as a means to introduce students to certain procedures for organising information and ideas in a coherent and persuasive way, in order to communicate with 'the absent addressee', it perhaps makes much more sense. It can facilitate the move towards 'reader-based' prose.

The general pedagogical point to be made here is that the best route to a desired learning outcome may not always be the direct one. Sometimes, in Widdowson's words (1979: 251), students can be:

more effectively prepared by a course … which concentrate[s] not so much on direct teaching as on setting up the kind of conditions which create a favourable set towards later learning.

One of the great dangers involved in the teaching of more social and institutional forms of discourse is that we will find ourselves pursuing a pedagogy of imposition and conformity. By taking the more indirect route provided by argumentative writing, we can allow learners to explore the conventions and norms of such discourses while still having the opportunity for self-expression. Learners may need transitional forms when they are making difficult transitions themselves. Through such pedagogical contrivances they can learn for themselves something of the enabling power of certain writing conventions and learn to adapt them to serve their own communicative purposes. Instead of seeing conventions and norms as barriers to their own intentions, they can learn to perceive them as the means of expressing those intentions and allowing them to interact with readers: 'Conventions are the contract on which writers and readers must agree if the text is to be comprehended … ' (Smith, 1982: 96).

Although the generic form of argumentative writing is to some extent a pedagogical contrivance, its purpose nevertheless must be genuine if it is to be of any use to the learner. This means that the topics dealt with must be significant, both in themselves and for the writer. The need to communicate and to extend communicative ability will otherwise be missing. A genuine sense of involvement and purpose releases in the learner the need for rhetorical skills. As Walter Nash (1989: 98) says:

> Rhetoric only begins to come into its own when the 'truths' it invokes are complex and conditional, and require interpretation: in short, when there is a case to be made.

What students bring with them to this transitional stage is their competence in relatively unplanned and spontaneous forms of speech and writing. They now face the task of planning their discourses on two fronts: they must organise on the referential front, that is in 'the use of language to refer and to predicate … to express propositions' and on the social or interactional front – the use of language to accomplish some kind of social or rhetorical act (Ochs, 1983: 134). As Ochs points out, we often find discourses which are planned with respect to reference, but unplanned with respect to the interactional dimension. On the other hand, we find discourses which meet the communicative needs of the situation but fail, for example, to identify an important referent. The reader or listener is left with a logical or informational gap.

This is not, of course, only a problem for young students. One of the great difficulties presented by institutional forms of writing may well be created by the absence of planning in one or other of these two important dimensions, usually in the area of communicative needs. The result can be the 'voiceless prose' of certain academic or bureaucratic texts. As Peter Elbow (1981: 287–8) comments:

> Writing with no voice is dead, mechanical, faceless. It lacks any sound. Writing with no voice may be saying something true, important, or new; it may be logically organized; it may even be a work of genius. But it is as though the words came through some kind of mixer rather than being uttered by a person. Extreme lack of voice is characteristic of bureaucratic memos, technical engineering writing, much sociology, many textbooks.

In the transitional stage which we call 'argumentative writing', learners, free from the over-constraining demands of authentic public genres, can try out their capacity to plan in the area of both reference and social voice. Let us now look at some examples of learners' discourses from this transitional stage in opinion work. The first example is the opening of an essay by a 16-year-old student whom we will call Sandra. The whole essay is not presented here, because it is rather long, but the style of the opening is representative of the entire piece.

CAN THE USE OF VIOLENCE BE JUSTIFIED IN THE GAINING OF POLITICAL POWER?

Whether the use of violence can be justified in the gaining of political power or not, is for you personally to decide. However one can define and express one's views about such activity as a brutal menace and a crippling defier of world peace. The realism of this factor looms feverishly amidst the ever increasing bureaucracy of nations, stretched far and wide across this riddled globe of hate and hardship. Those unaware of this germinating seed of rebellion are the ones who allow for the sprinkling of water across this enraging epidemic of sin and heartache. Every day, hour, minute and second we are painfully reminded of the horror, the suffering and isolation of those innocently trapped amidst this guilt ridden net of self pride and rebellion. This net that allows no one to escape unscathed. Every soul has embedded the scars of hatred, firmly sticking to them like an unremovable glue.

We have only to subject ourselves to watching television to be made aware and angered by the brutality and destruction of innocent lives. Only recently citizens of Paris were forced to contend and deal with

the suffocating effect of extremists bent on destruction to achieve
political ends. The old, young and the very weak at heart, found
themselves targets of a series of inexcusable bombings in the breathtaking city of Paris. Middle Eastern unrest unfortunately is never
confined to one minor sector of the world but filters, flowing
exuberantly across lands and seas, settling in various territories for a
short while. Once stimulated the toxifying flood of extreme harshness
continues. People find themselves ignoring the beauteous qualities of
Paris for instinctive survival has emerged to the forefront, encouraging
all to flee ...

We have never yet shown this text to a group of teachers who have not
begun to express a note of unease after the first few sentences. Sandra was
a highly intelligent student, and the rest of her essay shows that she had
an informed interest in current affairs. But, despite a certain kind of
eloquence, her essential message or meaning is unclear. Indeed, it is almost
as if the eloquence stands between us and the meaning, as a hindrance to
it. Sandra has a feeling for expressive language, a mature and rich
vocabulary; she can handle complex syntactical expressions; she uses many
literary devices. Or, rather, we can see her revelling in devices of what
Carter and Nash (1990:18) call 'literariness'. This is the exploitation of
features of language use more normally associated with literary contexts
but also found in what are conventionally thought of as non-literary
contexts.

Yet as an argumentative discourse, there is something wrong with it.
The high degree of literariness suggests a rhetorical strategy to overwhelm
the reader rather than convince her or him by logical argument. In this
respect, it has intertextual echoes from such discourses as advertising and
travel brochures (*the breathtaking city of Paris*, etc.) Her main rhetorical
procedure, in fact, reveals itself as a kind of desperate periphrasis, achieved
by means of many non-core vocabulary choices (see Carter, 1987), and a
great deal of tautological elaboration. Leech (1969: 138–9) has pointed to
the important connection between periphrasis and the desire for 'dignity
of expression' and he describes the periphrastic strategy in these terms:

> Periphrasis ... involves saying more than is warranted by the amount
> of meaning communicated. The principle of economy of expression
> discourages the use of periphrasis in most communicative situations.

Because she is exploring important public issues, Sandra clearly feels
that the periphrastic style will help her to achieve a voice of appropriate
gravity and seriousness, and she therefore avoids economy of expression:
The realism of this factor looms feverishly amidst the ever increasing bureaucracy

of nations, stretched far and wide across this riddled globe of hate and hardship.
However, as this is a piece of argumentative discourse, we are bound to be
struck by the extent to which Sandra's commitment to expressiveness
deflects her from the task of presenting a cogent line of argument. Our
suggestion is that her efforts to plan in the area of communicative 'voice'
have outpaced or displaced her ability to plan in the area of reference. Her
work demonstrates an early attempt to exploit the rhetorical resources of
the 'persuasive' voice: metaphor, emotive vocabulary, repetition and
parallelism, and so forth.

We now present a very different and, we suggest, a much more typical
example of the kind of work that is produced by many pupils as their
'opinion essay'. This essay is written by Tasleem, aged 14:

THE DEATH PENALTY

Alot of people think the death penalty should still be allowed. I
disagree.
The death penalty was used along time ago, even though in some
countries it is still used. eg. America.
If a murderer was jailed for life or more, I think it would be a good
punishment, better than assassinating them, for the crime they did. If
the murderer was assassinated I think that would be an easy way out.
It would be much more harder, living your whole life in jail than being
killed in less than a day. Spending your whole life in jail would be more
punishing.
If a murderer was going to be killed then what is the use of killing
another?
Some People think the death penalty should be brought back.
Because if a murderer was assassinated, other people would think
more about what they do. Not so many people would kill, if they knew
that themselves would be killed for doing it. Should the death penalty
be brought back?

English teachers we have consulted concur in finding Tasleem's work
very typical of a certain kind of student. As English teachers ourselves, we
have marked literally thousands of similar pieces. But what is the nature
of the problem? Like Sandra, Tasleem does not seem to have any major
problems with grammatical competence. She has produced a reasonably
complex set of hypothetical propositions; her errors are minor ones. Yet,
whether or not classroom preparation has included help with the content
of their essays, the final product of writers such as Tasleem is generally
sparse; the student seems to have little to say. Often their points read like

a series of topic sentences with little or no expansion of each one. Although Tasleem here uses the first person personal pronoun and tells the reader what she thinks, her writing is, as one teacher remarked, 'curiously anonymous'. It is not always entirely clear what she is trying to say, not because, like Sandra, she says too much, but because she says too little. Such texts are hard to read with interest because the writer seems unaware of any requirement to be interesting to a reader.

It seems that Tasleem's efforts, in contrast to Sandra's, have concentrated on the referential task at the expense of the development of a communicative voice as a writer. Her final sentence is designed, too late, to provoke a reader's response. But the major part of the essay represents her attempt to conduct a moral argument about the rights and wrongs of the death penalty. The work is dominated by her efforts, through the use of conditionals and comparatives and causal constructions, to weigh up the pros and cons of imprisonment or capital punishment. The referential planning is difficult enough to absorb her entire energy and the need to call up some interest in a potential reader, to be persuasive, or vivid, to communicate any urgency, is not met.

Classroom Implications

These examples and others we have analysed seemed to point to the need for classroom activities which focused more on the planning stages of argumentative writing, yet without adopting a didactic 'instructional' mode. In response to this perceived need we have worked with students to facilitate consciousness-raising about such issues as the need to communicate with an absent reader, and to help them to see the functional relevance of the norms and conventions of argumentative discourse, which can help to bridge the gap between their own ideas and the willing engagement with those ideas by a potential reader.

(1) The first activity was a simple consciousness-raising exercise in which we asked students to act as commentators or 'markers' of different examples of students' opinion work. How easy were they to follow? How persuasive were they? and so on. The questions were kept open to facilitate a more general discussion.

(2) A sample essay was now looked at in more detail by the entire class. The sample chosen was one in which the management of topic was poor. The writer had frequent resort to 'afterthought'. The students were asked to produce a series of headings and then to rearrange the writer's topics in what they considered a better order.

(3) Three very short video clips were shown. The first showed a rather violent family argument; the second a contentious discussion programme with an emotive topic ('Animal Rights'); the third was a more measured panel discussion between four 'experts'. The students were asked which of the three most closely resembled their view of 'opinion writing'. (Most chose the heated discussion programme!) We then asked the students to look more closely at how people on the videos presented their arguments, in particular for remarks which preceded a point and 'made way for it'. This was much easier to see in the slower panel discussion example, though all three had features of what we might call the 'metadiscourse' of argument. From the third example a list of these features was made: 'if I could just make one brief point ... '; ' ... three things to say about this ... ',' ... however ... ', and so on. We discussed how speakers 'make room for themselves' and indicate where they are going next by using such devices.[2]

(4) The students were then given a sample essay, written by us, on a typical opinion topic: 'Should Smoking be Banned in Public Places?' The essay was presented in two ways: (a) as a straightforward piece of writing; (b) in two columns, headed *Writes* and *Thinks*. In the first column the essay was written out with certain features highlighted by such things as 'signpost' markers, or circles. The second column spelled out the writer's thinking as she used these features to communicate with an absent reader. So, for example, the opening: *In the last twenty or thirty years ...* is accompanied by the 'thought': *I'm beginning in a very general sort of way, to put my reader in the picture. I'll get down to the details later.*

(5) Having been alerted to the idea of 'signposts' which guide the reader through your text, the students then played a game with conventional signal words or phrases, such as 'however', 'nevertheless'. About 20 or so of these were written on cards, each one twice, and students were asked to allot them to columns on larger cards, according to whether they were more or less likely to appear in a narrative or an opinion essay. A middle column was provided for words which could just as easily be in either. We chose narrative as a contrasting form of discourse and as the one students are most likely to feel at home with. The 'narrative' signals were almost all time signals; the 'opinion' signals usually indicated logical steps or sequential moves in an argument. The word 'likely' was used because of course there is no rule assigning these to one or another kind of discourse; only a degree of likelihood. There was discussion about the outcomes. Most students seemed to do this with great ease.[3]

(6)   The students were given sequencing activities using both kinds of discourse: narrative and argumentative. Again this was followed by discussion about the differences.

(7)   At this point, with older students, a list of conventional 'signal words' was given out and some specific teaching about their use was given.

Of course such activities were spread out over several lessons. We hoped by these means to give students:

(1)   An enhanced awareness of the communicative and referential demands of argumentative writing.

(2)   A repertoire of organising signals through which they could both express logical development in argumentation and negotiate an appropriate 'voice' for this kind of writing.

We now present a third piece of argumentative writing by a student:

IS WHALEING NECESSARY?

No one can see a television documentary of whale hunting and the cruel way in which they are killed without feeling revulsion, horror and a feeling of determination that this barbaric act should be outlawed by all countries involved, no matter what their reasons may be.

Greenpeace asked for a ban to be put on these countries, to make them stop whaleing. Iceland, Holland, Russia, Japan, Norway, America, South Korea and Great Britain.

Most of these countries stopped, including Iceland in 1977 and then Russia in 1986. But in spite of this Iceland said they would only whale for scientific research. Japan, Norway and South Korea had the same idea. 'This is still *too* much', Greenpeace.

Japan did whale because they have no oil fields, because the meat is a delicacy, the bone is a fertilizer, a good fertilizer and this job offers alot of work for the people of Japan, furthermore the money for one whale is excellent.

Nevertheless there are alternatives. Oil can very easily be imported or made out of vegetables. Fertilizers are very good, they do not have to be made out of whales plus the fact that other fertilizers are cheaper. The whalers could get other jobs, what is more hardly any Japanese eat whale meat because it is too much, at £70 per pound ...

This is, in fact, Tasleem herself writing a few weeks after the previous piece, having used some of the consciousness-raising activities described above, and having been given time to research her own chosen topic. We have used only the opening paragraphs, for reasons of space, but her second essay is nearly three times longer than her first, despite having been written in the same amount of time.

Her opening is interesting because it does what her previous work fails to do: it *summons* a reader to take interest. She now uses more of the 'expressive' language which we noted in Sandra's work, but, unlike Sandra, she is *deploying* such language for a more communicatively relevant purpose: it serves the message instead of overwhelming it. Towards the end of the essay, for example, we find this: *I would rather see whales swimming around in the sea, than to see huge metal ships surrounded by red sea.* Here, in this last image, Tasleem uses the literary device of metonymy to substantiate her argument for the reader. It is a device resembling those used by Sandra. But because the rhetorical voice is restrained by the referential purpose, it is not overplayed and emerges with effectiveness and dignity in the presentation of her case. Clearly, Tasleem still has some way to go, especially in the organisation and presentation of facts and figures. However, most teachers and students who have seen her two pieces of work have not recognised them as produced by the same student. The assumption has been that the second example is the work of a much more able student.

We hope we have demonstrated in this chapter that argumentative writing has a useful place in the syllabus because it allows learners to experience and explore the productive interaction of the conventional and the creative in planned discourse. We also hope we have shown that such learning modes as argumentative writing must be clearly and firmly set against the general developmental background of the extension of literacy, whereby individuals are able to move with ease between the different ends of the unplanned/planned continuum in order to achieve their varying communicative goals.

Acknowledgement

We are grateful to David Eccles of Beaumont Leys School, Leicester, for providing Tasleem's texts.

Notes

1. Obviously, there are similarities between the contrastive features of speech and writing and those of the unplanned/planned continuum. However, for our purposes here, we feel that the latter provides a more useful and fruitful model. In addition, many planned discourses are a complex admixture of speech and writing – as in lectures, sermons, etc. See Leech *et al.* (1982: Chapter 8).
2. The pedagogical relevance of discourse signals is well described in a recent essay by Walter Nash (1992: 99–115).

3. Of course, the clear division between narrative and argument suggested here is artificial and is used purely as a pedagogical contrivance. For discussions of the real complexities of their relationship see Andrews (1989a) and Nash (1989: Chapter 4).

Bibliography

ABEL, R. 1976, *Man is the Measure: A Cordial Invitation to the Central Problems of Philosophy.* New York: The Free Press.

ALEXANDER, R., ROSE, R. and WOODHEAD, C. 1992, *Curriculum Organisation and Classroom Practice in Primary Schools.* London: DES.

ALMOND, B. 1988, *Philosophy.* London: Penguin Books.

ANDREWS, R. (ed.) 1989a, *Narrative and Argument.* Milton Keynes: Open University Press.

—1989b, Introduction: new relationships between narrative and argument? In R. ANDREWS (ed.) *Narrative and Argument* (pp. 1–8). Milton Keynes: Open University Press.

—(ed.) 1992, *Rebirth of Rhetoric: Essays in Language, Culture and Education.* London: Routledge.

—1993, Developing argument. *The English & Media Magazine* 28, 34–8.

ANDREWS, R., COSTELLO, P.J.M. and CLARKE, S. 1993, *Improving the Quality of Argument, 5–16: Final Report.* Hull: University of Hull, Centre for Studies in Rhetoric.

ARISTOTLE 1982, *The Art of Rhetoric.* J. H. FREESE (trans.). Cambridge, MA: Harvard University Press.

Association for Science Education (ASE) 1994, *Models and Modelling in Science Education.* Hatfield: ASE.

BAKHTIN, M. 1981, *The Dialogic Imagination: Four Essays.* M. HOLQUIST (ed.) C. EMERSON and M. HOLQUIST (trans.). Austin, TX: University of Texas Press.

BARNES, M. 1989, *Religions in Conversation: Christian Identity and Religious Pluralism.* London: SPCK.

BAXTER, J. 1989, Children's understandings of familiar astronomical events. *International Journal of Science Education* (Special Issue) 11, 502–13.

BAYNHAM, M.J. 1988, Narrative and narrativity in the English of a first generation migrant community. PhD thesis, University of Reading.

BAZERMAN, C. 1988, Codifying the social scientific style: The APA Publication Manual as a behaviourist rhetoric. In *Shaping Written Knowledge: The Genre and Activity of the Experimental Article in Science* (pp. 257–77). Madison: University of Wisconsin Press.

BELENSKY, M., CLINCHY B., GOLDBERGER, N. and TARULE, J. 1986, *Women's Ways of Knowing: The Development of Self, Voice and Mind.* New York: Basic.

BENNETT, N. and CARRÉ, C. (eds) 1993, *Learning to Teach.* London: Routledge.

BERKENKOTTER, C., HUCKIN, T.N., and ACKERMAN, J. 1988, Conventions, conversations, and the writer: Case study of a student in a rhetoric PhD programme. *Research in the Teaching of English* 22, 9–44.

BERLAK, A. and BERLAK, H. 1981, *Dilemmas of Schooling: Teaching and Social Change*. London: Methuen.

BERNSTEIN, R.J. 1983, *Beyond Objectivism and Relativism*. Oxford: Blackwell.

BERRILL, D. 1991, Exploring underlying assumptions: Small group work of university undergraduates. *Educational Review* 43, 2, 143–56.

BEYER, B.K. 1985, Critical thinking: What is it? *Social Education* 49, 270–6.

BILLIG, M. 1987, *Arguing and Thinking: A Rhetorical Approach to Social Psychology*. Cambridge: Cambridge University Press.

—1991, *Ideology and Opinions*. London: Sage Publications.

BOLTON, G. 1979, *Towards a Theory of Drama in Education*. Essex: Longman.

BOULTER, C. 1992, Collaborating together to investigate questions: A model for primary science. Unpublished PhD thesis, University of Reading.

BRITTON, J. *et al.* 1975, *The Development of Writing Abilities, 11–18*. London: Macmillan.

BROCKRIEDE, W. 1974, Rhetorical criticism as argument. *Quarterly Journal of Speech* 60, 165–74.

BROOKFIELD, S.D. 1987, *Developing Critical Thinkers*. San Francisco, CA: Jossey-Bass.

BUBNER, R. 1982, Habermas's concept of critical theory. In J.B. THOMPSON and D. HELD (eds) *Habermas: Critical Debates* (pp. 42–56). London: Macmillan.

BUCHMANN, M. 1988, Argument and contemplation in teaching. *Oxford Review of Education* 14, 2, 201–14.

— 1993, Reason and romance in argument and conversation. In M. BUCHMANN and R. FLODEN (eds) *Detachment and Concern* (pp. 96–111). London: Cassell.

BUCHMANN, M. and FLODEN, R. (eds) 1993, *Detachment and Concern*. London: Cassell.

BURGESS, T. 1992, Liberal ironists and English teachers: The philosophy of Richard Rorty. In K. KIMBERLEY, M. MEEK and J. MILLER (eds) *New Readings: Contributions to an Understanding of Literacy* (pp. 66–76). London: A&C Black.

CAMPBELL, K.K. and JAMIESON, K.H. (eds) 1977, *Form and Genre: Shaping Rhetorical Action*. Falls Church, VA: Speech Communication Association.

CARLSON, A.C. 1994, How one uses evidence determines its value. *Western Journal of Communication* 58, 20–4.

CARMICHAEL, P., DRIVER, R., HOLDING, B., PHILLIPS, I., TWIGGER, D. and WATTS, M. 1990, *Research on Students' Conceptions in Science: A Bibliography*. Leeds: Children's Learning in Science Project.

CARTER, R. 1987, *Vocabulary*. London: Allen & Unwin.

CARTER, R. and NASH, W. 1990, *Seeing Through Language*. Oxford: Basil Blackwell.

CEDERBLOM, J. 1989, Willingness to reason and the identification of the self. In E.P. MAIMON, B.F. NODINE and F.W. O'CONNOR (eds) *Thinking, Reasoning, and Writing* (pp. 147–59). New York: Longman.

Central Council for Science Education (CASE) 1967, *Children and their Primary Schools* Vol. 1 (The Plowden Report). London: HMSO.

Children's Learning in Science Project (CLISP) 1990, *Teaching Schemes*. Leeds: Centre for Science and Mathematics Education.

City of Birmingham 1975, *Agreed Syllabus of Religious Instruction*. City of Birmingham: Educational Committee.

CLARKE, S. 1994, An area of neglect revisited. *Curriculum* 15, 1, 13–20.

CLARKE, S. and SINKER, J. 1992, *Arguments*. Cambridge: Cambridge University Press.

COE, R. 1987, An apology to form; or who took the form out of process? *College English* 49, 13–28.

COOK, A. 1988, *History/Writing*. Cambridge: Cambridge University Press.

CORSON, D. 1993, *Language, Minority Education and Gender: Linking Social Justice and Power*. Clevedon: Multilingual Matters.

COSTELLO, P.J.M. 1988, *Akrasia* and animal rights: Philosophy in the British primary school. *Thinking: The Journal of Philosophy for Children* 8, 1, 19–27.

—1989a, When reason sleeps: Arguments for the introduction of philosophy into primary schools. *Irish Educational Studies* 8, 1, 146–59.

—1989b, Supervising teachers of children's philosophy. In N.J. GEORGE and R. PROTHEROUGH (eds) *Supervision in Education, Aspects of Education* No. 39 (pp. 75–81). Hull: University of Hull Press.

—1993a, Artificial intelligence, determinism and the nature of courage: Primary perspectives on philosophical problems. *Curriculum* 14, 1, 35–47.

—1993b, Developing philosophical thinking in schools. In P. ABBS (ed.) *Socratic Education, Aspects of Education* No. 49 (pp. 49–65). Driffield: Studies in Education Ltd.

—1994a, The teaching and learning of argument. In M. BOTTERY, C. BROCK and M. RICHMOND (eds) *Politics and the Curriculum, Proceedings of the 27th Annual Conference of the British Comparative and International Education Society* (pp. 72–86). BCIES.

—1994b, Philosophy and children: A plea for diversity. *Values Education* 2, 1, 3–4.

—1995, Education, citizenship and critical thinking. *Early Child Development and Care* 107, 105–114.

COWIE, H. and RUDDOCK, J. 1988, *Cooperative Groupwork: An Overview*. London: BP Educational Service.

COX, C. and BOYSON, R. 1977, *Black Papers 1977*. London: Temple Smith.

COX, E. and CAIRNS, J.M. 1989, *Reforming Religious Education: The Religious Clauses of the 1988 Education Reform Act*. London: Kogan Press, The Bedford Way Series.

Department of Education and Science/Welsh Office (DES/WO) 1989, *English for Ages 5 to 16*. National Curriculum Proposals (The Cox Report). London: HMSO.

—1988, *Education Reform Act*. London: HMSO.

—1985, *Education for All* (The Swann Report). London: HMSO.

Department for Education (DFE) 1992, *Circular 9/92: Initial Teacher Training*. London: DFE.

DIAS, P., BEER, A., BROWN, J., PARE A. and PITTENGER, C. 1993, *Writing for Ourselves/Writing for Others*. Toronto: Nelson.

DIXON, J. 1975, *Growth Through English*. London: Oxford University Press.

DOWDEY, D. 1992, Citation and documentation across the curriculum. In M. SECOR and D. CHARNEY (eds) *Constructing Rhetorical Education* (pp. 330–51). Carbondale: Southern Illinois University Press.

DUNNE, R. 1992, A deliberate approach to learning to teach. In S. JENNINGS (ed.) *Models of Mentoring* (pp. 16–24). Exeter University: School of Education.

—1994, The acquisition of professional activity in teaching. In G. HARVARD and P. HODKINSON (eds), *Action and Reflection in Teacher Education* (pp. 105–24). New Jersey: Ablex Publishing Co.

DUNNE, R. and HARVARD, G. 1992a, Competence as the meaningful acquisition of professional activity in teaching. In D. SAUNDERS and P. RACE (eds), *Developing and Measuring Competence* (pp. 241–45). London: Kogan Page.

—1992b, The implications for course design and assessment in initial training of a competence-based programme. Paper presented at HMI hospitality conference on competence-based teacher education, Bromsgrove, Worcester, March 9–10, 1992.

—1992c, A model of how students learn to teach as the acquisition of professional activity. Paper presented at a Conference on Educational Research, University of Twente, Enschede, Netherlands, June 1992.

—1993, A model of teaching and its implications for mentoring. In D. MCINTYRE, H. HAGGER and M. WILKIN (eds) 1993, *Mentoring: Perspectives on School-Based Teacher Education* (pp. 85–94). London: Kogan Page.

DURROW, C. 1972, The myth of the soul. In J.R. BURR and M. GOLDINGER (eds) *Philosophy and Contemporary Issues* (pp. 291–99). New York: Macmillan.

ECO, U. 1979, *The Role of the Reader: Explorations in the Semiotics of Texts*. London: Hutchinson.

Editorial 1985, *British Journal of Religious Education* 8, 1–2.

—1988, *British Journal of Religious Education* 10, 119–21.

EDWARDS, D. and MERCER, N. 1987, *Common Knowledge: The Development of Understanding in the Classroom*. London: Routledge and Kegan Paul.

ELBOW, P. 1973, *Writing Without Teachers*. New York: Oxford University Press.

—1981, *Writing With Power*. Oxford: Oxford University Press.

ELLIS, R. 1985, *Understanding Second Language Acquisition*. Oxford: Oxford University Press.

ERICSSON, K. A. and SIMON, H. A. 1984, *Protocol Analysis: Verbal Reports on Data*. Cambridge: MIT Press.

EVANS, J.St.B.T. 1989, *Bias in Human Reasoning: Causes and Consequences*. Hove, UK: Lawrence Erlbaum.

FAIRCLOUGH, N. 1992, Discourse and text: Linguistic and intertextual analysis within discourse analysis. *Discourse and Society* 13, 2, 193–217.

FENSHAM, P. 1985, Science for all: A reflective essay. *Journal of Curriculum Studies* 17, 4, 415–35.

FENSTERMACHER, G. 1991, The concepts of method and manner in pedagogy. Paper presented at an international symposium: Research on Effective and Responsible Teaching, Fribourg, Switzerland, September 3–7, 1990.

FEYERABEND, P. 1975 (1982), *Against Method: Outline of an Anarchistic Theory of Knowledge*. London: Verso.

—1978 (1982), *Science in a Free Society*. London: Verso.

FLODEN, R. and BUCHMANN, M. 1993, Breaking with experience for guided adventures in learning. In M. BUCHMANN and R. FLODEN (eds) *Detachment and Concern* (pp. 34–49). London: Cassell.

FLOWER, L. 1979, Writer-based prose. *College English* 41, 19–37.

—1994, *The Construction of Negotiated Meaning: A Social Cognitive Theory of Writing*. Carbondale, IL: Southern Illinois Press.

FLOWER, L., COOK, D., DEEMS, J. and LAWRENCE, S. forthcoming, *Rival Hypotheses across the University: Mapping Images of Rival-Hypothesis in History and Biology*. (Technical Report). Berkeley: Center for the Study of Writing and

Literacy at University of California at Berkeley and at Carnegie Mellon University.

FLOWER, L., LONG, E., FLEMING, D., and WOJAHN, P. 1993, Learning to rival 'in school' and 'out': A window on the logic of learners. (Technical Report). Pittsburgh, PA: Mellon Institute for Scientific Literacy.

FLOWER, L., STEIN, V., ACKERMAN, J., KANTZ, M. J., MCCORMICK, K., and PECK, W. C. 1990, *Reading-To-Write: Exploring a Cognitive and Social Process*. New York: Oxford University Press.

FLOWER, L., WALLACE, D., NORRIS, L. and BURNETT, R (eds) 1994, *Making Thinking Visible: Writing, Collaborative Planning and Classroom Inquiry*. Urbana, IL: NCTE.

FOUCAULT, M. 1972, *The Archaeology of Knowledge*. A.M. SHERIDAN SMITH, (trans.). New York: Colophon/Harper & Row.

—1980, *Power/Knowledge*. Brighton: Harvester.

FOX, D. 1983, Personal theories of teaching. *Studies in Higher Education* 8, 2, 151–63.

FOX KELLER, E. 1985, *Reflections on Science and Gender*. London: Yale University Press.

GADAMER, H-G. 1975 (1988), *Truth and Method*. London: Sheed and Ward.

GALTON, M. 1981, Teaching groups in the junior school: A neglected art. *School Organisation* 2, 2 , 175–81.

GALTON, M., SIMON, B. and CROLL, P. 1980, *Inside the Primary School* (Oracle Report). London: Routledge and Kegan Paul.

GARDENER, S. 1986, Language and second chance education. In J. MCCAFFEREY and B. STREET (eds) *Literacy Research in the U.K.: Adult and School Perspectives* (pp. 105–19). Lancaster: Research and Practice in Adult Literacy.

GEE, J.P. 1989, Literacy, discourse, and linguistics. *Journal of Education* 171, 5–17.

GEERTZ, C. 1993, *Local Knowledge*. London: Fontana Press.

General Certificate of Secondary Education (GCSE) 1985, *The National Criteria: Religious Studies*.

GILBERT, J. and WATTS, M. 1983, Concepts, misconceptions and alternative conceptions: Changing perspectives in science education. *Studies in Science Education* 10, 61–98.

GRANNOTT, N. 1991, Separate minds, joint efforts and weird creatures: Patterns of interaction in the co-construction of knowledge. In R. WOZNIAK and K. FISCHER (eds) *Specific Environments: Thinking In Context*. Hillsdale, NJ: Erlbaum.

GRAVES, D. 1981, Renters and owners: Donald Graves on writing. *English Magazine* 8, 25.

GREIL, A.L. and RUDY, D.R. 1990, On the margins of the sacred. In T. ROBBINS & D. ANTHONY (eds) *In Gods We Trust* (pp. 219–32). New Brunswick, NJ: Transaction Publishers.

GUBB, J. 1987, Discursive Writing – a Small-scale Observation Study. In J. GUBB *et al.*, 1987, *The Study of Written Composition in England and Wales* (pp. 162–83). Windsor: NFER/Nelson.

HABERMAS, J. 1963 (1974), Dogmatism, reason and decision. In *Theory and Practice* (pp. 253–82). London: Heinemann.

—1968 (1972), *Knowledge and Human Interest*. London: Heinemann.

—1979, What is universal pragmatics? In *Communication and the Evolution of Society* (pp. 1–68). London: Heinemann.

Hampshire Agreed Syllabus 1978, *Paths to Understanding*. Basingstoke: MacMillan.

HARDING, J. (ed.) 1986, *Perspectives on Gender and Science*. London: Falmer.
HARDY, D.W. 1979, Truth in religious education: Further reflections on the implications of pluralism. *British Journal of Religious Education* 1, 102–19.
HARLEN, W. 1978, Does content matter in primary science? *School Science Review* 59, 209, 614–25.
HARRÉ, R. 1983, *Personal Being*. Oxford: Basil Blackwell.
—1985, *The Philosophies of Science*. Oxford: Oxford University Press.
—1993, Indexicals: What pronouns can tell us about the self. Paper presented at Carnegie Mellon University Visiting Lecture Series, Pittsburgh, PA.
—1989, Language games and texts of identity. In J. SHOTTER and K.J. GERGEN (eds) *Texts Of Identity* (pp. 20–35). London: Sage.
HARRIS, J. 1989, The idea of community in the study of writing. *College Composition and Communication* 40, 11–22.
HARVARD, G.R. 1990, Some exploratory uses of interactive video in teacher education: Designing and presenting interactive learning techniques and video sequences to primary student teachers. *Educational and Training Technology International* 7, 2, 153–73.
—1994, A model of how students learn how to teach and its implications for mentoring. In G. HARVARD and P. HODKINSON (eds) *Action and Reflection in Teacher Education* (pp.125–58). New Jersey: Ablex Publishing Co.
HARVARD, G., DAY, M. and DUNNE, R. 1991, Studying students' schemas of typical primary classroom incidents using interactive learning techniques and videodisc materials prior to beginning a teacher education course. *Interactive Learning International* 7, 101–18.
HARVARD, G. and DUNNE, R. 1992, The role of the mentor in developing teacher competence. *Westminster Studies in Education* 15, 33–44.
HARVARD, G. and HODKINSON, P. (eds) 1993, *Action and Reflection in Teacher Education*. New Jersey: Ablex Publishing Co.
HAYES, J.R. and SCHRIVER, K. forthcoming, *Persona Study*. (Technical Report). Berkeley: Centre for the Study of Writing and Literacy at University of California at Berkeley and at Carnegie Mellon University.
HIGGINS, L., MATHISON, M. and FLOWER, L. 1992, *The Rival-Hypothesis Stance*. (Technical Report). Berkeley: Center for the Study of Writing and Literacy at University of California at Berkeley and at Carnegie Mellon University.
HILL, B.V. 1990, Will and should the religious studies approach to schools in a pluralistic society foster religious relativism? *British Journal of Religious Education* 12, 126–36.
HILL, J. and ZEPEDA, O. 1993, Mrs Patricio's trouble: The distribution of responsibility in an account of personal experience. In J. HILL and J. IRVINE (eds) *Responsibility and Evidence in Oral Discourse* (pp. 197–225). Cambridge: Cambridge University Press.
HIRST, P.A. 1971–2, Christian education: A contradiction in terms? *Learning for Living* 11, 6–11.
HMSO 1967, *Children and Their Primary Schools* (The Plowden Report Vol. 1). London: HMSO.
HOFSTADTER, R. and METZGER, W.P. 1955, *The Development Of Academic Freedom in the United States*. New York: Columbia University Press.
HOLUB, R.C. 1991, *Jurgen Habermas: Critic in the the Public Sphere*. London: Routledge.

HORKHEIMER, M. and ADORNO, T. 1944 (1973), *Dialectics of Enlightenment*. London: Allen Lane.

HORKHEIMER, M. 1974, *Critique of Instrumental Reason*. New York: Continuum.

HOSPERS, J. 1989, *An Introduction to Philosophical Analysis*, 2nd Edn. London: Routledge.

HULL, G., and ROSE, M. 1989, Rethinking remediation: Toward a social-cognitive understanding of problematic reading and writing.*Written Communication* 6, 139–54.

—1990, 'This wooden shack place': The logic of an unconventional reading. *College Composition and Communication* 41, 287–98.

HULL, J.M. 1982, (ed.) *New Directions in Religious Education*. Lewes, Sussex: Falmer.

—1984, *Studies in Religion and Education*. Lewes, Sussex: Falmer.

HULMES, E. 1978, The problem of commitment. In W. OWEN COLE (ed.) *World Faiths in Education* (pp. 26–37). London: Allen & Unwin.

HUSSERL, E. 1954 (1970), *The Crisis of European Sciences and Transcendental Phenomenology*. D. CARR (trans.). Evanston: Northwestern University Press.

ILLICH, I. 1977, *Limits to Medicine*. Harmondsworth: Penguin.

JACOBY, S. 1993, The interactive evolution of graphic displays for a physics conference talk. Paper presented at Carnegie Mellon University, Pittsburgh, PA.

JANDA, M. 1990, Collaboration in a traditional classroom environment. *Written Communication* 7, 3 , 291–315.

JOHNSON, R. and BLAIR, J. 1985, Informal logic: The past five years 1978–1983. *American Philosophical Quarterly* 22, 181–96.

JOHNSON-LAIRD, P.N. and BYRNE, R.M.J. 1991, *Deduction*. London: Lawrence Erlbaum.

JONES, M. 1985, Education and racism. *Journal of Philosophy of Education* 19, 223–34.

—1986, The Swann Report on 'Education for All': A critique. *Journal of Philosophy of Education* 20, 107–12.

KAFKA, F., 1988, The Metamorphosis. In N. N. GLATZER (ed.) *The Collected Short Stories of Franz Kafka* (pp. 89–139). London: Penguin Books.

KAHANE, H. 1992, *Logic and Contemporary Rhetoric: The Use of Reason in Everyday Life*, 6th Edn. Belmont, CA: Wadsworth.

KAUFER, D. and GEISLER, C. 1989, Novelty in academic writing. *Written Communication* 8, 286–311.

—1991, A scheme for representing academic argument. *The Journal of Advanced Composition* 11, 107–22.

KLEIN, J.T. 1993, Blurring, cracking, and crossing: Permeation and the fracturing of discipline. In E. MESSER-DAVIDOW, D.R. SHUMWAY and D.J. SYLVAN (eds) *Knowledges: Historical and Critical Studies in Disciplinarity* (pp. 185–213). Charlottesville: University Press of Virginia.

KNIGHT, P. 1989, Empathy: Concept, confusion and consequences in a national curriculum. *Oxford Review of Education* 15, 41–53.

KOCH, S. 1976, Language communities, search cells, and the psychological studies. In W.J. ARNOLD (ed.) *Nebraska Symposium on Motivation 1975* (pp. 477–559). Lincoln: University of Nebraska Press.

KRESS, G. 1989, Texture and meaning. In R. ANDREWS (ed.) *Narrative and Argument* (pp. 9–21). Milton Keynes: Open University Press.

KRIEGER, D. 1991, *The New Universalism*. New York: Orbis.

KUHN, D. 1991, *The Skills of Argument*. Cambridge: Cambridge University Press.

—1992, Thinking as argument. *Harvard Educational Review* 62, 2, 155–78.
KUHN, T.S. 1962, *The Structure of Scientific Revolutions*. Chicago: University of Chicago Press.
LABOV, W. 1972, *Language in the Inner City*. Oxford: Blackwell.
LABOV, W. and FANSHEL, D. 1977, *Therapeutic Discourse*. New York: Academic Press.
LACAPRA, D. 1983, *Rethinking Intellectual History: Texts, Contexts, And Language*. Ithaca, NY: Cornell University Press.
LAKIN, S. and WELLINGTON, J. 1991, *Teaching the Nature of Science: A Study of Teachers' Views and their Implications for Science Education*. Sheffield: University of Sheffield.
LAKOFF, G. and JOHNSON, M. 1980, *Metaphors We Live By*. London: Chicago University Press.
LAMB, D. 1985, *Death, Brain Death and Ethics*. London: Croom Helm.
LATOUR, B. and WOOLGAR, S. 1979, *Laboratory Life: The Social Construction of Scientific Facts*. London: Sage.
LEECH, G. 1969, *A Linguistic Guide to English Poetry*. London: Longman.
LEECH, G., DEUCHAR, M. and HOOGENRAAD, R. 1982, *English Grammar for Today*. London: Macmillan.
LIEBES, T. and RIBAK, R. 1991, A mother's battle against TV news: A case study of political socialisation. *Discourse and Society* 2, 2, 203–22.
LINDSTROM, L. 1992, Context contests: debatable truth statements on Tanna (Vanuatu). In A. DURANTI and C. GOODWIN (eds) *Rethinking Context* (pp. 101–24). Cambridge: Cambridge University Press.
LIPMAN, M. 1988, *Philosophy Goes to School*. Philadelphia: Temple University Press.
—1991, *Thinking in Education*. Cambridge: Cambridge University Press.
LIPMAN, M., SHARP, A.M. and OSCANYAN, F.S. 1980, *Philosophy in the Classroom*, 2nd Edn. Philadelphia: Temple University Press.
London East Anglia Group (LEAG) June 1990/January 1991, *GCSE Religious Studies: A and B*. London: Stewart House.
LYOTARD, J.F. 1984, *The Postmodern Condition: A Report on Knowledge*. G. BEN-NINGTON and B. MASSUNI (trans.). Minneapolis, MN: University of Minnesota Press.
MCCARTHY, T. 1978 (1984), *The Critical Theory of Jurgen Habermas*. Cambridge, Massachusetts: MIT Press.
MCCORMICK, K. 1990, The cultural imperatives underlying cognitive acts. In L. FLOWER, V. STEIN, J. ACKERMAN, M. KANTZ and W. PECK (eds) *Reading-to-Write: Exploring a Social and Cognitive Process* (pp. 194–218). New York: Oxford University Press.
MCINTYRE, D., HAGGER, H. and WILKIN, M. (eds) 1993, *Mentoring: Perspectives on School-Based Teacher Education*. London: Kogan Page.
MARTIN, J. R. 1989, *Factual Writing: Exploring and Challenging Social Reality*. Oxford: Oxford University Press.
—1992, *English Text: System and Structure*. Amsterdam: John Benjamins.
MARVELL, J. 1976, Phenomenology and the future of religious education. *Learning for Living* 16, 4–8.
MARX, K. 1858 (1973), *Grundrisse*. London: Pelican.
MATLIN, M. 1983, *Cognition*. New York: Holt, Rinehart & Winston.
MEDWAY, P. 1981, *Finding a Language*. London: Writers and Readers Co-op.

MENDELSON, J. 1979, The Habermas-Gadamer Debate. *New German Critique* 18, 44–73.

MESSER-DAVIDOW, E., SHUMWAY, D.R. and SYLVAN, D.J. (eds) 1993, *Knowledges: Historical and Critical Studies in Disciplinarity*. Charlottesville: University Press of Virginia.

MILL, J.S. 1859 (1969), On the liberty of thought and discussion. In M. WARNOCK (ed.) *Utilitarianism*. London: Fontana.

MILLER, C. 1984, Genre as social action. *Quarterly Journal of Speech* 70, 151–67.

MILLER, R.B. 1986, How to win over a sceptic. *Thinking: The Journal of Philosophy for Children* 6, 3, 46–8.

MITCHELL, S. 1992, *Questions And Schooling: Classroom Discourse across the Curriculum*. (Occasional Paper No. 1). Hull: The University of Hull, Centre for Studies in Rhetoric.

—1994, *The Teaching and Learning of Argument in Sixth Forms and Higher Education: Final Report*. Hull: University of Hull, Centre for Studies in Rhetoric.

MOFFETT, J. 1968, *Teaching the Universe of Discourse*. Boston: Houghton Mifflin.

MOORE, D.S. and MCCABE, G.P. 1989, *Introduction to the Practice of Statistics*. New York: W.H. Freeman and Co.

NASH, W. 1989, *Rhetoric: The Wit of Persuasion*. Oxford: Blackwell.

—1992, *An Uncommon Tongue*. London: Routledge.

NEELANDS, J. 1992, *Learning Through Imagined Experience: The Role of Drama in the National Curriculum*. London: Hodder & Stoughton.

NISBETT, R. and ROSS, L. 1980, *Human Inference: Strategies and Shortcomings of Social Judgment*. Englewood Cliffs, NJ: Prentice-Hall.

Northern Examining Association (NEAB) 1992/3, *GCSE: Religious Studies Syllabus: A*. Eccles, Manchester: Orbit House.

Northamptonshire Agreed Syllabus for Religious Education (1980). Northamptonshire Local Education Authority.

NOVICK, P. 1988, *That Noble Dream: The 'Objectivity Question' and the American Historical Profession*. Cambridge: Cambridge University Press.

O'BANION, J. 1992, *Reorienting Rhetoric: The Dialectic of List and Story*. State College, PA: Pennsylvania State University Press.

O'HEAR, A. 1985, *What Philosophy Is: An Introduction to Contemporary Philosophy*. Harmondsworth: Penguin Books.

OCHS, E. and SCHIEFFELIN, B. 1983, Planned and unplanned discourse. In M. STUBBS (ed.) *Acquiring Conversational Competence* (pp. 129–57). London: Routledge.

OLSON, D.R. 1977, From utterance to text: The bias of language in speech and writing. *Harvard Educational Review* 47, 257–81.

OSBORNE, R. and FREYBERG, P. 1985, *Learning Science: The Implications of Children's Science*. London: Heinemann.

PAREKH, B. 1973, Social and political thought and the problem of ideology. In R. BENEWICK (ed.) *Knowledge and Belief in Politics* (pp. 57–87). London: Allen and Unwin.

Parliamentary Debates (Hansard) 496, 120.

PARRET, H. 1987, Argumentation and narrativity. In F.H. VAN EEMEREN, R. GROOTENDORST, J.A. BLAIR and C.A. WILLARD (eds) *Argumentation: Across the Lines of Discipline*. Dordrecht: Foris.

PECK, W.C. 1991, Community advocacy: Composing for action. PhD dissertation, Carnegie Mellon University, Pittsburgh, PA.

PERELMAN, C. 1981, *The Realm of Rhetoric*. W. KLUBACK (trans.). Notre Dame: University of Notre Dame Press.

POLANYI, M. 1967, *The Tacit Dimension*. London: Routledge and Kegan Paul.

POPPER, K.R. 1963, *Conjectures and Refutations: The Growth of Scientific Knowledge*. London: Routledge and Kegan Paul.

POSNER, G., STRIKE, K., HEWSON, P. and GERTZOG, W. 1982, Accommodation of scientific conception: Towards a theory of conceptual change. *Science Education*, 66, 2, 211–27.

POSTMAN, N. and WEINGARTNER, C. 1971, *Teaching as a Subversive Activity*. Harmondsworth: Penguin.

PRIOR, P. 1991, Contextualising writing and response in a graduate seminar. *Written Communication* 8, 267–310.

PYKE, N. 1993, Cheap talk allows children to catch up. *The Times Educational Supplement*, (19 February).

QUIRK, R., GREENBAUM, S., LEECH, G. and SVARTVIK, J. 1972, *A Grammar of Contemporary English*. London: Longman.

REIFF, J. and KIRSCHT, J. 1992, Inquiry as human process: Interviews with researchers across the disciplines. *Journal of Advanced Composition* 12, 359–72.

REITHER, J.A. 1985, Writing and knowing: Toward defining the writing process. *College English* 47, 620–28.

RICOEUR, P. 1970, *Freud and Philosophy*. New Haven and London: Yale University Press.

RORTY, R. 1989, *Contingency, Irony, and Solidarity*. Cambridge: Cambridge University Press.

ROSENFIELD, L.W. 1968, The anatomy of critical discourse. *Speech Monographs 35*, 50–69.

ROWE, A.J. 1986, Critical openness and religious education. *British Journal of Religious Education 8*, 62–4.

ROYCE, J.R. 1976, Psychology is multi-: Methodological, variate, epistemic, world view, systemic, paradigmatic, theoretic, and disciplinary. In W.J. ARNOLD (ed.) *Nebraska Symposium on Motivation 1975* (pp. 1–63). Lincoln: University of Nebraska Press.

RUDOLPH, F. 1977, *Curriculum: A History of the American Undergraduate Curriculum since 1936*. San Francisco: Jossey-Bass.

—1990, *The American College and University: A History*. New York: Vintage (Original work published 1962).

RUSCIO, K.P. 1987, Many sectors, many professions. In B.R. CLARK (ed.) *The Academic Profession: National, Disciplinary and Institutional Settings* (pp. 331–68). Berkeley: University of California Press.

RUSHDIE, S. 1988, *The Satanic Verses*. London: Penguin.

RUSSELL, D.R. 1991, *Writing in the Academic Disciplines, 1870–1990: A Curricular History*. Carbondale, IL: Southern Illinois University Press.

RUSSELL, T. 1983, Analysing arguments in science classroom discourse: Can teachers' questions distort scientific authority? *Journal of Research in Science Teaching 20*, 1, 27–45.

RYLE, G. 1949, *The Concept of Mind*. Harmondsworth: Penguin Books.

SAUNDERS, D. and RACE, P. 1992, *Developing and Measuring Competence*. London: Kogan Page.

SCHMERSAHL, C.B. and STAY, B.L. 1992, Looking under the table: The shapes of writing in college. In M. SECOR and D. CHARNEY (eds) *Constructing Rhetorical Education* (pp. 140–9). Carbondale IL: Southern Illinois University Press.

SCHÖN, D.A. 1987, *Educating the Reflective Practitioner*. San Francisco: Jossey-Bass.

School Curriculum and Assessment Authority (SCAA) 1994a, *English in the National Curriculum: Draft Proposals*. London: HMSO.

School Curriculum and Assessment Authority (SCAA) 1994b, *GCSE Criteria for Religious Studies*. London: HMSO.

Schools Council 1971, *Working Paper 36: Religious Education in Secondary Schools*. London: Evans/Methuen Educational.

—1974 , *Nuffield 5–13*. London: McDonald.

Science Processes and Concept Exploration (SPACE) 1991, *Research Reports*. Liverpool: Liverpool University Press.

SECOR, M.J. 1987, Recent research in argumentation theory. *The Technical Writing Teacher* 14 , 337–54.

SHOEMAKER, S. 1963, *Self-Knowledge and Self-Identity*. New York: Cornell University Press.

SIEGEL, H. 1988, *Educating Reason: Rationality, Critical Thinking, and Education*. New York: Routledge.

—1989, Epistemology, critical thinking, and critical thinking pedagogy. *Argumentation* 3, 127–40.

SMART, N. 1968, *Secular Education: The Logic of Religion*. London: Faber.

SMITH, F. 1982, *Writing and the Writer*. Oxford: Heinemann.

SPENDER, D. 1980, *Man Made Language*. London: Routledge and Kegan Paul.

SPIVEY, N.N., MATHISON, M.A., GOGGIN, M.D. and GREENE, S. 1992, *Writing From Academic Sources: Acquiring Discourse Knowledge for Writing and Learning*. (Final Report). Berkeley: Center for the Study of Writing and Literacy at University of California, Berkeley, and at Carnegie Mellon University.

STONE, L. 1979, The revival of narrative: Reflections on a new old history. *Past and Present* 85, 3–24.

TALYZINA, N. 1981, *The Psychology of Learning*. Moscow: Progress Press.

TANNEN, D. 1991, *You Just Don't Understand Me*. London: Virago.

THOMPSON, N.H. (ed.) 1988, *Religious Pluralism and Religious Education*. Birmingham, Alabama: Religious Education Press.

TIZARD, B. and HUGHES, M. 1984, *Young Children Talking*. London: Fontana.

TRACY, K. 1988, A discourse analysis of four discourse studies. *Discourse Processes* 11, 243–59.

TRIM, J.L.M. 1989, Communicative effectiveness: A unifying concept for language teaching across the curriculum. In C.S. BUTLER, R.A. CARDWELL and J. CHANNELL (eds) *Language and Literature – Theory and Practice* (pp. 39–50). University of Nottingham Monographs in the Humanities.

VEYSEY, L.R. 1965, *The Emergence of the American University*. Chicago, IL: University of Chicago Press.

VOSS, J.F., ENGSTLER-SCHOOLER, T., FINCHER-KIEFER, R. and NEY, L. 1989, *On the Evaluation of Arguments*. Paper presented at the meeting of the Psychonomics Society, Atlanta, GA, November 1989.

VOSS, J.F., FINCHER-KIEFER, R., WILEY, J. and SILFIES, L.N. 1993, On the processing of arguments. *Argumentation* 7, 165–82.

VOSS, J.F. and MEANS, M.L. 1991, Learning to reason via instruction in argumentation. *Learning and Instruction* 1, 337–50.

VYGOTSKY, L. 1986, *Thought and Language*. Cambridge, Mass: Harvard University Press.

WALY, P. and COOK, S.W. 1965, Effect of attitude on judgments of plausibility. *Journal of Personality and Social Psychology* 2, 745–49.

WARNOCK, M. 1975, The neutral teacher. In M.J. TAYLOR (ed.) *Progress and Problems in Moral Education* (pp. 103–12). Slough, Berkshire: NFER.

Westhill Project: R.E. 5–16 (The) 1990, *How Do I Teach R.E.?* Cheltenham: Stanley Thornes & Hulton.

WHALING, F. (ed.) 1984, *Contemporary Approaches to the Study of Religions: Volume 1*. New York: Monton Publishers.

WHALLEY, M.J. 1987, Unexamined lives: The case for philosophy in schools. *British Journal of Educational Studies* 35, 3, 260–80.

WHYLD, J. 1983, *Sexism in the Secondary Curriculum*. London: Harper and Row.

WIDDOWSON, H.G. 1972, A linguistic approach to written communication. *The Use of English* 23, 206–11.

WIDDOWSON, H.G. 1979, *Explorations in Applied Linguistics*. Oxford: Oxford University Press.

WILLARD, C.A. 1989, *A Theory of Argumentation*. Alabama: The University of Alabama Press.

WILLIAMSON, M. 1988, A model for investigating the functions of written language in different disciplines. In D.A. JOLLIFFE (ed.) *Writing in Academic Disciplines* (pp. 89–132). Norwood, NJ: Ablex Publishing Company.

WILSON, S.M. and WINEBURG, S.S. 1988, Peering at history through disciplinary lenses: The role of disciplinary perspectives in teaching history. *Disciplinary Perspectives in Teaching* 89, 45–59.

WINCH, P. 1972 (1977), Understanding a primitive society. In F.R. DALLMAYR (ed.) *Understanding and Social Inquiry* (pp. 159–88). London: University of Notre Dame Press.

WISE, G. 1980, *American Historical Explanations: A Strategy for Grounded Inquiry*, 2nd Edn., rev. Minneapolis, MN: University of Minnesota.

WOLFGANG, M.E. 1967, Criminal homicide and the subculture of violence. In M.E. WOLFGANG (ed.) *Studies in Homicide* (pp. 3–12). New York: Harper and Row.

WOOD, P. 1990, Indoctrination and religious education in infant schools. *British Journal of Religious Education* 12, 160–6.

Index

Subjects

academic discipline(s) 6, 10-22, 116, 128, 131-46, 160
Alternative Conceptions Movement 2, 86-8
anecdote 36, 107, 166-7, 169-70
argument,
— as appropriation and transformation 138-45
— and conceptual change 5, 84, 94-6
— conditions for 53
— definitions of 1-2, 5, 25-6, 53-4, 60-1, 90-2, 99-100, 107, 113, 132
— dialogic 1, 42, 91-2, 94-6, 110
— didactic 90-2, 94, 96, 98
— as display 100
— evaluations of 3, 7, 10, 12, 17, 147-59, 160-71
— everyday 39, 44, 161
— as games 24-34
— goals 7, 18-9, 173, 175, 200
— and narrative 4, 5, 35-49, 101, 109-10, 173, 206
— as opposition 134-8
— to persuade 1, 26, 108, 147-8, 174-83, 188, 193
— and philosophy 112-4
— on basis of possibility 173-4, 178-9, 182
— on basis of probability 173-4, 177-8, 182
— as publication 145-6
— quality of 3, 23, 158-9
— rhetorical 1, 90, 95, 166
— reading of 34, 147-8
— socratic 91-2, 94, 96, 98
— functions of 24, 133
— virtual 39-41, 43-4, 47-8

— to win 1, 26
assessment 5, 8, 10, 16, 22n, 70, 85, 100-2, 105-8, 113, 129-30, 132, 136, 151-9, 189-90
audio-tape 4, 6, 102-11
authority 4, 13, 29, 37-9, 82, 141

belief 3, 5, 20, 52, 72-3, 75, 114, 134, 144-6, 163, 168-70

change 1, 13, 20, 132, 148
claims 147-8, 163, 172, 174-5, 179-80, 182-3
common sense 7, 134-6, 138-9, 144
consensus 1-2, 21, 44, 46, 62, 96, 132, 138, 144-5 ∙
constructivism 85, 88-91, 93-6
context 3, 11, 17-8, 21, 87, 89, 92, 103, 108, 131, 174, 177, 179
conversation 26, 36, 47, 55, 58, 78, 131, 173, 183n, 198
critical attitude/thinking 4-5, 50-3, 98, 151
cultural pluralism 5, 69, 73, 78
culture 35-6, 78, 101, 133

debate 3, 26, 28, 33, 35, 102, 104, 113-4
dialogue 5, 14, 36, 49, 68-83, 85, 107, 112, 137-8, 143, 180, 198
discourse(s) 17, 131-2, 134-46
— unplanned/planned 196-200 207
discourse/disciplinary community 15, 16, 20, 22n, 79, 147-8, 157
dogmatic attitude/thinking 4-5, 50-3, 57, 59
dogma/dogmatism 68, 74-6, 78, 80, 82
drama 82

Names